10th Workshop on Multiword Expressions

(MWE 2014)

Held at the 14th Conference of the European Chapter of the Association for Computational Linguistics

Gothenburg, Sweden
26 – 27 April 2014

ISBN: 978-1-63266-403-7

Printed from e-media with permission by:

Curran Associates, Inc.
57 Morehouse Lane
Red Hook, NY 12571

Some format issues inherent in the e-media version may also appear in this print version.

Printed by Curran Associates, Inc. (2014)

Association for Computational Linguistics
209 N. Eighth Street
Stroudsburg, Pennsylvania 18360

Phone: 1-570-476-8006
Fax: 1-570-476-0860

acl@aclweb.org

Additional copies of this publication are available from:

Curran Associates, Inc.
57 Morehouse Lane
Red Hook, NY 12571 USA
Phone: 845-758-0400
Fax: 845-758-2634
Email: curran@proceedings.com
Web: www.proceedings.com

Introduction

The 10th Workshop on Multiword Expressions (MWE 2014) took place on April 26 and 27, 2014 in Gothenburg, Sweden in conjunction with the 14th Conference of the European Chapter of the Association for Computational Linguistics (EACL 2014) and was endorsed by the Special Interest Group on the Lexicon of the Association for Computational Linguistics (SIGLEX), as well as SIGLEX's Section dedicated to the study and research of Multiword Expressions (SIGLEX-MWE). Moreover, this year's edition of the MWE workshop was also supported by the IC1207 COST[1] action PARSEME[2] dedicated to Parsing and Multiword Expressions. This European initiative, which started in 2013, gathers 29 European COST member countries, one COST cooperating state and 3 non-COST institutions from the USA and Brazil. Its objective is to increase and enhance the information and communication technology support of the European multilingual heritage by bringing about a substantial progress in the understanding and modelling of MWEs within advanced multilingual NLP techniques, notably deep parsing. The special track of the MWE 2014 workshop endorsed by PARSEME gathered 8 papers where links between lexical and grammatical aspects of MWEs, as well as their role in deep parsing and NLP applications, such as machine translation, were addressed.

The workshop has been held almost every year since 2003 in conjunction with ACL, EACL, NAACL, COLING and LREC. It provides an important venue for interaction, sharing of resources and tools and collaboration efforts for advancing the computational treatment of Multiword Expressions (MWEs), attracting the attention of an ever-growing community working on a variety of languages and MWE types.

MWEs include idioms (storm in a teacup, sweep under the rug), fixed phrases (in vitro, by and large, rock'n roll), noun compounds (olive oil, laser printer), compound verbs (take a nap, bring about), among others. These, while easily mastered by native speakers, are a key issue and a current weakness for natural language parsing and generation, as well as real-life applications depending on some degree of semantic interpretation, such as machine translation, just to name a prominent one among many. However, thanks to the joint efforts of researchers from several fields working on MWEs, significant progress has been made in recent years, especially concerning the construction of large-scale language resources. For instance, there is a large number of recent papers that focus on acquisition of MWEs from corpora, and others that describe a variety of techniques to find paraphrases for MWEs. Current methods use a plethora of tools such as association measures, machine learning, syntactic patterns, web queries, etc.

In the call for papers we solicited submissions about major challenges in the overall process of MWE treatment, both from the theoretical and the computational viewpoint, focusing on original research related (but not limited) to the following topics:

- Manually and automatically constructed resources
- Representation of MWEs in dictionaries and ontologies
- MWEs and user interaction

- Multilingual acquisition
- Multilingualism and MWE processing
- Models of first and second language acquisition of MWEs
- Crosslinguistic studies on MWEs
- The role of MWEs in the domain adaptation of parsers
- Integration of MWEs into NLP applications
- Evaluation of MWE treatment techniques
- Lexical, syntactic or semantic aspects of MWEs

Submission modalities included Long Papers and Short Papers. From a total of 36 submissions, 14 were long papers and 22 were short papers, and we accepted 6 long papers for oral presentation and 2 as posters. We further accepted 6 short papers for oral presentation and 8 as posters. The overall acceptance rate is 58%. The workshop also featured 3 invited talks.

Acknowledgements

We would like to thank the members of the Program Committee for the timely reviews and the authors for their valuable contributions. We also want to thank PARSEME which funded travel and stay for at least 20 participants from the Action's member countries.

Valia Kordoni, Agata Savary, Markus Egg, Eric Wehrli, Stefan Evert
Co-Organizers

EUROPEAN COOPERATION
IN SCIENCE AND TECHNOLOGY

Organizers:

Valia Kordoni, Humboldt Universität zu Berlin (Germany)
Markus Egg, Humboldt Universität zu Berlin (Germany)
Agata Savary, special track organizer, Université François Rabelais Tours (France)
Eric Wehrli, special track organizer, Université de Genève (Switzerland)
Stefan Evert, Friedrich-Alexander-Universität Erlangen-Nürnberg (Germany)

Program Committee:

Iñaki Alegria, University of the Basque Country (Spain)
Dimitra Anastasiou, University of Bremen (Germany)
Doug Arnold, University of Essex (UK)
Eleftherios Avramidis, DFKI GmbH (Germany)
Tim Baldwin, University of Melbourne (Australia)
Núria Bel, Universitat Pompeu Fabra (Spain)
Chris Biemann, Technische Universität Darmstadt (Germany)
Francis Bond, Nanyang Technological University (Singapore)
Lars Borin, University of Gothenburg (Sweden)
António Branco, University of Lisbon (Portugal)
Miriam Butt, Universität Konstanz (Germany)
Aoife Cahill, ETS (USA)
Ken Church, IBM Research (USA)
Matthieu Constant, Université Paris-Est Marne-la-Vallée (France)
Paul Cook, University of Melbourne (Australia)
Béatrice Daille, Nantes University (France)
Koenraad De Smedt, University of Bergen (Norway)
Gaël Dias, University of Caen Basse-Normandie (France)
Gülşen Eryiğit, Istanbul Technical University (Turkey)
Tomaž Erjavec, Jožef Stefan Institute (Slovenia)
Joaquim Ferreira da Silva, New University of Lisbon (Portugal)
Roxana Girju, University of Illinois at Urbana-Champaign (USA)
Chikara Hashimoto, National Institute of Information and Communications Technology (Japan)
Ulrich Heid, Universität Hildesheim (Germany)
Kyo Kageura, University of Tokyo (Japan)
Ioannis Korkontzelos, University of Manchester (UK)
Brigitte Krenn, Austrian Research Institute for Artificial Intelligence (Austria)
Cvetana Krstev, University of Belgrade (Serbia)
Marie-Catherine de Marneffe, The Ohio State University (USA)
Takuya Matsuzaki, National Institute of Informatics (Japan)
Preslav Nakov, Qatar Computing Research Institute (Qatar)
Malvina Nissim, University of Bologna (Italy)

Joakim Nivre, Uppsala University (Sweden)
Diarmuid Ó Séaghdha, University of Cambridge (UK)
Jan Odijk, University of Utrecht (The Netherlands)
Yannick Parmentier, Université d'Orléans (France)
Pavel Pecina, Charles University in Prague (Czech Republic)
Scott Piao, Lancaster University (UK)
Adam Przepiórkowski, Institute of Computer Science, Polish Academy of Sciences (Poland)
Victoria Rosén, University of Bergen (Norway)
Carlos Ramisch, Aix-Marseille University (France)
Manfred Sailer, Goethe University Frankfurt am Main (Germany)
Magali Sanches Duran, University of São Paulo (Brazil)
Violeta Seretan, University of Geneva (Switzerland)
Ekaterina Shutova, University of California, Berkeley (USA)
Jan Šnajder, University of Zagreb (Croatia)
Pavel Straňák, Charles University in Prague (Czech Republic)
Sara Stymne, Uppsala University (Sweden)
Stan Szpakowicz, University of Ottawa (Canada)
Beata Trawinski, Institut für Deutsche Sprache (IDS), Mannheim (Germany)
Yulia Tsvetkov, Carnegie Mellon University (USA)
Yuancheng Tu, Microsoft (USA)
Ruben Urizar, University of the Basque Country (Spain)
Gertjan van Noord, University of Groningen (The Netherlands)
Aline Villavicencio, Federal University of Rio Grande do Sul (Brazil)
Veronika Vincze, Hungarian Academy of Sciences (Hungary)
Martin Volk, University of Zurich (Switzerland)
Tom Wasow, Stanford University (USA)
Shuly Wintner, University of Haifa (Israel)
Dekai Wu, The Hong Kong University of Science & Technology (Hong Kong)

Invited Speakers:

Ekaterina Shutova, ICSI, UC Berkeley (USA)
Preslav Nakov, Qatar Computing Research Institute (Qatar)
One more invited speaker to be confirmed

Table of Contents

Conference Program

Saturday, April 26, 2014

8:45–9:00 Opening Remarks

Oral Session 1: Detection and Extraction of MWEs

9:00–9:30 *Breaking Bad: Extraction of Verb-Particle Constructions from a Parallel Subtitles Corpus*
Aaron Smith

9:30–10:00 *A Supervised Model for Extraction of Multiword Expressions, Based on Statistical Context Features*
Meghdad Farahmand and Ronaldo Martins

Oral Session 2: PARSEME I – Parsing MWEs

10:00–10:30 *VPCTagger: Detecting Verb-Particle Constructions With Syntax-Based Methods*
István Nagy T. and Veronika Vincze

10:30–11:00 Coffee Break

11:00–12:00 Invited Talk 1: TBA

Oral Session 2: PARSEME I – Parsing MWEs (continued)

12:00–12:30 *The Relevance of Collocations for Parsing*
Eric Wehrli

12:30–14:00 Lunch

Oral Session 3: Short papers – PARSEME II

14:00–14:20 *Parsing Modern Greek verb MWEs with LFG/XLE grammars*
Niki Samaridi and Stella Markantonatou

14:20–14:40 *Evaluation of a Substitution Method for Idiom Transformation in Statistical Machine Translation*
Giancarlo Salton, Robert Ross and John Kelleher

14:40–15:00 *Encoding MWEs in a conceptual lexicon*
Aggeliki Fotopoulou, Stella Markantonatou and Voula Giouli

Saturday, April 26, 2014 (continued)

15:00–15:30 **Poster Booster Session (4 minutes per poster)**

German Compounds and Statistical Machine Translation. Can they get along?
Carla Parra Escartín, Stephan Peitz and Hermann Ney

Extracting MWEs from Italian corpora: A case study for refining the POS-pattern methodology
Sara Castagnoli, Malvina Nissim and Francesca Masini

Mickey Mouse is not a Phrase: Improving Relevance in E-Commerce with Multiword Expressions
Prathyusha Senthil Kumar, Vamsi Salaka, Tracy Holloway King and Brian Johnson

Encoding of Compounds in Swedish FrameNet
Karin Friberg Heppin and Miriam R L Petruck

Extraction of Nominal Multiword Expressions in French
Marie Dubremetz and Joakim Nivre

Towards an Empirical Subcategorization of Multiword Expressions
Luigi Squillante

Contexts, Patterns, Interrelations - New Ways of Presenting Multi-word Expressions
Kathrin Steyer and Annelen Brunner

Detecting change and emergence for multiword expressions
Martin Emms and Arun Jayapal

An Approach to Take Multi-Word Expressions
Claire Bonial, Meredith Green, Jenette Preciado and Martha Palmer

15:30–16:00 Coffee Break

16:00–17:30 Poster Session

Sunday, April 27, 2014

9:30–10:30 Invited Talk 2: TBA

10:30–11:00 Coffee Break

Oral Session 5: Short papers – MWEs in multilingual applications

11:00–11:20 *Paraphrasing Swedish Compound Nouns in Machine Translation*
Edvin Ullman and Joakim Nivre

11:20–11:40 *Feature Norms of German Noun Compounds*
Stephen Roller and Sabine Schulte im Walde

11:40–12:00 *Identifying collocations using cross-lingual association measures*
Lis Pereira, Elga Strafella, Kevin Duh and Yuji Matsumoto

Oral Session 6: Issues in lexicon construction and Machine Translation

12:00–12:30 *Unsupervised Construction of a Lexicon and a Repository of Variation Patterns for Arabic Modal Multiword Expressions*
Rania Al-Sabbagh, Roxana Girju and Jana diesner

12:30–14:00 Lunch

14:00–14:30 *Issues in Translating Verb-Particle Constructions from German to English*
Nina Schottmüller and Joakim Nivre

14:30–15:30 Invited Talk 3: TBA

15:30–15:45 Closing remarks

Breaking Bad: Extraction of Verb-Particle Constructions from a Parallel Subtitles Corpus

Aaron Smith
Department of Linguistics and Philology
Uppsala University
Box 635, 75126 Uppsala, Sweden
aaron.smith.4159@student.uu.se

Abstract

The automatic extraction of verb-particle constructions (VPCs) is of particular interest to the NLP community. Previous studies have shown that word alignment methods can be used with parallel corpora to successfully extract a range of multi-word expressions (MWEs). In this paper the technique is applied to a new type of corpus, made up of a collection of subtitles of movies and television series, which is parallel in English and Spanish. Building on previous research, it is shown that a precision level of $94 \pm 4.7\%$ can be achieved in English VPC extraction. This high level of precision is achieved despite the difficulties of aligning and tagging subtitles data. Moreover, many of the extracted VPCs are not present in online lexical resources, highlighting the benefits of using this unique corpus type, which contains a large number of slang and other informal expressions. An added benefit of using the word alignment process is that translations are also automatically extracted for each VPC. A precision rate of $75 \pm 8.5\%$ is found for the translations of English VPCs into Spanish. This study thus shows that VPCs are a particularly good subset of the MWE spectrum to attack using word alignment methods, and that subtitles data provide a range of interesting expressions that do not exist in other corpus types.

1 Introduction

In this paper, a method for the automatic extraction of English verb-particle constructions (VPCs) from parallel corpora is described and assessed. The method builds on previous research, particularly that of Caseli et al. (2010), adapting their approach specifically to VPC extraction and applying it to a different kind of corpus, based on subtitles from popular movies and television series, which is parallel in English and Spanish. The use of a parallel corpus also allows translations of VPCs to be obtained; an evaluation of the success rate of this process is also presented.

The paper is structured in the following manner: Section 2 discusses previous research and introduces key terminology, Section 3 describes the corpus and details the methodology and Section 4 explains the evaluation process. Results are then presented in Section 5, before discussion and future work in Section 6, and finally conclusions in Section 7.

2 Background

Amongst the many factors that contribute to the difficulty faced by NLP systems in processing multi-word expressions (MWEs), their sheer multifariousness is surely one of the most challenging. MWEs are combinations of simplex words that display idiosyncrasies in their syntax, semantics, or frequency (Caseli et al., 2010; Kim and Baldwin, 2010). They include nominal compounds such as *distance learning*, phrasal verbs such as *loosen up* and *rely on*, idioms such as *we'll cross that bridge when we come to it* and collocations such as *salt and pepper*, as well as instances which cannot so easily be classified such as *by the by* and *ad hoc* (Copestake et al., 2010). Due to their diverse and often non-compositional nature, MWEs constitute a big problem in many NLP tasks, from part-of-speech (PoS) tagging to parsing to machine translation (Chatterjee and Balyan, 2011, Constant et al., 2013).

In this paper the focus is on VPCs, a subset of phrasal verbs consisting of a verb and a particle, which, according to Villavicencio (2005), can be either prepositional, as in *hold on*, adverbial, as in *back away*, adjectival, as in *cut short*, or verbal, as in *let be*. The definitions of phrasal verbs, VPCs and prepositional verbs are often confusing, with several competing terminologies. Greenbaum and Quirk (1990), for example, use a different system than that defined here: they use the term *multi-word verbs* where this study uses phrasal verbs, and *phrasal verbs* for those which are called VPCs here. In their system phrasal verbs are thus, along with prepositional verbs, a subset of multi-word verbs. The confusion between the different categories is often heightened by the fact that VPCs and prepositional verbs can be tricky to distinguish. The terminology used in this paper follows that of Villavicencio (2005): VPCs and prepositional verbs are a subset of the broader category of phrasal verbs.

The two most fundamental MWE-related tasks in NLP can be classified as *identification* and *extraction*. Identification, in the context of VPCs, is described in Kim and Baldwin (2010) as "the detection of individual VPC token instances in corpus data", while in extraction "the objective is to arrive at an inventory of VPCs types/lexical items based on analysis of token instances in corpus data". These tasks have relevance in different applications: identification is important in any form of text processing, whereas extraction is important for the creation of lexical resources and for text generation. Note that there is also a strong link between the two: lexical resources listing MWEs can naturally be used to identify their instances in a text.

In the present study the focus lies on VPC extraction: the goal is ultimately to create a list of valid VPCs. It is not the case that every verb can be combined with every possible particle – this would make our lives a lot easier (though perhaps less interesting). Villavicencio (2005) discusses the availability of VPCs in various lexical resources, including dictionaries, corpora, and the internet. She finds 3156 distinct VPCs across three electronic dictionaries, and extends that total to 9745 via automatic extraction from British National Corpus. She goes on to use the semantic classification of verbs defined by Levin (1993) to create lists of candidate VPCs based on their semantic properties, before using the internet as a gigantic corpus to attest them. The conclusion is that semantic classes are a good predictor of verbs' VPC productivity.

The current study owes a large debt to the work of Caseli et al. (2010). They proposed a method for identifying MWEs in bilingual corpora as a by-product of the word alignment process. Moreover, their method was able to extract possible translations for the MWEs in question, thus providing an efficient way to improve the coverage of bilingual lexical resources. Zarriess and Kuhn (2009) had previously argued that MWE patterns could be identified from one-to-many alignments in bilingual corpora in conjunction with syntactic filters. Caseli et al. (2010) draw on a previous study by Villada Moirón and Tiedemann (2006), who extract MWE candidates using association measures and head dependence heuristics before using alignment for ranking purposes.

An interesting variation on the word alignment extraction method was investigated by Liu (2011), who in fact use a monolingual corpus along with techniques designed for bilingual word alignment. They create a replica of the monolingual corpus, and align each sentence to its exact copy. They then adapt a word alignment algorithm (specifically IBM model 3), adding the constraint that a word cannot be aligned to its copy in the parallel corpus. This facilitates the extraction of collocations, and the authors show that their method elicits significant gains in both precision and recall over its competitors. A more recent attempt to use parallel corpora in the extraction of MWEs was made by Pichotta and DeNero (2013). They focused on English phrasal verbs, and devised a method of combining information from translations into many languages. They conclude that using information from multiple languages provides the most effective overall system.

A key finding of Caseli et al. (2010) was that their method achieved its highest levels of precision for phrasal verbs. For this reason the present study will focus specifically on VPCs, in a sense narrowing the previous study to focus on part of its most successful element. Like that study, this work will also find and evaluate candidate translations for each extracted English phrase. The corpus used in that study was composed of articles from a Brazilian scientific magazine. Based on the observation that VPCs are often less formal than their non-VPC counterparts (consider for example *The experiments back up the theory* v. *The experiments support the theory*), the current work evaluates the methodology on a spoken text corpus, specifically subtitles from movies and television series. It is expected that this type of corpus will have a high density of VPCs, and moreover that they will often be informal, slang, and even profanities that would not be found in most corpus types. Indeed, the name of one of the most successful television series of recent times, *Breaking Bad*, is a perfect example of a slang VPC that would not be found in most lexical resources.

3 Methodology

The methodology in this study, adapted from that of Caseli et al. (2010), consists of four stages: PoS tagging, extraction, filtering and grouping, which are explained in turn in Sections 3.1–3.4. The corpus used is the OpenSubtitles2012 corpus (Tiedemann, 2012), a collection of documents from http://www.opensubtitles.org/, consisting of subtitles from movies and television series. As it based on user uploads there can be several sets of subtitles for the same movie, normally varying only slightly from each other. The corpus is tokenised, true-cased and sentence-aligned, and various word alignments are also provided. The section of the corpus used in this study, which is parallel in English and Spanish, contains 39,826,013 sentence pairs, with 342,833,112 English tokens and 299,880,802 Spanish tokens.

3.1 PoS Tagging

First of all, both the English and Spanish data are PoS tagged using TreeTagger (Schmid, 1994). An advantage of TreeTagger is that as well as PoS tags, it also provides lemma information for each word, which will be useful later in identifying different conjugations of the same VPCs. Subtitles, being a form of spoken text, are inherently difficult to tag; the overall accuracy of the TreeTagger is likely to be low on this data type. It should be noted however that PoS taggers generally have a high accuracy for verbs compared to other parts of speech.

3.2 Extraction

Using the `aligned.grow-diag-final-and` alignment file provided with the corpus, all word alignments containing more than one word in either language are extracted. This alignment file has been created by first word-aligning the parallel data sets in both directions using GIZA++ (Och and Ney, 2000), before merging them according to the algorithm in Och and Ney (2003). By varying the parameters to this algorithm to trade between precision and recall, various other alignment files have also been produced and made available as part of the OpenSubtitles2012 corpus.

The first alignment from the raw extraction process (for illustration purposes – there is nothing particularly special about this entry) is as follows:

```
've/VHP/have got/VVN/get ///
 tengo/VLfin/tener
```

The English *'ve got* is aligned to the Spanish *tengo* ("I have"), along with the respective PoS tags and lemmas. In total there are 53,633,153 such alignments in the corpus, many of which are repetitions. Identical entries are counted and sorted, before filtering is applied to find candidate VPCs.

3.3 Filtering

This is achieved by looking for all instances where the first English word has a verb tag (any tag beginning with *V*), the second is a particle (indicated by the tag *RP*), and the Spanish translation is also a verb. A minimum frequency of five is also effected; this is higher than the threshold of two applied by Caseli et al. (2010). There are several reasons for this: the larger corpus size here, the fact that PoS tagging is expected to be less accurate on this corpus, and the fact that some movies have more than one set of subtitles, leading to some almost identical sections in the corpus. This filtering is rather strict: to make it through this stage a VPC must occur at least five times in the corpus in exactly the same conjugation with the same translation. Some genuine VPCs might therefore be filtered away at this stage; those that occur few times and in different conjugations will be lost. The value of five was chosen early on in the study and left unchanged, based on some initial observations of lines that were repeated two or three times in the corpus and taking into account the other factors mentioned above. This parameter can of course be adjusted to increase recall, with the expected damage to the precision score; a more detailed investigation of this effect would be an interesting extension to the present study.

The filtered list contains a total of 18186 entries, the first of which is:

```
10900 come/VV/come on/RP/on ///
 vamos/VLfin/ir
```

This looks promising so far: the English entry *come on* is a valid VPC, and the Spanish translation *vamos* ("let's go") is a good translation. There is still more work to do, however, as at this stage the list contains many instances of the same VPCs in different conjugations and with different translations. There are also, due to the fact that the original corpus was in true case, some instances of repetitions of the same VPC with different casing.

3.4 Grouping

The remaining data is lower-cased, before entries are grouped based on their lemmas, adding together the respective counts. By doing this some information is lost: certain VPCs may only naturally appear in certain conjugations, or may have different meanings depending on the conjugation they appear in. This therefore undoubtedly introduces some error into the evaluation process, but for the purposes of simplification of analysis is a crucial step.

Grouping reduces the list of VPC-translation pairs to 6833 entries, 37.6% of the number before grouping. This large reduction shows that the VPCs that occur many times in one conjugation tend to also appear in several other conjugations. The grouping process merges these to a single entry, leading to the observed reduction. Amongst the remaining 6833 entries, there are 1424 unique English VPCs. The next challenge is to evaluate the accuracy of the results.

4 Evaluation

The evaluation of the extracted candidate VPCs and their translations is in three parts: first, an evaluation of whether the candidates are in fact valid English VPCs; secondly, whether they already exist in certain online resources; and thirdly whether the Spanish translations are valid. Evaluating all 6833 candidates is not feasible in the time-frame of this study, thus the following approach is taken: a random selection of 100 VPC candidates is chosen from the list of 1424 VPCs, then for each of these candidates the highest probability translation (that with the highest count in the corpus) is found.

4.1 Validity of VPC Candidates

The 100 candidate VPCs are judged by a native English speaker as either valid or not, following the definitions and rules set out in Chapter 16 of Greenbaum and Quirk (1990) (note however their different terminology as mentioned in Section 2). One of the major difficulties in this evaluation is that VPCs are productive; it can be difficult even for a native speaker to judge the validity of a VPC candidate. Consider for example the unusual VPC *ambulance off*; while this almost certainly would not appear in any lexical resources, nor would have been uttered or heard by the vast majority, native speaker intuition says that it could be used as a VPC in the sense of 'carry away in an ambulance'. This should therefore be judged valid in the evaluation. It is important to remember here that one of the main reasons for using the subtitles corpus in the first place is to find unusual VPCs not usually found in other corpora types or lexical resources; candidates cannot simply be ruled out because they have never been seen or heard before by the person doing the evaluation. *Ambulance off* does actually appear in the corpus, in the sentence *A few of a certain Billy-boy's friends were ambulanced off*, though it is not part of the 100 candidate VPCs evaluated in this study.

At the evaluation stage, the aim is to judge whether the candidate VPCs could in theory validly be employed as VPCs, not to judge whether they were in fact used as VPCs in the corpus. The corpus itself was however a useful resource for the judge; if a borderline VPC candidate was clearly used at least once as a VPC in the corpus, then it was judged valid. Not all VPC candidates were checked against the corpus however, as many could be judged valid without this step. It is worth noting that some genuine VPCs could have found themselves on the candidate list despite not actually having been employed as VPCs in the corpus, though this probably happens very infrequently.

4.2 Existence in Current Lexical Resources

Once valid VPCs have been identified by the judge from the list of 100 candidates in the previous step, they are checked against two online resources: Dictionary.com (http://dictionary.reference.com/) and The Free Dictionary (http://www.thefreedictionary.com/). Both these resources contain substantial quantities of MWEs; The Free Dictionary even has its own 'idioms' section containing many slang expressions. A VPC is considered to be already documented if it appears anywhere in either of the two dictionaries.

4.3 Accuracy of Translations

The final stage of evaluation was carried out by a native Spanish speaker judge from Mexico with a near-native level of English. The judge was asked to asses whether each of the Spanish translation candidates could be employed as a translation of the English VPC in question. The original corpus was used for reference purposes in a similar manner to the evaluation of the VPC candidates: not every example was looked up but in borderline cases it served as a useful reference.

5 Results

5.1 Validity of VPC Candidates

Amongst the 100 randomly selected VPC candidates, 94 were judged valid by a native speaker. The normal approximation gives a 95% confidence interval of $94 \pm 4.7\%$. In the original list of 1424 candidates, the number of true VPCs is therefore expected to lie in the range between 1272 and 1405. This precision rate is in line with the figure of 88.94–97.30% stated in Table 9 of Caseli et al. (2010). Note however that the two figures are not directly comparable; in their study they looked at all combinations of verbs with particles *or* prepositions, and judged whether they were true MWEs. Their analysis thus likely includes many prepositional verbs as well as VPCs. Remember here that only combinations of verbs with particles were considered, and it was judged whether they were true VPCs. The current study shows however that high levels of precision can be achieved in the extraction of phrasal verbs, even given a more difficult corpus type.

Amongst the VPC candidates judged valid, four appeared in slightly unusual form in the list: *teared up*, *brung down*, *fessed up* and *writ down*. In all four cases the problem seems to stem from the lemmatiser: it fails to convert the past tense *teared* to the infinitive *tear* (note that "tear" has two quite separate meanings with corresponding pronunciations – one with "teared" as past tense and one with "tore"), it fails to recognise the dialectal variation *brung* (instead of *brought*), it fails to recognise the slang verb *fess* (meaning "confess"), and it fails to recognise an old variation on the past tense of *write*, which was *writ* rather than *wrote*. These mistakes of the lemmatiser are not punished; there were marked valid as long as they were genuine VPCs. This reinforces a difficulty of working with subtitle corpora: verbs might be used in unusual forms which cause difficulties for existing automatic text-analysis tools. It is of course also the reason why subtitles are in fact so interesting as corpus material.

It is illuminating to analyse why certain VPC candidates were judged invalid; this can highlight problems with the method, the evaluation, or even the corpus, which may help future studies. The six VPC candidates in question are *base on, bolt out, bowl off, bury out, hide down* and *imprint on*. These false positives all contain valid verbs, but combined with the particle do not make valid VPCs. In several cases the confusion arises between a preposition and a particle; it appears the tagger has incorrectly labelled the second token as a particle instead of a preposition in the cases *base on*, *bolt out*, *bury out* and *imprint on*. This seems to occur particularly when the preposition occurs at the very end of a sentence, for example in *that's what these prices are based on*, or when there is a two-word preposition such as in phrases like *he bolted out of the room*. It is easy to see how the tagger could have interpreted these prepositions as particles; very similar examples can be found where we do indeed have a VPC, such as *that was a real mess up* or *he was shut out of the discussion* (the particles 'up' and 'out' here appear in the same positions as the prepositions in the previous examples). The candidate VPC *hide down* is a somewhat similar case, appearing in phrases such as *let's hide down there*. The tagger incorrectly labels 'down' as a particle instead of an adverb. A clue that this is the wrong interpretation comes from the fact that when the phrase is spoken out loud the emphasis is placed on *hide*.

The final false positive to be explained is *bowl off*. This verb appears in the phrase *they'd bowl you off a cliff*, which occurs no less than eleven times in the corpus, each time aligned to a single Spanish verb. Here we see how a problem with the corpus leads to errors in the final list of candidates. This appears to be a case where several sets of subtitles exist for the same movie, and the tagger and aligner are making the same faulty decision each time they see this phrase, allowing the incorrect VPC to bypass the filters. One possible resolution to this problem could be to simply exclude all identical lines above a certain length from the corpus. This is however somewhat unsatisfactory, as having multiple copies of the same subtitles does provide some information; the fact that several users have all chosen to transcribe a particular section of a movie in a certain way should increase our credence in the fact that it is both valid English and an accurate reflection of what was actually said. Another option might therefore be to alter the parameter determining the minimum number of times a particular alignment must occur to be included in the analysis. A more thorough investigation of the trade off between precision and recall, which can be altered both by varying this parameter and by invoking more or less strict word alignment algorithms, could be the subject of a further study.

It is reasonable to ask the question as to why the accuracy of VPC extraction is so high in comparison to other MWE types. A possible reason for this is that VPCs in one language, such as English, tend to be translated to a verb construction in another language, such as Spanish. They can thus said to be cross-linguistically consistent (although not in the stronger sense that a VPC always translates to a VPC – many languages indeed do not have VPCs). This is not true of all MWE types; in many cases complex constructions may be required to translate a certain type of MWE from one language to another. Another contributing factor may be that PoS taggers have good accuracy for verbs compared to other PoS categories, which makes the filtering process more precise.

5.2 Existence in Current Lexical Resources

One of the aims of this study was to show that subtitles data contain interesting VPCs that are rarely seen in other types of corpora, even those that contain a considerable number of idioms and slang expressions. Of the 94 validated VPCs from Section 5.1, 80 were found on either Dictionary.com or The Free Dictionary. 14 of the 100 randomly selected VPC candidates were thus valid previously undocumented VPCs (see Table 1), with a 95% confidence interval of $14 \pm 6.8\%$. This gives us a range of valid previously undocumented VPCs amongst the total 1424 extracted between 103 and 296.

beam up	make whole
clamber up	reach over
dance around	shorten up
grab up	single up
grill up	spin up
lift up	storm off
poke up	torch out

Table 1: The 14 validated VPCs that do not appear in either of the online resources.

Interestingly, nine of the 14 previously undocumented VPCs in the sample take the particle 'up', suggesting that this type of VPC may be particularly under-represented in lexical resources. This particle often adds an aspectual meaning to the verb in question, rather than creating a completely new idiomatic sense. That is certainly the case with several of the VPCs listed in Table 1; *shorten up*, *grab up* and *grill up*, for example, could be replaced by *shorten*, *grab* and *grill* respectively without a dramatic change in sense. This particle may therefore be somewhat more productive than the others observed in Table 1; *whole*, *out*, *over*, *around*, and *off* cannot be so freely added to verbs to make new VPCs.

5.3 Accuracy of Translations

The translations of 75 of the 94 validated VPCs from Section 5.1 were judged valid by a native Spanish speaker. This equates to a 95% confidence interval of $75 \pm 8.5\%$ of the original selection of 100 VPC candidates that are valid and have correct translations. As with the original list of English VPCs, there were some issues in the Spanish translations stemming from the lemmatiser. Certain verbs appeared in forms other than the infinitive; as before these mistakes were not punished in the evaluation. The point here was not to judge the quality of the lemmatisation, which was primarily used as a tool to simplify the evaluation.

The precision rate of $75 \pm 8.5\%$ obtained in this study is higher than the range 58.61–66.91% quoted in Caseli et al. (2010), though there is a small overlap of 0.41% (note that their range is bounded by the number of examples judged correct by two judges and those judged correct by only one of the judges, and is not a statistical confidence interval in the same sense). Their analysis again differs somewhat here, however, as they consider translations of many different types of MWE; they do not present an analysis of how this figure breaks down with different MWE types. The results presented here suggest that high precision rates can be achieved for VPC translations using this alignment method. Although the precision is a little lower than for VPC extraction, it is still likely to be practically quite useful in the creation of bilingual lexical resources for NLP tasks.

6 Discussion and Future Work

The methodology described in this paper consisted of four stages – PoS tagging, extraction, filtering and grouping. Analysis of false positive candidate VPCs extracted from the corpus demonstrated that improvements at various points along this pipeline could be effected to boost the final results. A common error at the first stage was prepositions being tagged as particles. It was always likely that PoS tagging on difficult data like subtitles would be less than perfect, and for this reason it is not surprising that errors of this nature arose. Training a PoS-tagger on labelled subtitles data, something which is not currently available, would be an obvious way to improve the accuracy here.

An important factor at the extraction stage was that some sections of the corpus were essentially duplicates of each other, due to the fact that there could be several user uploads of the same movie. This could lead to certain VPCs being validated despite being very rare in reality. A solution here might be to try to remove duplicates from the corpus, and there are several conceivable ways of doing this. One could impose a limit of one set of subtitles per movie, though this would require access to a version of the corpus with more information than that used in this study, and would raise the question of which version to choose, bearing in mind that both the English and Spanish subtitles may have several versions. A more brute method would be to directly remove duplicate lines from the corpus, that is to say all lines where both the English and Spanish are identical in every respect. A preliminary study (not shown here) shows that keeping all other parameters equal, this reduces the number of candidate VPC-translation pairs from 6833 to 3766 (a reduction of 45%), with a reduction in the number of unique VPCs from 1424 to 852 (a reduction of 40%). One would of course hope that the precision rate be higher amongst the candidate VPCs, though given the large reduction of candidates, the overall number of valid VPCs extracted would surely be lower. A lowering of the frequency threshold might therefore be required in order to extract more VPCs; a future study will look into this trade-off.

Another methodological choice made in this study was the order in which various parts of the methodology were carried out: grouping came after filtering in the four-stage process, but these could equally be switched. A preliminary study (not shown here) shows that applying the grouping algorithm before the frequency threshold increases the number of candidate VPCs to 12,945 (an increase of 89%), with 2052 unique VPCs (an increase of 44%). However, there is a corresponding decrease in precision from $94 \pm 4.7\%$ to $85 \pm 7.0\%$ (though the confidence intervals do overlap here). A more thorough investigation would be required to confirm this effect, and to test what happens to the number of previously undocumented VPCs and precision of translations.

The frequency threshold was set to five in this work: each candidate VPC had to appear at least five times in the same conjugation to be accepted. This number was chosen at the beginning of the study and never altered; it is clear however that it plays a big role in the final number of candidate VPCs and the precision rate therein. An interesting extension to this work would be to analyse the relationship between this threshold and precision: at what frequency level does the precision become acceptable? This could be analysed from both the point of view of VPC candidates and their translations: the level may not be the same for both. This would of course require a large amount of empirical evaluation that may be expensive and hard to carry out in practise. The highest frequency translations for each of the randomly selected VPC candidates were evaluated in this study; it would also be interesting to look at the precision rate for all translations. Caseli et al. (2010) found that the range of accurate translations reduced from 58.61–66.92% for the most frequent translations to 46.08–54.87% for all possible translations across a larger spectrum of MWEs.

The results presented in this study would be stronger if confirmed by other judges; the more the better but ideally at least three. It should be remembered however that the criteria for judging was whether the VPC candidate could in any circumstance be used as a genuine VPC. Only one positive example is required to prove this for each VPC candidate, and no number of negative examples proves the reverse. The difficulty for the judge is therefore not really that he or she will accidentally label an invalid candidate as valid, but the opposite: sometimes it is simply difficult to think up a valid phrase with the VPC in question, but once it appears in the mind of the judge he is certain that it is valid. The same can be true of translation: it may be difficult to think of a sense of the English VPC in which the Spanish verb is valid, even if that sense does exist. The results presented here can thus be viewed as a minimum: the addition of further judges is unlikely to lead to a reduction in precision, but could lead to an increase. One area where further evaluation could lead to less-impressive results is the number of undocumented VPCs. Validated VPCs were checked against two resources in this study: The Free Dictionary and Dictionary.com. It would be interesting to do further tests against other resources, such as the English Resource Grammar and Lexicon (www.delph-in.net/erg/).

This study did not consider recall, choosing instead to focus on precision and a comparison of extracted VPCs with existing resources. It would however be useful for many applications to have an idea of the percentage of VPCs in the corpus that end up in the final list, although a full analysis would require a labelled subtitles corpus. Caseli et al. (2010) present a method to estimate recall when a labelled corpus is not available. Generally speaking however it can be assumed that the normal inverse relation between precision and recall holds here. The exact dynamic of this relation can be adjusted in the filtering process: by letting VPCs with lower frequency through recall is bound to increase, but at the same time reduce the high levels of precision as more false positives end up in the final list. The balance between precision and recall can also be adjusted during the alignment process; the effect this would have on VPC extraction is unclear. An evaluation of this effect could be carried out by re-running the study using each of the different alignment tables provided with the OpenSubtitles corpus.

Only one language pair was considered in this study, namely English and Spanish. Pichotta and DeNero (2013) have shown that combining information from many languages – albeit in conjunction with a different extraction method – can improve VPC extraction accuracy. One way to further increase the precision achieved via the alignment methods in this study may be to use a similar combination technique. The latest version of the OpenSubtitles corpus contains 59 different languages, and this multitude of data could potentially be put to better use to obtain yet more VPCs. The choice of English and Spanish is also relevant via the fact that English has VPCs while Spanish does not – this may be an important factor. Whether better results could be obtained using two languages with VPCs, such as English and German, for example, is another interesting question that may be the subject of a follow up study.

7 Conclusions

This study has demonstrated that word alignment methods and a PoS tag based filter on a large parallel subtitles corpus can be used to achieve high precision extraction of VPCs and their translations. Despite the difficulties associated with the corpus type, which hinder both the tagging and the word alignment processes, a precision of $94 \pm 4.7\%$ was found for the extraction of valid English VPCs from a parallel corpus in English and Spanish. $14 \pm 6.8\%$ of the extracted VPC candidates were both valid and previously undocumented in two large online resources, while several more appeared in unusual dialectal forms, highlighting the unique nature of the corpus type. Analysing the Spanish translations extracted along with the VPCs, $75 \pm 8.5\%$ were judged valid by a native Spanish speaker. This represents a large increase in precision over similar previous studies, highlighting the benefits of focusing on VPCs rather than a larger range of MWE types.

Acknowledgements

This work benefited greatly from discussions with my fellow students on the Language Technology: Research and Development course at Uppsala University. I am particularly grateful to Nina Schottmüller and Marie Dubremetz for their detailed suggestions, and our teacher Joakim Nivre for his significant input to this paper. I would also like to thank the three anonymous reviewers for their valuable feedback.

References

H. M. Caseli, C. Ramisch, M. G. V. Nunes, and A. Villavicencio. 2010. Alignment-based extraction of multiword expressions. *Language Resources & Evaluation*, 44:59–77.

N. Chatterjee and R. Balyan. 2011. Context Resolution of Verb Particle Constructions for English to Hindi Translation. *25th Pacific Asia Conference on Language, Information and Computation*, 140–149.

M. Constant and J. Le Roux and A. Signone. 2013. Combining Compound Recognition and PCFG-LA

Parsing with Word Lattices and Conditional Random Fields. In *ACM Transactions on Speech and Language Processing*, 10(3).

A. Copestake, F. Lambeau, A. Villavicencio, F. Bond, T. Baldwin, I. Sag, and D. Flickinger. 2002. Multiword expressions: linguistic precision and reusability. In *Proceedings of LREC*, 1941–1947.

C. M. Darwin and L. S. Gray. 1999. Going After the Phrasal Verb: An Alternative Approach to Classification. *TESOL Quarterly*, 33(1).

S. Greenbaum and R. Quirk. 1990. *A Student's Grammar of the English Language*. Pearson Education Limited, Harlow, UK.

S. N. Kim and T. Baldwin. 2010. How to pick out token instances of English verb-particle constructions. *Language Resources & Evaluation*, 44:97–113.

B. Levin. 1993. *English Verb Classes and Alternations – A Preliminary Investigation*. The Chicago Press.

Z. Liu, H. Wang, H. Wu, and S. Li. 2011. Two-Word Collocation Extraction Using Monolingual Word Alignment Method. In *ACM Transactions on Intelligent Systems and Technology*, 3(487–495).

F. J. Och and H. Ney. 2000. Improved Statistical Alignment Models. In *Proceedings of the 38th Annual Meeting of the ACL*, 440–447.

F. J. Och and H. Ney. 2003. A Systematic Comparison of Various Statistical Alignment Models. *Computational Linguistics*, 29(19–51).

K. Pichotta and J. DeNero. 2013. Identifying Phrasal Verbs Using Many Bilingual Corpora. In *Proceedings of the 2013 Conference on Empirical Methods in Natural Language Processing*, 636–646.

H. Schmid. 1994. Probabilistic Part-of-Speech Tagging Using Decision Trees. In *Proceedings of International Conference on New Methods in Language Processing*, Manchester, UK.

J. Tiedemann. 2012. Parallel Data, Tools, and Interfaces in OPUS. In *Proceedings of the 8th International Conference on Language Resources and Evaluation (LREC 2012)*, 2214–2218.

B. Villada Moirón and J. Tiedemann. 2006. Identifying Idiomatic Expressions using Automatic Word-Alignment. In *Proceedings of the Workshop on Multi-Word-Expressions in a Multilingual Context (EACL-2006)*, 33–40.

A. Villavicencio. 2005. The availability of verb particle constructions in lexical resources: How much is enough? *Computer Speech And Language*, 19:415–432.

S. Zarriess and J. Kuhn. 2009. Exploiting Translational Correspondences for Pattern-Independent MWE Identication. In *Proceedings of the Workshop on Multiword Expressions*, Suntec, Singapore 23–30

A Supervised Model for Extraction of Multiword Expressions Based on Statistical Context Features

Meghdad Farahmand
The Computer Science Center
University of Geneva
Switzerland
meghdad.farahmand@unige.ch

Ronaldo Martins
UNDL Foundation
Geneva - Switzerland
r.martins@undl.ch

Abstract

We present a method for extracting Multiword Expressions (MWEs) based on the immediate context they occur in, using a supervised model. We show some of these contextual features can be very discriminant and combining them with MWE-specific features results in a relatively accurate extraction. We define context as a sequential structure and not a bag of words, consequently, it becomes much more informative about MWEs.

1 Introduction

Multiword Expressions (MWEs) are an important research topic in the area of Natural Language Processing (NLP). Efficient and effective extraction and interpretation of MWEs is crucial in most NLP tasks. They exist in many types of text and cause major problems in all kinds of natural language processing applications (Sag et al., 2002). However, identifying and lexicalizing these important but hard to identify structures need to be improved in most major computational lexicons (Calzolari et al., 2002). Jackendoff (1997) estimates that the number of MWEs is equal to the number of single words in a speaker's lexicon, while Sag et al. (2002) believe that the number is even greater than this. Moreover, as a language evolves, the number of MWEs consistently increases. MWEs are a powerful way of extending languages' lexicons. Their role in language evolution is so important that according to Baldwin and Kim (2010), "It is highly doubtful that any language would evolve without MWEs of some description".

The efficient identification and extraction of MWEs can positively influence many other NLP tasks, e.g., part of speech tagging, parsing, syntactic disambiguation, semantic tagging, machine translation, and natural language generation. MWEs also have important applications outside NLP. For instance in document indexing, information retrieval (Acosta et al., 2011), and cross lingual information retrieval (Hull and Grefenstette, 1996).

In this paper we present a method of extracting MWEs which is relatively different from most of the state of the art approaches. We characterize MWEs based on the statistical properties of the immediate context they occur in. For each possible MWE candidate we define a set of contextual features (e.g., prefixes, suffixes, etc.). The contextual feature vector is then enriched with a few MWE-specific features such as the frequency of its components, type frequency of the candidate MWE, and the association between these two (which is learned by a supervised model). Subsequently the MWEhood of the extracted candidates is predicted based on this feature representation, using a Support Vector Machine (SVM). The system reaches a relatively high accuracy of predicting MWEs on unseen data.

1.1 Previous Work

Attempts to extract MWEs are of different types. The most common techniques are primarily focused on collocations. Some of these techniques are rule-based and symbolic e.g., (Seretan, 2011; Goldman et al., 2001; Nerima et al., 2003; Baldwin, 2005; Piao et al., 2003; McCarthy et al., 2003; Jacquemin et al., 1997). Some rely on lexicons (Michiels and Dufour, 1998; Li et al., 2003) and (Pearce, 2001) that uses WordNet to evaluate the candidate MWE based on anti-collocations. Other approaches are hybrid in the sense that they benefit from both statistical and linguistic information. For instance (Seretan and Wehrli, 2006; Baldwin and Villavicencio, 2002; Piao and McEnery, 2001; Dias, 2003).

There are also fully statistical approaches. For instance (Pecina, 2010; Evert, 2005; Lapata and

Lascarides, 2003; Smadja et al., 1996), or the early work **Xtract** (Smadja, 1993).

Other approaches consider all types of MWEs (Zhang et al., 2006). Some of these approaches build upon generic properties of MWEs, for instance semantic non-compositionality (Van de Cruys and Moirón, 2007).

A different approach is presented in (Widdows and Dorow, 2005). The authors present a graph-based model to capture and assess fixed expressions in form of *Noun and/or Noun*.

There are also bilingual models which are mostly based on the assumption that a translation of the MWE in a source language exists in a target language. For instance (de Medeiros Caseli et al., 2010; Ren et al., 2009), and (Moirón and Tiedemann, 2006) which measures MWEs candidates' idiomaticity based on translational entropy. Another example is (Duan et al., 2009) which is a hybrid model that aims at extracting bilingual (English-Chinese) MWEs . It combines Multiple Sequence Alignment Model with some filtering based on hard rules to obtain an improved extraction.

A more generic model is presented in (Ramisch, 2012) where the author develops a flexible platform that can accept different types of criteria (from statistical to deep linguistic) in order to extract and filter MWEs. However, in this work, as the author claims, the quality of the extracted MWEs is highly dependent on the level of deep linguistic analysis, and thereby, the role of statistical criterion is less significant.

1.2 Motivation

We propose an original method to extract multiword expressions based on statistical contextual features, e.g., a set of immediate prefixes, suffixes, circumfixes, infixes to circumfixes, etc., (see Sec. 2). These features are used to form a feature representation, which together with a set of annotations train a supervised model in order to predict and extract MWEs from a large corpus.

We observed some discriminant behavior in contextual features (such as prefixes, suffixes, circumfixes, etc.) of a set of manually selected MWEs. A supervised model is then applied to learn MWEhood based on these features.

In general, modeling lexical and syntactic (and not semantic) characteristics of continuous MWEs is the focus of this paper. In order for the MWE decomposability condition to hold, we consider bigrams and above (up to size 4). Idiomaticity at some level is a necessary prerequisite of MWEs. Hereby, we consider idiomaticity at lexical, syntactic and statistical levels, and leave the semantic idiomaticity to the future work.

Relatively similar models have been previously applied to problems similar to MWEs, for instance named entity recognition (Nadeau and Sekine, 2007; Ratinov and Roth, 2009).

The focus on contextual features allows some degree of generalization, i.e., we can apply this model to a family of languages.[1] However, this work focuses only on English MWEs.

2 Proposed System

We prepared a corpus that comprises 100K Wikipedia documents for each of the mentioned languages.[1] After cleaning and segmenting the corpus, we extracted all possible n-grams (up to size 7) and their token and type frequencies. Then two basic statistical filters were applied in order to systematically decrease the size of our immense n-gram set: (i) *Frequency* filter, where we filter an n-gram if its frequency is less than the ratio between *tokens* and *types*, where for a given size of n-grams, the total number of n-grams and the number of distinct n-grams of that size, are considered *tokens* and *types*, respectively. (ii) *Redundancy* filter where we consider an n-gram to be redundant if it is subsumed by any other n'-gram, where $n' > n$. This gives us a pruned set of n-grams which we refer to as the *statistically significant* set. Table 1 presents a count-wise description of the filtering results on the English corpus.

	raw	frq flt	rdund flt
1-grams	1782993	64204	64204
2-grams	14573453	1117784	1085787
3-grams	38749315	3797456	3394414
4-grams	53023415	5409794	3850944
5-grams	53191941	2812650	2324912
6-grams	47249534	1384821	568645
7-grams	39991254	757606	757606

[1]We are adapting our model so that it can handle clusters of similar languages. So far we have processed the following 9 widely-spoken languages: English, German, Dutch, Spanish, French, Italian, Portuguese, Polish, and Russian. However, to study the efficiency of the presented model applied to languages other than English, remains a future work.

Table 1: Number of extracted n-grams for EN. First column indicates raw data, second and third columns indicate the number of n-grams after frequency and redundancy filters respectively.

For the set of significant n-grams a set of statistical features are extracted which will be described shortly. Fig. 1 illustrates the workflow of the system.

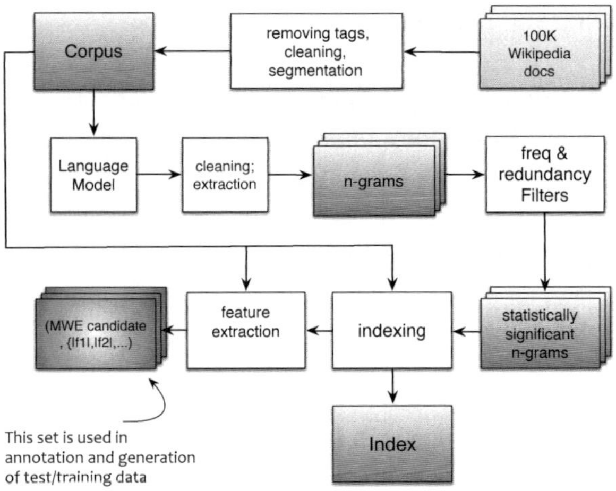

Figure 1: Schematic of pre-processing, n-gram extraction and filtering. Blended and plain nodes represent resources, and operations respectively.

While studying the English corpus and different MWEs therein, it was observed that often, MWEs (as well as some other types of syntactic units) are followed, preceded or surrounded by a limited number of high frequency significant n-gram types. Moreover, our manual evaluation and constituency tests reveal that generally when a frequent significant prefix co-occurs with a frequent significant suffix, they form a circumfix whose significant infixes are (i) many, (ii) can mostly be considered syntactic unit, specifically when it comes to bi/trigrams. Table 2 illustrates a randomly selected sample of infixes of such circumfix (*the..of*). Remarkably, the majority of them are idiomatic at least at one level.

franz liszt academy	official list
most important albums	closest relatives
ministry of commerce	protestant church
executive vice president	peak period
famous italian architect	manhattan school
blessed virgin mary	rise and fall
world cup winner	former head

Table 2: Examples of bi/trigrams surrounded by the circumfix *the..of*

The immediate proximity of these particular context features to MWEs keeps emerging while evaluating similar circumfixes. We believe it suggests the presence of a discriminant attribute that we model with features 5-8 (see Table 3) and learn using a supervised model. Nevertheless, the fact that MWEs share these features with other types of syntactic units encourages introducing more MWE-specific features (namely, MWE's frequency, the frequency of its components, and their associations), then enforcing the learning model to recognize a MWE based on the combination of these two types of features. Note that the association between the type frequency of a MWE, and the frequency of its components is implicitly learned by the supervised model throughout the learning phase. A candidate MWE can be represented as:

$$\mathbf{y} = (x_1, ..., x_m, x_{m+1}, ..., x_n) \in \mathbb{N}_0 \quad (1)$$

Where $x_1, ..., x_m$ are *contextual*, and $x_{m+1}, ..., x_n$ are *specific* features ($m = 8$, and $n = 11$). These features are described in Table 3.

	contextual features
x_1	# set of all possible prefixes of **y**
x_2	# set of distinct prefixes of **y**
x_3	# set of all possible suffixes of **y**
x_4	# set of distinct suffixes of **y**
x_5	# set of all possible circumfixes of **y**
x_6	# set of distinct circumfixes of **y** (**C**)
x_7	# set of all possible infixes to members of **C**
x_8	# set of distinct infixes to members of **C**
	specific features
x_9	the size of **y**
x_{10}	number of occurrences of **y** in the corpus
x_{11}	list of frequencies of the components of **y**

Table 3: Description of the extracted features

A prefix of $\mathbf{y}$ is the longest n-gram immediately before $\mathbf{y}$, if any or the boundary marker #, otherwise. A suffix of $\mathbf{y}$ is the longest n-gram immediately after $\mathbf{y}$, if any or the boundary marker #, otherwise. A circumfix ($c_i \in \mathbf{C}$) of $\mathbf{y}$ is the pair (p, s) where p and s are respectively the prefix and the suffix of a given occurrence of $\mathbf{y}$. An Infix of c_i is an n-gram that occurs between p and s.

Components to generate candidate MWEs, filter them and extract their relevant features were very memory and CPU intensive. To address the performance issues we implemented parallel programs and ran them on a high performance cluster.

3 Experimental Results

A set of $\approx$ 10K negative and positive English MWE examples were annotated. This set does not particularly belong in any specific genre, as the examples were chosen randomly from across a general-purpose corpus. This set comprises an equal number of positive and negative annotations. Part of it was annotated manually at UNDL foundation,[2] and part of it was acquired from the manually examined MWE lexicon presented in (Nerima et al., 2003). The set of positive and negative annotated n-grams is detailed in Table 4. The bias toward bigrams is due to the fact that the majority of manually verified MWEs that could be obtained are bigrams.

size	+ examples	− examples
2-grams	4,632	5,173
3-grams	500	22
4-grams	68	15

Table 4: Annotations' statistics

This set was divided into 1/3 test and 2/3 training data, which were selected randomly but were evenly distributed with respect to positive and negative examples. The test set remains completely unseen to the model during the learning phase. We then train a linear SVM:

$$h(y) = \mathbf{w}^{\mathsf{T}}\,\mathbf{y} + b \qquad (2)$$

Where $h(y)$ is a discriminant hyperplane, $\mathbf{w}$ is the weight vector, and $\mathbf{y}$ is a set of MWE examples, where each example is defined as: $\mathbf{y}_j = x_1, ..., x_{11}$. Table 5 shows the results of the model's multiple runs on five different pairs of training and test sets.

[2]The Universal Networking Digital Language Foundation: http://www.undlfoundation.org/

	precision (%)	recall (%)	accuracy(%)
run 1	84.8	96.8	89.7
run 2	82.5	97.4	88.4
run 3	83.6	97.8	89.3
run 4	84.1	97.5	89.5
run 5	83.4	97.1	88.9

Table 5: Performance of the SVM which learns the MWEhood based on contextual and specific features ($x_1 - x_{11}$)

Table 6 illustrates the trained model's predictions on a set of randomly selected test examples. The overall performance of the model is shown in the form of a precision-recall curve in Fig. 2.

n-grams classified as MWE	
spend time	genetically modified
hijack a plane	fish tank
top dog	toy car
factory outlet	motorcycle racing
season nine	vintage car
video conference	chestnut tree
kill your	entry fee
safety precaution	quantum leap
version shown	make an appeal
flood damage	drug dealer
bargaining chip	lung transplant
grant her	tone like
postgraduate student	make a phone call
raise the price	ozone layer
n-grams classified as non-MWE	
score is	and dartmouth
the tabular	capped a
on sale	clarified his
liver was	the cancan
the regulating	an ending
the rabi	warns the
this manuscript	a few
an exponential	an institution
the petal	blades are
or ended	difficulties he
and workmen	the guidance
the eyelids	the examined
the vices	the episodes
they work	monument is

Table 6: Sample SVM's output on unseen data.

A t-test ranks the significance of the defined features in classifying n-grams into MWE, and non-MWE classes, as illustrated in Fig. 3. The most

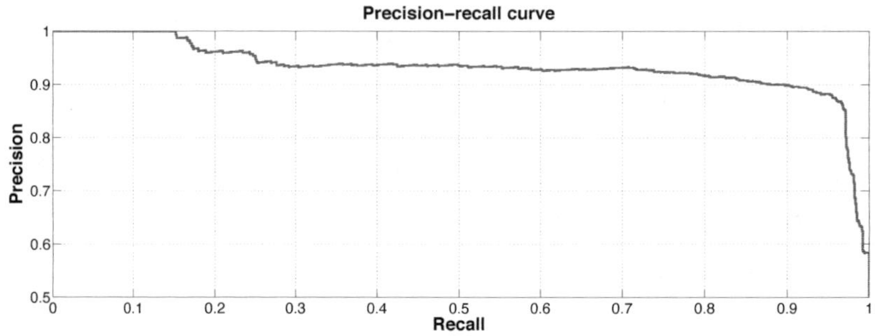

Figure 2: Precision-recall curve

important features are the size of examples (x_9), and the frequencies of their components (x_{11}). The significance of x_9 is due to the fact that in the training set majority of MWEs are bigrams. Therefore, by the SVM, being a bigram is considered as a substantial feature of MWEs. Nevertheless since the number of negative and positive examples which are bigrams are approximately the same, the bias toward x_9 in discriminating MWEs from non-MWE balances out. However its association with other features which is implicitly learned still has an impact on discriminating these two classes. x_7 and x_8 are the next two important features, as we expected. These two are the features whose magnitude suggests the presence or lack of contexts such as (*the..of*).

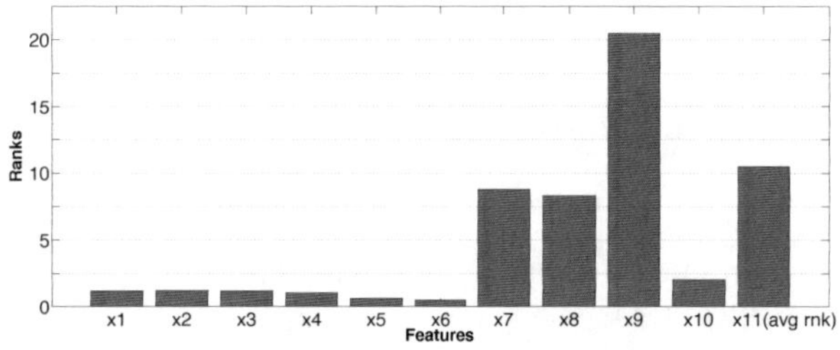

Figure 3: Ranks of the features that represent their discriminant impact.

The class separability of MWE (1), and non-MWE (-1) examples can be seen in Fig. 4, where the bidimentional projection of the examples of two classes is visualized. A star plot of a sample of 50 manually annotated examples is shown in Fig. 5. In many cases, but not always, non-MWEs can be discriminated from MWEs, in this eleven dimensional visualization. Same pattern was observed in the visualization of 500 examples (which would be hard to demonstrate in the present paper's scale).

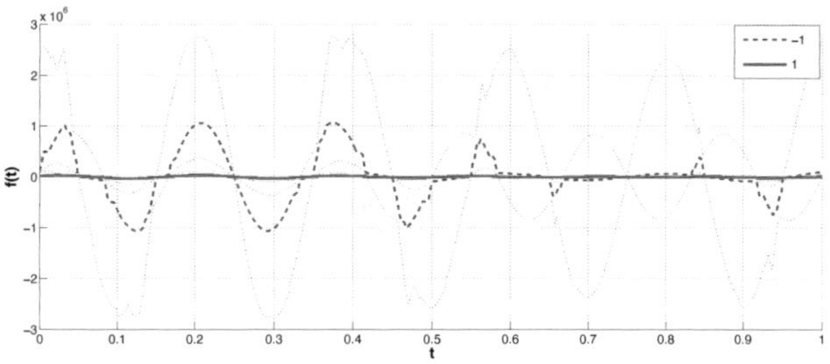

Figure 4: Andrews curve for the training examples. Bold line in the middle, and bold dotted line represent the median of MWE and non-MWE classes respectively.

4 Conclusions and Future Work

We presented a method to extract MWEs based on the immediate context they occur in, using a supervised model. Several contextual features were extracted from a large corpus. The size of the corpus had a profound effect on the effectiveness of these features. The presented MWE extraction model reaches a relatively high accuracy on an unseen test set. In future work, the efficiency of this approach on languages other than English will be studied. Furthermore, other features - specifically deep linguistic ones e.g., degree of constituency as described in (Ponvert et al., 2011) or POS tags, will be added to the feature representation of MWE candidates. Finally context-based probabilistic scores which are linguistically motivated can be investigated and compared with the supervised model. Another interesting work would be to introduce kernels so that we can go from statistics of contextual features to training the supervised model directly on the textual context.

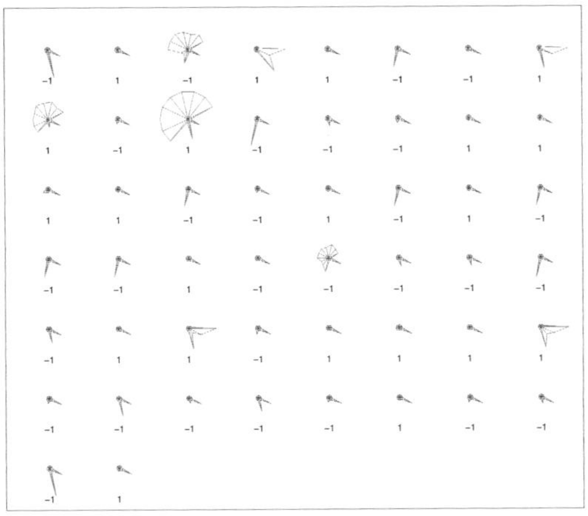

Figure 5: Star plot of 50 MWE (1), and non-MWE (−1) examples

References

Otavio Acosta, Aline Villavicencio, and Viviane Moreira. 2011. Identification and treatment of multiword expressions applied to information retrieval. *Kordoni et al*, pages 101–109.

Timothy Baldwin and Su Nam Kim. 2010. Multiword expressions. *Handbook of Natural Language Processing, second edition. Morgan and Claypool.*

Timothy Baldwin and Aline Villavicencio. 2002. Extracting the unextractable: A case study on verb-particles. In *proceedings of the 6th conference on Natural language learning-Volume 20*, pages 1–7. Association for Computational Linguistics.

Timothy Baldwin. 2005. Deep lexical acquisition of verb–particle constructions. *Computer Speech & Language*, 19(4):398–414.

Nicoletta Calzolari, Charles J Fillmore, Ralph Grishman, Nancy Ide, Alessandro Lenci, Catherine MacLeod, and Antonio Zampolli. 2002. Towards best practice for multiword expressions in computational lexicons. In *LREC*.

Helena de Medeiros Caseli, Carlos Ramisch, Maria das Graças Volpe Nunes, and Aline Villavicencio. 2010. Alignment-based extraction of multiword expressions. *Language resources and evaluation*, 44(1-2):59–77.

Gaël Dias. 2003. Multiword unit hybrid extraction. In *Proceedings of the ACL 2003 workshop on Multiword expressions: analysis, acquisition and treatment-Volume 18*, pages 41–48. Association for Computational Linguistics.

Jianyong Duan, Mei Zhang, Lijing Tong, and Feng Guo. 2009. A hybrid approach to improve bilingual multiword expression extraction. In *Advances in Knowledge Discovery and Data Mining*, pages 541–547. Springer.

Stefan Evert. 2005. *The statistics of word cooccurrences*. Ph.D. thesis, Dissertation, Stuttgart University.

Jean-Philippe Goldman, Luka Nerima, and Eric Wehrli. 2001. Collocation extraction using a syntactic parser. In *Proceedings of the ACL Workshop on Collocations*, pages 61–66.

David A Hull and Gregory Grefenstette. 1996. Querying across languages: a dictionary-based approach to multilingual information retrieval. In *Proceedings of the 19th annual international ACM SIGIR conference on Research and development in information retrieval*, pages 49–57. ACM.

Ray Jackendoff. 1997. *The architecture of the language faculty*. Number 28. MIT Press.

Christian Jacquemin, Judith L Klavans, and Evelyne Tzoukermann. 1997. Expansion of multi-word terms for indexing and retrieval using morphology and syntax. In *Proceedings of the eighth conference on European chapter of the Association for Computational Linguistics*, pages 24–31. Association for Computational Linguistics.

Mirella Lapata and Alex Lascarides. 2003. Detecting novel compounds: The role of distributional evidence. In *Proceedings of the tenth conference on European chapter of the Association for Computational Linguistics-Volume 1*, pages 235–242. Association for Computational Linguistics.

Wei Li, Xiuhong Zhang, Cheng Niu, Yuankai Jiang, and Rohini Srihari. 2003. An expert lexicon approach to identifying english phrasal verbs. In *Proceedings of the 41st Annual Meeting on Association for Computational Linguistics-Volume 1*, pages 513–520. Association for Computational Linguistics.

Diana McCarthy, Bill Keller, and John Carroll. 2003. Detecting a continuum of compositionality in phrasal verbs. In *Proceedings of the ACL 2003 workshop on Multiword expressions: analysis, acquisition and treatment-Volume 18*, pages 73–80. Association for Computational Linguistics.

Archibald Michiels and Nicolas Dufour. 1998. Defi, a tool for automatic multi-word unit recognition, meaning assignment and translation selection. In *Proceedings of the first international conference on language resources & evaluation*, pages 1179–1186.

Begona Villada Moirón and Jörg Tiedemann. 2006. Identifying idiomatic expressions using automatic word-alignment. In *Proceedings of the EACL 2006 Workshop on Multi-wordexpressions in a multilingual context*, pages 33–40.

David Nadeau and Satoshi Sekine. 2007. A survey of named entity recognition and classification. *Lingvisticae Investigationes*, 30(1):3–26.

Luka Nerima, Violeta Seretan, and Eric Wehrli. 2003. Creating a multilingual collocation dictionary from large text corpora. In *Proceedings of the tenth conference on European chapter of the Association for Computational Linguistics-Volume 2*, pages 131–134. Association for Computational Linguistics.

Darren Pearce. 2001. Synonymy in collocation extraction. In *Proceedings of the Workshop on WordNet and Other Lexical Resources, Second meeting of the North American Chapter of the Association for Computational Linguistics*, pages 41–46. Citeseer.

Pavel Pecina. 2010. Lexical association measures and collocation extraction. *Language resources and evaluation*, 44(1-2):137–158.

Scott Songlin Piao and Tony McEnery. 2001. Multiword unit alignment in english-chinese parallel corpora. In *the Proceedings of the Corpus Linguistics 2001*, pages 466–475.

Scott SL Piao, Paul Rayson, Dawn Archer, Andrew Wilson, and Tony McEnery. 2003. Extracting multiword expressions with a semantic tagger. In *Proceedings of the ACL 2003 workshop on Multiword expressions: analysis, acquisition and treatment-Volume 18*, pages 49–56. Association for Computational Linguistics.

Elias Ponvert, Jason Baldridge, and Katrin Erk. 2011. Simple unsupervised grammar induction from raw text with cascaded finite state models. In *ACL*, pages 1077–1086.

Carlos Ramisch. 2012. A generic framework for multiword expressions treatment: from acquisition to applications. In *Proceedings of ACL 2012 Student Research Workshop*, pages 61–66. Association for Computational Linguistics.

Lev Ratinov and Dan Roth. 2009. Design challenges and misconceptions in named entity recognition. In *Proceedings of the Thirteenth Conference on Computational Natural Language Learning*, pages 147–155. Association for Computational Linguistics.

Zhixiang Ren, Yajuan Lü, Jie Cao, Qun Liu, and Yun Huang. 2009. Improving statistical machine translation using domain bilingual multiword expressions. In *Proceedings of the Workshop on Multiword Expressions: Identification, Interpretation, Disambiguation and Applications*, pages 47–54. Association for Computational Linguistics.

Ivan A Sag, Timothy Baldwin, Francis Bond, Ann Copestake, and Dan Flickinger. 2002. Multiword expressions: A pain in the neck for NLP. In *Computational Linguistics and Intelligent Text Processing*, pages 1–15. Springer.

Violeta Seretan and Eric Wehrli. 2006. Accurate collocation extraction using a multilingual parser. In *Proceedings of the 21st International Conference on Computational Linguistics and the 44th annual meeting of the Association for Computational Linguistics*, pages 953–960. Association for Computational Linguistics.

Violeta Seretan. 2011. *Syntax-based collocation extraction*, volume 44. Springer.

Frank Smadja, Kathleen R McKeown, and Vasileios Hatzivassiloglou. 1996. Translating collocations for bilingual lexicons: A statistical approach. *Computational linguistics*, 22(1):1–38.

Frank Smadja. 1993. Retrieving collocations from text: Xtract. *Computational linguistics*, 19(1):143–177.

Tim Van de Cruys and Begona Villada Moirón. 2007. Semantics-based multiword expression extraction. In *Proceedings of the Workshop on a Broader Perspective on Multiword Expressions*, pages 25–32. Association for Computational Linguistics.

Dominic Widdows and Beate Dorow. 2005. Automatic extraction of idioms using graph analysis and asymmetric lexicosyntactic patterns. In *Proceedings of the ACL-SIGLEX Workshop on Deep Lexical Acquisition*, pages 48–56. Association for Computational Linguistics.

Yi Zhang, Valia Kordoni, Aline Villavicencio, and Marco Idiart. 2006. Automated multiword expression prediction for grammar engineering. In *Proceedings of the Workshop on Multiword Expressions: Identifying and Exploiting Underlying Properties*, pages 36–44. Association for Computational Linguistics.

VPCTagger: Detecting Verb-Particle Constructions With Syntax-Based Methods

István Nagy T.[1] and **Veronika Vincze**[1,2]
[1]Department of Informatics, University of Szeged
Árpád tér 2., 6720 Szeged, Hungary
nistvan@inf.u-szeged.hu
[2]Hungarian Academy of Sciences, Research Group on Artificial Intelligence
Tisza Lajos krt. 103., 6720 Szeged, Hungary
vinczev@inf.u-szeged.hu

Abstract

Verb-particle combinations (VPCs) consist of a verbal and a preposition/particle component, which often have some additional meaning compared to the meaning of their parts. If a data-driven morphological parser or a syntactic parser is trained on a dataset annotated with extra information for VPCs, they will be able to identify VPCs in raw texts. In this paper, we examine how syntactic parsers perform on this task and we introduce VPCTagger, a machine learning-based tool that is able to identify English VPCs in context. Our method consists of two steps: it first selects VPC candidates on the basis of syntactic information and then selects genuine VPCs among them by exploiting new features like semantic and contextual ones. Based on our results, we see that VPCTagger outperforms state-of-the-art methods in the VPC detection task.

1 Introduction

Verb-particle constructions (VPCs) are a subclass of multiword expressions (MWEs) that contain more than one meaningful tokens but the whole unit exhibits syntactic, semantic or pragmatic idiosyncracies (Sag et al., 2002). VPCs consist of a verb and a preposition/particle (like *hand in* or *go out*) and they are very characteristic of the English language. The particle modifies the meaning of the verb: it may add aspectual information, may refer to motion or location or may totally change the meaning of the expression. Thus, the meaning of VPCs can be compositional, i.e. it can be computed on the basis of the meaning of the verb and the particle (*go out*) or it can be idiomatic; i.e. a combination of the given verb and particle results in a(n unexpected) new meaning (*do in* "kill"). Moreover, as their syntactic surface structure is very similar to verb – prepositional phrase combinations, it is not straightforward to determine whether a given verb + preposition/particle combination functions as a VPC or not and contextual information plays a very important role here. For instance, compare the following examples: *The hitman* ***did in*** *the president* and *What he* ***did in*** *the garden was unbelievable*. Both sentences contain the sequence *did in*, but it is only in the first sentence where it functions as a VPC and in the second case, it is a simple verb-prepositional phrase combination. For these reasons, VPCs are of great interest for natural language processing applications like machine translation or information extraction, where it is necessary to grab the meaning of the text.

The special relation of the verb and particle within a VPC is often distinctively marked at several annotation layers in treebanks. For instance, in the Penn Treebank, the particle is assigned a specific part of speech tag (RP) and it also has a specific syntactic label (PRT) (Marcus et al., 1993), see also Figure 1. This entails that if a data-driven morphological parser or a syntactic parser is trained on a dataset annotated with extra information for VPCs, it will be able to assign these kind of tags as well. In other words, the morphological/syntactic parser itself will be able to identify VPCs in texts.

In this paper, we seek to identify VPCs on the basis of syntactic information. We first examine how syntactic parsers perform on Wiki50 (Vincze et al., 2011), a dataset manually annotated for different types of MWEs, including VPCs. We then present our syntax-based tool called VPCTagger to identify VPCs, which consists of two steps: first, we select VPC candidates (i.e. verb-preposition/particle pairs) from the text and then we apply a machine learning-based technique to classify them as genuine VPCs or not. This

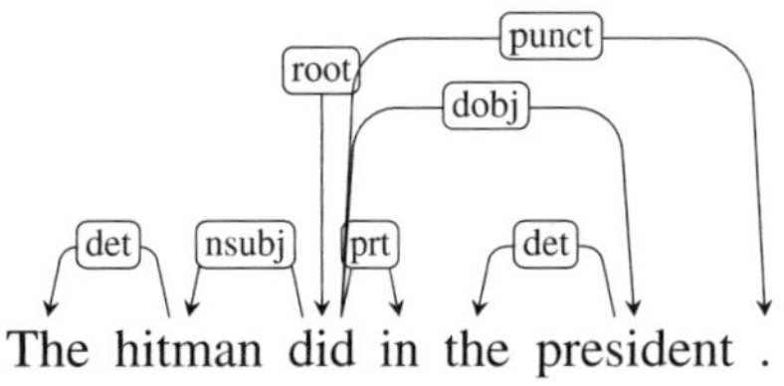

Figure 1: A dependency parse of the sentence "The hitman did in the president".

method is based on a rich feature set with new features like semantic or contextual features. We compare the performance of the parsers with that of our approach and we discuss the reasons for any possible differences.

2 Related Work

Recently, some studies have attempted to identify VPCs. For instance, Baldwin and Villavicencio (2002) detected verb-particle constructions in raw texts with the help of information based on POS-tagging and chunking, and they also made use of frequency and lexical information in their classifier. Kim and Baldwin (2006) built their system on semantic information when deciding whether verb-preposition pairs were verb-particle constructions or not. Nagy T. and Vincze (2011) implemented a rule-based system based on morphological features to detect VPCs in raw texts.

The (non-)compositionality of verb-particle combinations has also raised interest among researchers. McCarthy et al. (2003) implemented a method to determine the compositionality of VPCs and Baldwin (2005) presented a dataset in which non-compositional VPCs could be found. Villavicencio (2003) proposed some methods to extend the coverage of available VPC resources.

Tu and Roth (2012) distinguished genuine VPCs and verb-preposition combinations in context. They built a crowdsourced corpus of VPC candidates in context, where each candidate was manually classified as a VPC or not. However, during corpus building, they applied lexical restrictions and concentrated only on VPCs formed with six verbs. Their SVM-based algorithm used syntactic and lexical features to classify VPCs candidates and they concluded that their system achieved good results on idiomatic VPCs, but the classification of more compositional VPCs is more challenging.

Since in this paper we focus on syntax-based VPC identification more precisely, we also identify VPCs with syntactic parsers, it seems necessary to mention studies that experimented with parsers for identifying different types of MWEs. For instance, constituency parsing models were employed in identifying contiguous MWEs in French and Arabic (Green et al., 2013). Their method relied on a syntactic treebank, an MWE list and a morphological analyzer. Vincze et al. (2013) employed a dependency parser for identifying light verb constructions in Hungarian texts as a "side effect" of parsing sentences and report state-of-the-art results for this task.

Here, we make use of parsers trained on the Penn Treebank (which contains annotation for VPCs) and we evaluate their performance on the Wiki50 corpus, which was manually annotated for VPCs. Thus, we first examine how well these parsers identify VPCs (i.e. assigning VPC-specific syntactic labels) and then we present how VPCTagger can carry out this task. First, we select VPC candidates from raw text and then, we classify them as genuine VPCs or not.

3 Verb-particle Constructions in English

As mentioned earlier, verb-particle constructions consist of a verb and a particle. Similar constructions are present in several languages, although there might be different grammatical or orthographic norms for such verbs in those languages. For instance, in German and in Hungarian, the particle usually precedes the verb and they are spelt as one word, e.g. *aufmachen* (up.make) "to open" in German or *kinyitni* (out.open) "to open" in Hungarian. On the other hand, languages like Swedish, Norwegian, Icelandic and Italian follow the same pattern as English; namely, the verb precedes the particle and they are spelt as two words (Masini, 2005). These two typological classes require different approaches if we would like identify VPCs. For the first group, morphology-based solutions can be implemented that can identify the internal structure of compound words. For the second group, syntax-based methods can also be successful, which take into account the syntactic relation between the verb and the particle.

Many of the VPCs are formed with a motion verb and a particle denoting directions (like *go out*, *come in* etc.) and their meaning reflects this: they denote a motion or location. The meaning of VPCs belonging to this group is usually transparent and thus they can be easily learnt by second language learners. In other cases, the particle adds some aspectual information to the meaning of the verb: *eat up* means "to consume totally" or *burn out* means "to reach a state where someone becomes exhausted". These VPCs still have a compositional meaning, but the particle has a non-directional function here, but rather an aspectual one (cf. Jackendoff (2002)). Yet other VPCs have completely idiomatic meanings like *do up* "repair" or *do in* "kill". In the latter cases, the meaning of the construction cannot be computed from the meaning of the parts, hence they are problematic for both language learners and NLP applications.

Tu and Roth (2012) distinguish between two sets of VPCs in their database: the *more compositional* and the *more idiomatic* ones. Differentiating between compositional and idiomatic VPCs has an apt linguistic background as well (see above) and it may be exploited in some NLP applications like machine translation (parts of compositional VPCs may be directly translated while idiomatic VPCs should be treated as one unit). However, when grouping their data, Tu and Roth just consider frequency data and treat one VPC as one lexical entry. This approach is somewhat problematic as many VPCs in their dataset are highly ambiguous and thus may have more meanings (like *get at*, which can mean "criticise", "mean", "get access", "threaten") and some of them may be compositional, while others are not. Hence, clustering all these meanings and classifying them as either compositional or idiomatic may be misleading. Instead, VPC and non-VPC uses of one specific verb-particle combination could be truly distinguished on the basis of frequency data, or, on the other hand, a word sense disambiguation approach may give an account of the compositional or idiomatic uses of the specific unit.

In our experiments, we use the Wiki50 corpus, in which VPCs are annotated in raw text, but no semantic classes are further distinguished. Hence, our goal here is not the automatic semantic classification of VPCs because we believe that first the identification of VPCs in context should be solved and then in a further step, genuine VPCs might be classified as compositional or idiomatic, given a manually annotated dataset from which this kind of information may be learnt. This issue will be addressed in a future study.

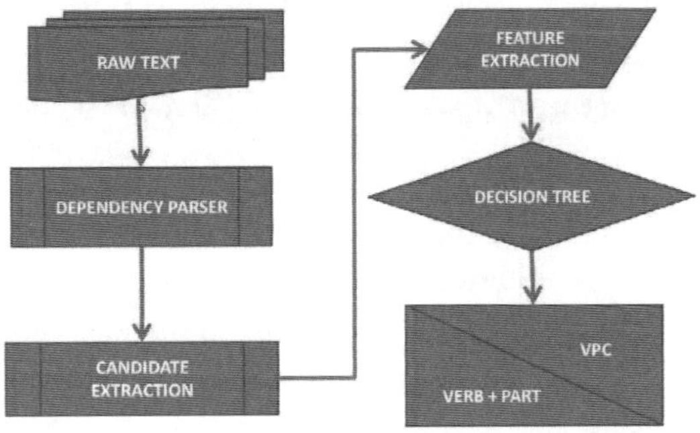

Figure 2: System Architecture

4 VPC Detection

Our goal is to identify each individual VPC in running texts; i.e. to take individual inputs like *How did they get on yesterday?* and mark each VPC in the sentence. Our tool called VPCTagger is based on a two-step approach. First, we syntactically parse each sentence, and extract potential VPCs with a syntax-based candidate extraction method. Afterwards, a binary classification can be used to automatically classify potential VPCs as VPCs or not. For the automatic classification of candidate VPCs, we implemented a machine learning approach, which is based on a rich feature set with new features like semantic and contextual features. Figure 2 outlines the process used to identify each individual VPC in a running text.

4.1 Corpora

To evaluate of our methods, we made use of two corpora. Statistical data on the corpora can be seen in Table 1. First, we used Wiki50 (Vincze et al., 2011), in which several types of multiword expressions (including VPCs) and Named Entities were marked. This corpus consists of 50 Wikipedia pages, and contains 466 occurrences of VPCs.

Corpus	Sentences	Tokens	VPCs	#
Wiki50	4,350	114,570	466	342
Tu&Roth	1,348	38,132	878	23

Table 1: Statistical data on the corpora.

In order to compare the performance of our system with others, we also used the dataset of Tu and Roth (2012), which contains 1,348 sentences taken from different parts of the British National Corpus. However, they only focused on VPCs in this dataset, where 65% of the sentences contain a phrasal verb and 35% contain a simplex verb-preposition combination. As Table 1 indicates, the Tu&Roth dataset only focused on 23 different VPCs, but 342 unique VPCs were annotated in the Wiki50 corpus.

4.2 Candidate Extraction

In this section, we concentrate on the first step of our approach, namely how VPC candidates can be selected from texts. As we mentioned in Section 1, our hypothesis is that the automatic detection of VPCs can be basically carried out by dependency parsers. Thus, we examined the performance of two parsers on VPC-specific syntactic labels.

As we had a full-coverage VPC annotated corpus where each individual occurrence of a VPC was manually marked, we were able to examine the characteristics of VPCs in a running text and evaluate the effectiveness of the parsers on this task. Therefore, here we examine dependency relations among the manually annotated gold standard VPCs, provided by the Stanford parser (Klein and Manning, 2003) and the Bohnet parser (Bohnet, 2010) for the Wiki50 corpus. In order to compare the efficiency of the parsers, both were applied using the same dependency representation. We found that only 52.57% and 58.16% of the annotated VPCs in Wiki50 had a verb-particle syntactic relation when we used the Stanford and Bohnet parsers, respectively. As Table 2 shows, there are several other syntactic constructions in which VPCs may occur.

Edge type	Stanford		Bohnet	
	#	%	#	%
prt	235	52.57	260	58.16
prep	23	5.15	107	23.94
advmod	56	12.52	64	14.32
sum	314	70.24	431	96.42
other	8	1.79	1	0.22
none	125	27.97	15	3.36
sum	447	100.00	447	100.00

Table 2: Edge types in the Wiki50 corpus. prt: particle. prep: preposition. advmod: adverbial modifier. other: other dependency labels. none: no direct syntactic connection between the verb and particle.

Therefore, we extended our candidate extraction method, where besides the *verb-particle* dependency relation, the *preposition* and *adverbial modifier* syntactic relations were also investigated among verbs and particles. With this modification, 70.24% and 96.42% of VPCs in the Wiki50 corpus could be identified. In this phase, we found that the Bohnet parser was more successful on the Wiki50 corpus, i.e. it could cover more VPCs, hence we applied the Bohnet parser in our further experiments.

Some researchers filtered LVC candidates by selecting only certain verbs that may be part of the construction. One example is Tu and Roth (2012), where the authors examined a verb-particle combination only if the verbal components were formed with one of the previously given six verbs (i.e. *make*, *take*, *have*, *give*, *do*, *get*).

Since Wiki50 was annotated for all VPC occurrences, we were able to check what percentage of VPCs could be covered if we applied this selection. As Table 3 shows, the six verbs used by Tu and Roth (2012) are responsible for only 50 VPCs on the Wiki50 corpus, so it covers only 11.16% of all gold standard VPCs.

Table 4 lists the most frequent VPCs and the verbal components on the Wiki50 corpus. As can be seen, the top 10 VPCs are responsible for only 17.41% of the VPC occurrences, while the top 10 verbal components are responsible for 41.07% of the VPC occurrences in the Wiki50 corpus. Furthermore, 127 different verbal component occurred in Wiki50, but the verbs *have* and *do* – which are used by Tu and Roth (2012) – do not appear in the corpus as verbal component of VPCs. All this indicates that applying lexical restrictions and focusing on a reduced set of verbs will lead to the exclusion of a considerable number of VPCs occurring in free texts and so, real-world tasks would hardly profit from them.

verb	#
take	27
get	10
give	5
make	3
have	0
do	0
sum	**50**

Table 3: The frequency of verbs on the Wiki50 corpus used by Tu and Roth (2012).

VPC	#	verb	#
call for	11	set	28
point out	9	take	27
carry out	9	turn	26
set out	8	go	21
grow up	8	call	21
set up	7	come	15
catch up	7	carry	13
turn on	7	look	13
take up	6	break	10
pass on	6	move	10
sum	**78**	**sum**	**184**

Table 4: The most frequent VPCs and verbal components on the Wiki50 corpus.

4.3 Machine Learning Based Candidate Classication

In order to perform an automatic classification of the candidate VPCs, a machine learning-based approach was implemented, which will be elaborated upon below. This method is based on a rich feature set with the following categories: orthographic, lexical, syntactic, and semantic. Moreover, as VPCs are highly ambiguous in raw texts, contextual features are also required.

- Orthographic features: Here, we examined whether the candidate **consists of two or more tokens**. Moreover, if the particle component **started with 'a'**, which prefix, in many cases, etymologically denotes a movement (like *across* and *away*), it was also noted and applied as a feature.

- Lexical features: We exploited the fact that the **most common verbs** occur most frequently in VPCs, so we selected fifteen verbs from the most frequent English verbs [1]. Here, we examined whether the lemmatised verbal component of the candidate was one of these fifteen verbs. We also examined whether the particle component of the potential VPC occurred among the **common English particles**. Here, we apply a manually built particle list based on linguistic considerations. Moreover, we also checked whether a potential VPC is contained in the **list of typical English VPCs** collected by Baldwin (2008).

- Syntactic features: the **dependency label** between the verb and the particle can also be exploited in identifying LVCs. As we typically found when dependency parsing the corpus, the syntactic relation between the verb and the particle in a VPC is `prt`, `prep` or `advmod` – applying the Stanford parser dependency representation, hence these syntactic relations were defined as features. If the candidate's **object was a personal pronoun**, it was also encoded as another syntactic feature.

- Semantic features: These features were based on the fact that the meaning of VPCs may typically reflect a motion or location like *go on* or *take away*. First, we examine that the verbal component is a **motion verb** like *go* or *turn*, or the **particle indicates a direction** like *out* or *away*.

  Moreover, the **semantic type of the prepositional object, object and subject** in the sentence can also help to decide whether the candidate is a VPC or not. Consequently, the `person`, `activity`, `animal`, `artifact` and `concept` semantic senses were looked for among the upper level hyperonyms of the nominal head of the prepositional object, object and subject in Princeton WordNet 3.1[2].

When several different machine learning algorithms were experimented on this feature set, the preliminary results showed that decision trees performed the best on this task. This is probably due to the fact that our feature set consists of a few compact (i.e. high-level) features. The J48 classifier of the WEKA package (Hall et al., 2009) was trained with its default settings on the above-mentioned feature set, which implements the C4.5 (Quinlan, 1993) decision tree algorithm. Moreover, Support Vector Machines (SVM) (Cortes and Vapnik, 1995) results are also reported to compare the performance of our methods with that of Tu and Roth (2012).

As the investigated corpora were not sufficiently large for splitting them into training and test sets of appropriate size, we evaluated our models in a cross validation manner on the Wiki50 corpus and the Tu&Roth dataset.

[1] http://en.wikipedia.org/wiki/Most_common_words_in_English

[2] http://wordnetweb.princeton.edu/perl/webwn

As Tu and Roth (2012) presented only the accuracy scores on the Tu & Roth dataset, we also employed an accuracy score as an evaluation metric on this dataset, where positive and negative examples were also marked. But, in the case of Wiki50 corpus, where only the positive VPCs were manually annotated, the $F_{\beta=1}$ score was employed and interpreted on the positive class as an evaluation metric. Moreover, all potential VPCs were treated as negative that were extracted by the candidate extraction method but were not marked as positive in the gold standard. Thus, in the resulting dataset negative examples are over-represented.

As Table 2 shows, the candidate extraction method did not cover all manually annotated VPCs in the Wiki50 corpus. Hence, we treated the omitted LVCs as false negatives in our evaluation.

As a baseline, we applied a context-free dictionary lookup method. In this case, we applied the same VPC list that was described among the lexical features. Then we marked candidates of the syntax-based method as VPC if the candidate VPC was found in the list. We also compared our results with the rule-based results available for Wiki50 (Nagy T. and Vincze, 2011) and also with the 5-fold cross validation results of Tu and Roth (2012).

5 Results

Table 5 lists the results obtained using the baseline dictionary lookup, rule-based method, dependency parsers and machine learning approaches on the Wiki50 corpus. It is revealed that the dictionary lookup method performed worst and achieved an F-score of 35.43. Moreover, this method only achieved a precision score of 49.77%. However, the rule-based method achieved the highest precision score with 91.26%, but the dependency parsers also got high precision scores of about 90% on Wiki50. It is also clear that the machine learning-based approach, the VPCTagger, is the most successful method on Wiki50: it achieved an F-score 10 points higher than those for the rule-based method and dependency parsers and more than 45 points higher than that for the dictionary lookup.

In order to compare the performance of our system with others, we evaluated it on the Tu&Roth dataset (Tu and Roth, 2012). Table 6 compares the results achieved by the dictionary lookup and the rule-based method on the Tu&Roth dataset. Moreover, it also lists the results of Tu and Roth (2012) and the VPCTagger evaluated in the 5-fold cross validation manner, as Tu and Roth (2012) applied this evaluation schema. As in the Tu&Roth dataset positive and negative examples were also marked, we were able to use accuracy as evaluation metric besides the $F_{\beta=1}$ scores. It is revealed that the dictionary lookup and the rule-based method achieved an F-score of about 50, but our method seems the most successful on this dataset, as it can yield an accuracy 3.32% higher than that for the Tu&Roth system.

Method	Prec.	Rec.	F-score
Dictionary Lookup	49.77	27.5	35.43
Rule-based	**91.26**	58.52	71.31
Stanford Parser	91.09	52.57	66.67
Bohnet Parser	89.04	58.16	70.36
ML J48	85.7	**76.79**	**81.0**
ML SVM	89.07	65.62	75.57

Table 5: Results obtained in terms of precision, recall and F-score.

Method	Accuracy	F-score
Dictionary Lookup	51.13	52.24
Rule Based	56.92	43.84
VPCTagger	**81.92**	**85.69**
Tu&Roth	78.6%	–

Table 6: 5-fold cross validation results on the Tu&Roth dataset in terms of accuracy and F-score.

6 Discussion

The applied machine learning-based method extensively outperformed our dictionary lookup and rule-based baseline methods, which underlines the fact that our approach can be suitably applied to VPC detection in raw texts. It is well demonstrated that VPCs are very ambiguous in raw text, as the dictionary lookup method only achieved a precision score of 49.77% on the Wiki50 corpus. This demonstrates that the automatic detection of VPCs is a challenging task and contextual features are essential. In the case of the dictionary lookup, to achieve a higher recall score was mainly limited by the size of the dictionary used.

As Table 5 shows, VPCTagger achieved an F-score 10% higher than those for the dependency parsers, which may refer to the fact that our machine learning-based approach performed well on this task. This method proved to be the most balanced as it got roughly the same recall, precision and F-score results on the Wiki50 corpus. In addition, the dependency parsers achieve high precision with lower recall scores.

Moreover, the results obtained with our machine learning approach on the Tu&Roth dataset outperformed those reported in Tu and Roth (2012). This may be attributed to the inclusion of a rich feature set with new features like semantic and contextual features that were used in our system.

As Table 6 indicates, the dictionary lookup and rule-based methods were less effective when applied on the Tu&Roth dataset. Since the corpus was created by collecting sentences that contained phrasal verbs with specific verbs, this dataset contains a lot of negative and ambiguous examples besides annotated VPCs, hence the distribution of VPCs in the Tu&Roth dataset is not comparable to those in Wiki50, where each occurrence of a VPCs were manually annotated in a running text. Moreover, in this dataset, only one positive or negative example was annotated in each sentence, and they examined just the verb-particle pairs formed with the six verbs as a potential VPC. However, the corpus probably contains other VPCs which were not annotated. For example, in the sentence *The agency* ***takes on*** *any kind of job – you just name the subject and give us some indication of the kind of thing you want to know, and then we* ***go out*** *and* ***get it for*** *you.*, the only phrase *takes on* was listed as a positive example in the Tu&Roth dataset. But two examples, (*go out* – positive and *get it for* – negative) were not marked. This is problematic if we would like to evaluate our candidate extractor on this dataset as it would identify all these phrases, even if it is restricted to verb-particle pairs containing one of the six verbs mentioned above, thus yielding false positives already in the candidate extraction phase.

In addition, this dataset contains 878 positive VPC occurrences, but only 23 different VPCs. Consequently, some positive examples were overrepresented. But the Wiki50 corpus may contain some rare examples and it probably reflects a more realistic distribution as it contains 342 unique VPCs.

A striking difference between the Tu & Roth database and Wiki50 is that while Tu and Roth (2012) included the verbs *do* and *have* in their data, they do not occur at all among the VPCs collected from Wiki50. Moreover, these verbs are just responsible for 25 positive VPCs examples in the Tu & Roth dataset. Although these verbs are very frequent in language use, they do not seem to occur among the most frequent verbal components concerning VPCs. A possible reason for this might be that VPCs usually contain a verb referring to movement in its original sense and neither *have* nor *do* belong to motion verbs.

An ablation analysis was carried out to examine the effectiveness of each individual feature types of the machine learning based candidate classification. Besides the feature classification described in Section 4.3, we also examined the effectiveness of the contextual features. In this case, the feature which examined whether the candidates object was a personal pronoun or not and the semantic type of the prepositional object, object and subject were treated as contextual features. Table 7 shows the usefulness of each individual feature type on the Wiki50 corpus. For each feature type, a J48 classifier was trained with all of the features except that one. Then we compared the performance to that got with all the features. As the ablation analysis shows, each type of feature contributed to the overall performance. We found that the lexical and orthographic features were the most powerful, the semantic, syntactic features were also useful; while contextual features were less effective, but were still exploited by the model.

Features	**Prec.**	**Rec.**	**F-score**	Diff.
All	**85.7**	**76.79**	**81.0**	–
Semantic	86.55	66.52	75.22	-5.78
Orthographic	83.26	65.85	73.54	-7.46
Syntax	84.31	71.88	77.6	-3.4
Lexical	89.68	60.71	72.41	**-8.59**
Contextual	86.68	74.55	80.16	-0.84

Table 7: The usefulness of individual features in terms of precision, recall and F-score using the Wiki50 corpus.

The most important features in our system are lexical ones, namely, the lists of the most frequent English verbs and particles. It is probably due to the fact that the set of verbs used in VPCs is rather limited, furthermore, particles form a closed word class that is, they can be fully listed, hence the particle component of a VPC will necessarily come from a well-defined set of words.

Besides the ablation analysis, we also investigated the decision tree model produced by our experiments. The model profited most from the syntactic and lexical features, i.e. the dependency label provided by the parsers between the verb and the particle also played an important role in the classification process.

We carried out a manual error analysis in order to find the most typical errors our system made. Most errors could be traced back to POS-tagging or parsing errors, where the particle was classified as a preposition. VPCs that include an adverb (as labeled by the POS tagger and the parser) were also somewhat more difficult to identify, like *come across* or *go back*. Preposition stranding (in e.g. relative clauses) also resulted in false positives like in *planets he had an adventure on*.

Other types of multiword expressions were also responsible for errors. For instance, the system classified *come out* as a VPC within the idiom *come out of the closet* but the gold standard annotation in Wiki50 just labeled the phrase as an idiom and no internal structure for it was marked. A similar error could be found for light verb constructions, for example, *run for office* was marked as a VPC in the data, but *run for* was classified as a VPC, yielding a false positive case. Multiword prepositions like *up to* also led to problems: in *he taught up to 1986*, *taught up* was erroneously labeled as VPC. Finally, in some cases, annotation errors in the gold standard data were the source of mislabeled candidates.

7 Conclusions

In this paper, we focused on the automatic detection of verb-particle combinations in raw texts. Our hypothesis was that parsers trained on texts annotated with extra information for VPCs can identify VPCs in texts. We introduced our machine learning-based tool called VPCTagger, which allowed us to automatically detect VPCs in context. We solved the problem in a two-step approach. In the first step, we extracted potential VPCs from a running text with a syntax-based candidate extraction method and we applied a machine learning-based approach that made use of a rich feature set to classify extracted syntactic phrases in the second step. In order to achieve a greater efficiency, we defined several new features like semantic and contextual, but according to our ablation analysis we found that each type of features contributed to the overall performance.

Moreover, we also examined how syntactic parsers performed in the VPC detection task on the Wiki50 corpus. Furthermore, we compared our methods with others when we evaluated our approach on the Tu&Roth dataset. Our method yielded better results than those got using the dependency parsers on the Wiki50 corpus and the method reported in (Tu and Roth, 2012) on the Tu&Roth dataset.

Here, we also showed how dependency parsers performed on identifying VPCs, and our results indicate that although the dependency label provided by the parsers is an essential feature in determining whether a specific VPC candidate is a genuine VPC or not, the results can be further improved by extending the system with additional features like lexical and semantic features. Thus, one possible application of the VPCTagger may be to help dependency parsers: based on the output of VPCTagger, syntactic labels provided by the parsers can be overwritten. With backtracking, the accuracy of syntactic parsers may increase, which can be useful for a number of higher-level NLP applications that exploit syntactic information.

In the future, we would like to improve our system by defining more complex contextual features. We also plan to examine how the VPCTagger improve the performance of higher level NLP applications like machine translation systems, and we would also like to investigate the systematic differences among the performances of the parsers and VPCTagger, in order to improve the accuracy of parsing. In addition, we would like to compare different automatic detection methods of multiword expressions, as different types of MWEs are manually annotated in the Wiki50 corpus.

Acknowledgments

István Nagy T. was partially funded by the National Excellence Program TÁMOP-4.2.4.A/2-11/1-2012-0001 of the State of Hungary, co-financed by the European Social Fund. Veronika Vincze was funded in part by the European Union and the European Social Fund through the project FuturICT.hu (grant no.: TÁMOP-4.2.2.C-11/1/KONV-2012-0013).

References

Timothy Baldwin and Aline Villavicencio. 2002. Extracting the unextractable: A case study on verb-particles. In *Proceedings of the 6th Conference on Natural Language Learning - Volume 20*, COLING-02, pages 1–7, Stroudsburg, PA, USA. Association for Computational Linguistics.

Timothy Baldwin. 2005. Deep lexical acquisition of verb-particle constructions. *Computer Speech and Language*, 19(4):398–414, October.

Timothy Baldwin. 2008. A resource for evaluating the deep lexical acquisition of English verb-particle constructions. In *Proceedings of the LREC Workshop Towards a Shared Task for Multiword Expressions (MWE 2008)*, pages 1–2.

Bernd Bohnet. 2010. Top accuracy and fast dependency parsing is not a contradiction. In *Proceedings of Coling 2010*, pages 89–97.

Corinna Cortes and Vladimir Vapnik. 1995. *Support-vector networks*, volume 20. Kluwer Academic Publishers.

Spence Green, Marie-Catherine de Marneffe, and Christopher D. Manning. 2013. Parsing models for identifying multiword expressions. *Computational Linguistics*, 39(1):195–227.

Mark Hall, Eibe Frank, Geoffrey Holmes, Bernhard Pfahringer, Peter Reutemann, and Ian H. Witten. 2009. The WEKA data mining software: an update. *SIGKDD Explorations*, 11(1):10–18.

Ray Jackendoff. 2002. English particle constructions, the lexicon, and the autonomy of syntax. In Nicole Deh, Ray Jackendoff, Andrew McIntyre, and Silke Urban, editors, *Verb-Particle Explorations*, pages 67–94, Berlin / New York. Mouton de Gruyter.

Su Nam Kim and Timothy Baldwin. 2006. Automatic identification of English verb particle constructions using linguistic features. In *Proceedings of the Third ACL-SIGSEM Workshop on Prepositions*, pages 65–72.

Dan Klein and Christopher D. Manning. 2003. Accurate unlexicalized parsing. In *Annual Meeting of the ACL*, volume 41, pages 423–430.

Mitchell P. Marcus, Beatrice Santorini, and Mary Ann Marcinkiewicz. 1993. Building a Large Annotated Corpus of English: The Penn Treebank. *Computational Linguistics*, 19(2):313–331.

Francesca Masini. 2005. Multi-word expressions between syntax and the lexicon: The case of Italian verb-particle constructions. *SKY Journal of Linguistics*, 18:145–173.

Diana McCarthy, Bill Keller, and John Carroll. 2003. Detecting a continuum of compositionality in phrasal verbs. In *Proceedings of the ACL 2003 Workshop on Multiword Expressions: Analysis, Acquisition and Treatment - Volume 18*, MWE '03, pages 73–80, Stroudsburg, PA, USA. Association for Computational Linguistics.

István Nagy T. and Veronika Vincze. 2011. Identifying Verbal Collocations in Wikipedia Articles. In *Proceedings of the 14th International Conference on Text, Speech and Dialogue*, TSD'11, pages 179–186, Berlin, Heidelberg. Springer-Verlag.

Ross Quinlan. 1993. *C4.5: Programs for Machine Learning*. Morgan Kaufmann Publishers, San Mateo, CA.

Ivan A. Sag, Timothy Baldwin, Francis Bond, Ann Copestake, and Dan Flickinger. 2002. Multiword Expressions: A Pain in the Neck for NLP. In *Proceedings of CICLing 2002*, pages 1–15, Mexico City, Mexico.

Yuancheng Tu and Dan Roth. 2012. Sorting out the Most Confusing English Phrasal Verbs. In *Proceedings of the First Joint Conference on Lexical and Computational Semantics - Volume 1: Proceedings of the Main Conference and the Shared Task, and Volume 2: Proceedings of the Sixth International Workshop on Semantic Evaluation*, SemEval '12, pages 65–69, Stroudsburg, PA, USA. Association for Computational Linguistics.

Aline Villavicencio. 2003. Verb-particle constructions and lexical resources. In *Proceedings of the ACL 2003 Workshop on Multiword Expressions: Analysis, Acquisition and Treatment - Volume 18*, MWE '03, pages 57–64, Stroudsburg, PA, USA. Association for Computational Linguistics.

Veronika Vincze, István Nagy T., and Gábor Berend. 2011. Multiword Expressions and Named Entities in the Wiki50 Corpus. In *Proceedings of RANLP 2011*, pages 289–295, Hissar, Bulgaria, September. RANLP 2011 Organising Committee.

Veronika Vincze, János Zsibrita, and István Nagy T. 2013. Dependency Parsing for Identifying Hungarian Light Verb Constructions. In *Proceedings of the Sixth International Joint Conference on Natural Language Processing*, pages 207–215, Nagoya, Japan, October. Asian Federation of Natural Language Processing.

The Relevance of Collocations for Parsing

Eric Wehrli
LATL-CUI
University of Geneva
Eric.Wehrli@unige.ch

Abstract

Although multiword expressions (MWEs) have received an increasing amount of attention in the NLP community over the last two decades, few papers have been dedicated to the specific problem of the interaction between MWEs and parsing. In this paper, we will discuss how the collocation identification task has been integrated in our rule-based parser and show how collocation knowledge has a positive impact on the parsing process. A manual evaluation has been conducted over a corpus of 4000 sentences, comparing outputs of the parser used with and without the collocation component. Results of the evaluation clearly support our claim.

1 Introduction

Collocations and more generally multiword expressions (MWEs) have received a large and increasing amount of attention in the NLP community over the last two decades, as attested by the number of workshops, special interest groups, and –of course– publications. The importance of this phenomenon is now clearly recognized within the NLP community.

It is fair to say that collocation extraction has been the main focus of attention, and a great deal of research has been devoted to developing techniques for collocation extraction from corpora (Church & Hanks, 1990; Smadja, 1993; Evert, 2004; Seretan & Wehrli, 2009, among many others). Much less attention has been paid to the interaction between collocations and the parsing process[1]. In this paper, we will argue (i) that collocation detection should be considered as a component of the parsing process, and (ii) that contrary to a common view, collocations (and more generally MWEs) do not constitute a problem or a hurdle for NLP (cf. Green et al., 2011; Sag et al., 2002), but rather have a positive impact on parsing results.

Section 2 shows how collocation identification has been integrated into the parsing process. An evaluation which compares the results of the parse of a corpus **with** and **without** the collocation identification component will be discussed in section 3.

2 Parsing collocations

That syntactic information is useful – indeed necessary – for a proper identification of collocations is widely acknowledged by now. More controversial, however, is the dual point, that is

[1]Preprocessing, that is, the detection of MWEs during tokenisation (ie. before parsing) is used in several systems – for instance, ParGram (Butt et al., 1999), or more recently, Talismane (Urieli, 2013). However, this technique can only be successfully applied to MWEs whose components are adjacent (or near-adjacent), leaving aside most of the cases that will be discussed below.

that collocation identification is useful for parsing.

Several researchers (cf. Seretan et al., 2009; Seretan, 2011, and references given there) have convincingly argued that collocation identification crucially depends on precise and detailed syntactic information. One main argument supporting that view is the fact that in some collocations, the two constituents can be far away from each other, or in reverse order, depending on grammatical processes such as extraposition, relativization, passive, etc. Based on such considerations, we developed a collocation extraction system based on our Fips multilingual rule-based parser(cf. Wehrli, 2007; Wehrli et al., 2010). Although quite satisfactory in terms of extraction precision, we noticed some shortcomings in terms of recall, due to the fact that the parser would not always return the most appropriate structure. A closer examination of some of the cases where the parser failed to return the structure containing a collocation – and therefore failed to identify it – showed that heuristics had (wrongly) favoured an alternative structure. Had the parser known that there was a collocation, the correct structure could have received a higher score.

These observations led us to revise our position and consider that parsing and the identification of collocations are in fact interrelated tasks. Not only does collocation identification rely on syntactic dependencies, and thus on parsed data, but the parser can fruitfully use collocational knowledge to favour some analyses over competing ones. A new version of the Fips parser has since been developed, in which collocations are identified as soon as the relevant structure is computed, that is as soon as the second term of the collocation is attached to the structure.

The collocation identification process is triggered by the (left or right) attachment of a lexical element marked [+partOfCollocation][2]. Governing nodes are iteratively considered, halting at the first node of major category (noun, verb, adjective, adverb). If that second node is itself marked [+partOfCollocation], then we check whether the two terms correspond to a known collocation.

Consider first some simple cases, as illustrated in (1).

(1)a. He had no **loose change**.

b. Paul **took up** a new **challenge**.

The collocation *loose change* in sentence (1a) is identified when the adjective *loose* is (left-) attached to the noun *change*. Both elements are lexically marked [+partOfCollocation], the procedure looked up the collocation database for a $[_{\texttt{NP}}\ [_{\texttt{AP}}$ loose] change] collocation. In the second example (1b), the procedure is triggered by the attachment of the noun *challenge* to the determiner phrase (DP) *a*, which is already attached as direct object subconstituent of the verb *took (up)*. As pointed out above, the procedure checks the governing nodes until finding a node of major category – in this case the verb. Both the verb and the noun are marked [+partOfCollocation], so that the procedure looks up the database for a collocation of type verb-direct object.

Let us now turn to somewhat more complex cases, such as the ones illustrated (2):

(2)a. Which **record** did Paul **break**?

b. The **record** Paul has just **broken** was very old.

c. This **record** seems difficult to **break**.

d. This **record**, Paul will **break** at the next Olympic Games.

[2]The collocation identification process only concerns lexicalized collocations, that is collocations that we have entered into the parser's lexical database.

e. Which **record** did Paul consider difficult to **break**?

f. The **record** will be **broken**.

g. The **record** is likely to be **broken**.

h. Ce **défi**, Jean le considère comme difficile à **relever**.
"This **challenge**, Jean considers [it] as difficult to **take up**"

Sentence (2a) is a *wh*-interrogative clause, in which the direct object constituent occurs at the beginning of the sentence. Assuming a generative grammar analysis, we consider that such preposed constituents are connected to so-called canonical positions. In this case, the fronted element being a direct object, the canonical position is the typical direct object position in an English declarative sentence, that is a postverbal DP position immediately dominated by the VP node. The parser establishes such a link and returns the structure below, where $[_{DP}\ e]_i$ stands for the empty category (the "trace") of the preposed constituent *which record*.

(3) $[_{CP}\ [_{DP}$ which record$]_i$] did $[_{TP}\ [_{DP}$ Paul] break $[_{DP}\ e]_i$]

In such cases, the collocation identification process is triggered by the insertion of the empty constituent in the direct object position of the verb. Since the empty constituent is connected to the preposed constituent, such examples can be easily treated as a minor variant of case (1b).

All so-called *wh*-constructions[3] are treated in a similar fashion, that is relative clause (2b) and topicalization (2c). Sentence (2d) concerns the *tough*-movement construction, that is constructions involving adjectives such as *tough, easy, difficult*, etc. governing an infinitival clause. In such constructions, the matrix subject is construed as the direct object of the infinitival verb. In dealing with such structures, the parser will hypothesize an abstract *wh*-operator in the specifier position of the infinitival clause, which is linked to the matrix subject. Like all *wh*-constituents, the abstract operator will itself be connected to an empty constituent later on in the analysis, giving rise to a chain connecting the subject of the main clause and the direct object position of the infinitival clause. The structure as computed by the parser is given in (4), with the chain marked by the index *i*.

(4) $[_{TP}\ [_{DP}$ this record$]_i$ seems $[_{AP}$ difficult $[_{CP}\ [_{DP}\ e]_i\ [_{TP}$ to $[_{VP}$ break $[_{DP}\ e]_i$]]]]]

Finally, examples (2f,g) concern the passive construction, in which we assume that the direct object is promoted to the subject position. In the tradition of generative grammar, we could say that the "surface" subject is interpreted as the "deep" direct object of the verb. Given such an analysis of passive, the parser will connect the subject constituent of a passive verb with an empty constituent in direct object position, as illustrated in (5).

(5) $[_{TP}\ [_{DP}$ the record$]_i$ will $[_{VP}$ be $[_{VP}$ broken $[_{DP}\ e]_i$]]]

The detection of a verb-object collocation in a passive sentence is thus triggered by the insertion of the empty constituent in direct object position. The collocation identification procedure checks whether the antecedent of the (empty) direct object and the verb constitute a (verb-object) collocation.

2.1 Why collocations help

The parser can benefit from collocation knowledge in two ways. The improvement comes either from a better choice of lexical element (in

[3]See Chomsky (1977) for a general analysis of *wh*-constructions.

case of ambiguous words), or from a more felicitous phrase attachment. Both cases are illustrated below, by means of examples taken from our evaluation corpus. Consider first collocations of the noun-noun type containing syntactically ambiguous words (in the sense that they can be assigned more than one lexical category) as in (6):

(6)a. balancing act
eating habits
nursing care
living standards
working conditions

b. austerity measures
opinion polls
tax cuts
protest marches

As illustrated by Chomsky's famous example *Flying planes can be dangerous*, *-ing* forms of English transitive verbs are quite systematically ambiguous, between a verbal reading (gerund) and an adjectival reading (participle use). The examples given in (6a) are all cases of collocations involving a present participle modifying a noun. All those examples were wrongly interpreted as gerunds by the parser running without the collocation identification procedure. The noun-noun collocations in (6b) all have a noun head which is ambiguous between a nominal and a verbal reading. Such examples were also wrongly interpreted with the verbal reading when parsed without the identification procedure.

The second way in which collocational knowledge can help the parser has to do with structural ambiguities. This concerns particularly collocations which include a prepositional phrase, such as the noun-preposition-noun collocations, as in (7):

(7) bone of contention
state of emergency
struggle for life
flag of convenience

The attachment of prepositional phrases is known to be a very difficult task for parsers (cf. Church & Patil, 1982). So, knowing that a particular prepositional phrase is part of a collocation (and giving priority to such analyses containing collocations over other possible analyses) is an effective way to solve many cases of PP attachments.

3 Evaluation

To evaluate the effect of collocational knowledge on parsing, we compared the results produced by the parser **with** and **without** the collocation identification procedure. The corpus used for this evaluation consists of 56 articles taken from the magazine *The Economist*, corresponding to almost 4000 sentences. We first compared the number of complete analyses achieved by both runs, with the results in Figure 1[4]:

with collocations	without collocations
70.3%	69.2%

Figure 1: Percentage of complete analyses

Although the number of complete parses (sentences for which the parser can assign a complete structure) varies very slightly (a little more than a percent point better for the version with collocation identification, at 70.3%), the content of the analyses may differ in significant ways, as the next evaluation will show.

A manual evaluation of the results was conducted over the corpus, using a specific user interface. To simplify the evaluation, we selected the POS-tagging mode of the parser, and further

[4]By complete analysis, we mean a single constituent covering the whole sentence. When the Fips parser fails to achieve a complete analysis, it returns a sequence of chunks (usually 2 or 3) covering the whole sentence.

diff.	diff N vs V	with coll.	without coll.
416	148	116	32

Figure 3: Differences with and without collocation

restricted the output to the triple (word, pos-tag, position)[5]. For the POS tagset, we opted for the universal tagset (cf. Petrov et al., 2012). Both output files could then easily be manually compared using a specific user interface as illustrated in figure 2 below, where differences are displayed in red.

Notice that in order to facilitate the manual evaluation, we only took into account differences involving the NOUN and VERB tags. In the screenshot the two result files are displayed, on the left the results obtained by the parser with (W) the collocation identification component, on the right the results obtained with the parser without (WO) the collocation identification component. For each file, one line contains the input lexical item (simple word or compound), its tag, and its position with respect to the beginning of file (article). Differences (restricted here to NOUN vs VERB tags) between the two files are indicated in red. For each difference, the user selects the best choice, using the **Better left** or **Better right** button or the **Skip** button if the difference is irrelevant (or if neither tag is correct). After each choice, the next difference is immediately displayed.

The results are given in figure 3. Column 1 gives the total number of differences, column 2 the number of differences for the NOUN vs VERB tags, columns 3 and 4 show how many times the result (NOUN / VERB) is better with the collocation component (column 3) or without it (column 4).

This manual evaluation clearly shows that the quality of the parses improves significantly when the parser "knows" about collocations, that is when collocation detection takes place during the parse. The comparison of the results obtained with and without collocation knowledge shows a total 416 differences of POS-tags, of which 148 concern the difference between Noun vs Verb tags. In 116 cases (nearly 80%) the choice was better when the parser had collocational knowledge, while in 32 cases (approx. 21%) the choice was better without the collocational knowledge.

The fact that in a little over 20% of the cases the parser makes a better choice without collocational knowledge may seem a bit odd or counter-intuitive. Going through several such cases revealed that in all of them, the parser could not achieve a full parse and returned a sequence of chunks. It turns out that in its current state, the Fips parser does not use collocational knowledge to rank chunks. Nor can it identify collocations that spread over two chunks. Clearly something to be updated.

4 Concluding remarks and future work

In this paper, we have argued that collocation identification and parsing should be viewed as interrelated tasks. One the one hand, collocation identification relies on precise and detailed syntactic information, while on the other hand the parser can fruitfully use collocation knowledge in order to rank competing analyses and, more interestingly, to disambiguate some otherwise difficult cases.

This preliminary study focused primarily on the NOUN vs VERB ambiguity, an ambiguity which is very common in English and which may have a devastating effect when the wrong reading is chosen. For instance, in a translation task, such mistakes are very likely to lead to incomprehensible results.

[5]Using Fips in POS-tagging mode only means that the output will restricted to word and POS-tags. The analysis itself is identical whether we use Fips in parsing mode or in Pos-tagging mode.

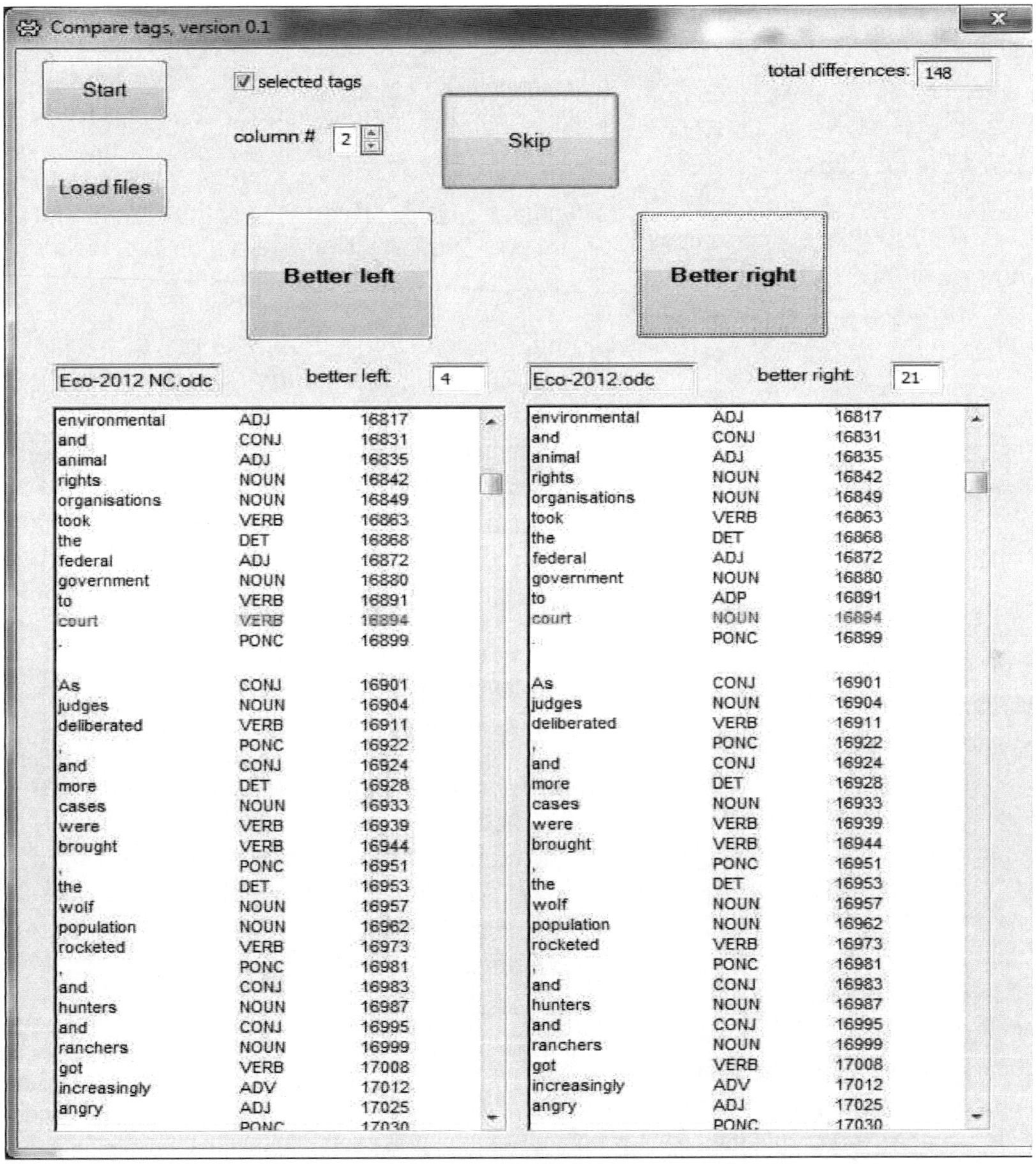

Figure 2: Manual evaluation user interface

In future work, we intend (i) to perform a evaluation over a much larger corpus, (ii) to take into account all types of collocations, and (iii) to consider other languages, such as French, German or Italian.

5 References

Butt, M., T.H. King, M.-E. Niño & F. Segond, 1999. *A Grammar Writer's Cookbook*, Stanford, CSLI Publications.

Church, K. & P. Hanks, 1990. "Word association norms, mutual information, and lexicography", *Computational Linguistics* 16(1), 22-29.

Church, K. & R. Patil, 1982. "Coping with Syntactic Ambiguity or How to Put the Block in the Box on the Table", *American Journal of Computational Linguistics*, vol. 8, number 3-4, 139-150.

Chomsky, N. 1977. "On Wh-Movement", in Peter Culicover, Thomas Wasow, and Adrian Akmajian, eds., *Formal Syntax*, New York: Academic Press, 71-132.

Evert, S., 2004. *The Statistics of Word Cooccurrences: Word Pairs and Collocations*, PhD dissertation, IMS, University of Stuttgart.

Green S., M.-C. de Marneffe, J. Bauer & Ch.D. Manning, 2011. "Multiword Expression Identification with Tree Substitution Grammars: A Parsing *tour de force* with French", *Proceedings of the 2011 Conference on Empirical Methods in Natural Language Processing*, 725-735.

Petrov, S., D. Das & R. McDonald, 2012. "A Universal Part-of-Speech Tagset", *Proceedings of LREC-2011*.

Sag, I., T. Baldwin, F. Bond, A. Copestake & D. Flickinger (2002), "Multiword Expressions: A Pain in the Neck for NLP", Proceedings of Cicling 2002, Springer-Verlag.

Seretan, V., 2011. *Syntax-Based Collocation Extraction*, Springer Verlag.

Seretan, V. & E. Wehrli, 2009. "Multilingual Collocation Extraction with a Syntactic Parser", *Language Resources and Evaluation* 43:1, 71-85.

Smadja, F., 1993. "Retrieving collocations from text: Xtract", *Computational Linguistics* 19(1), 143-177.

Urieli, A., 2013. *Robust French Syntax Analysis: reconciling statistical methods and linguistic knowledge in the Talismane toolkit*, PhD dissertation, University of Toulouse. [http://redac.univ-tlse2.fr/applications/talismane/biblio/URIELI-thesis-2013.pdf]

Wehrli, E., 2007. "Fips, a deep linguistic multilingual parser" in *Proceedings of the ACL 2007 Workshop on Deep Linguistic Processing*, Prague, Czech Republic, 120-127.

Wehrli, E., V. Seretan & L. Nerima, 2010. "Sentence Analysis and Collocation Identification" in *Proceedings of the Workshop on Multiword Expressions: from Theory to Applications* (MWE 2010), Beijing, China, 27-35.

Parsing Modern Greek verb MWEs with LFG/XLE grammars

Niki Samaridi
National and Kapodistrian University of Athens
nsamaridi@gmail.com

Stella Markantonatou
Institute for Language and Speech Processing/ 'Athena' RIC
marks@ilsp.athena-innovation.gr

Abstract

We report on the first, still on-going effort to integrate verb MWEs in an LFG grammar of Modern Greek (MG). Text is lemmatized and tagged with the ILSP FBT Tagger and is fed to a MWE filter that marks Words_With_Spaces in MWEs. The output is then formatted to feed an LFG/XLE grammar that has been developed independently. So far we have identified and classified about 2500 MWEs, and have processed 40% of them by manipulating only the lexicon and not the rules of the grammar.

Research on MG MWEs (indicatively, Anastasiadi-Simeonidi, 1986; Fotopoulou, 1993; Mini et al., 2011) has developed collections of MWEs and discussed classification, syntax and semantics issues. To the best of our knowledge, this is the first attempt to obtain deep parses of a wide range of types of MG verb MWEs with rich syntactic structure.

1 The parsing system

We take advantage of the mature ILSP FBT Tagger (Papageorgiou et al., 2000) that is an adaptation of the Brill tagger trained on MG text. It uses a PAROLE compatible tagset of 584 tags. The tagger works on the output of a sentence detection and tokenisation tool and assigns a lemma and a set of tags corresponding to an exhaustive morphological analysis of tokens (Fig. 1). The tagger is a black box for our system and allows for no preprocessing of MWEs, as it would be possible if the XFST/XLE component was used (Attia, 2006). We have been working on a system that aims to move as much as possible of the parsing burden from the LFG/XLE component to a MWE recognizer (the 'filter') at the same time allowing for 'natural' LFG analyses. Oflazer et al. (2004) discuss a similar preprocessing step but they focus on the retrieval and not on the deep parsing of verb MWEs. Our filter, implemented in Perl, scans the output of the tagger for strings containing verb MWEs and feeds a script ('formatter') that yields a format readable by an LFG/XLE grammar.

1.1 The filter lexicon

The filter consults the 'filter lexicon' where each verb MWE entry is specified for the following:

1. Compositionality. Certain verb MWEs can take a compositional interpretation. For instance, the free subject, flexible (Sag et al, 2001) verbal

MWE κάνω μαύρα μάτια να σε δω (9) has no compositional interpretation while the semi-fixed MWE τις_αρπάζω (2) “to be beaten up”, can take the compositional interpretation “grab/steal them-FEM”. The filter lexicon specifies which MWEs will be eventually assigned both MWE and compositional XLE parses.

2. The lemmatized form of Words_With_Spaces (WWS) whether they are independent fixed MWEs or substrings of a MWE. For instance, the lemmatised WWS μαύρος_μάτι would be stored for WWS μαύρα μάτια of the MWE (9).

3. PoS of the WWS. For instance, we have classified the WWS ταπί-και-**ψύχραιμος** ‘penniless and calm’(6) as adjective; however, only the second conjunct (ψύχραιμος ‘calm’) is an adjective while the first conjunct ταπί is an indeclinable non-Greek word that occurs with this type of MWE only. Regarding distribution, the conjunction behaves as an adjective. In general, we have relied on distribution criteria in order to assign PoS to WWSs.

4. Morphological constraints on the lemmatized constituents of a WWS that uniquely identify fixed or semi-fixed MWE substrings. For instance, for the adjective μαύρα in the WWS μαύρα μάτια (9) the lemma of the adjective μαύρος is stored together with the tags adjective-plural-accusative-neutral-basic.

5. Multiple WWSs if different word orders of the same WWS occur, for instance πίνει [το αίμα του κοσμάκη]$_{WWS}$ [gloss: drink the blood of people] and πίνει [του κοσμάκη το αίμα]$_{WWS}$ ‘takes a lot of money from people by applying force’.

1.2 The filter

The filter, implemented in Perl, reads the tagged sentence from an xml file (the output of the tagger), checks it for MWEs and feeds it to the formatter if no MWE or a MWE that can take a compositional interpretation is found. Strings containing MWEs are preprocessed by the filter: their fixed parts are replaced with the corresponding WWS and morphological constraints and the resulting new string is sent to the formatter. The filter can identify all word permutations available to a listed MWE.

2 An outline of the LFG analysis

The output of the formatter is parsed with an LFG grammar of MG. The grammar includes sublexical rules that parse the output of the tagger and ensure information flow from the tagger to XLE. The sub-lexical trees can be seen in the c-structure of Fig. 1. MG MWEs are rich in syntactic structure despite any simplifications that might result from the usage of WWSs. In agreement with Gross (1998a; 1998b) and Mini et al. (2011) who argue that MWEs and compositional structures can be treated with more or less the same grammar, we have so far manipulated only the lexicon but not the grammar rules. Identification of phrasal constituents within the MWEs relies on possible permutations and the ability of XPs to intervene between two words, thus indicating the border between two constituents. Grammatical functions are identified with diagnostics that apply to compositional expressions such as morphological marking and WH questions. The types of syntactic structure we have treated thus far are:

1. **Fixed verb WWS** (Table 1:1): no inflection or word permutation.

(1) πάρε πέντε
take-2-sg-IMP five-numeral
‘You are silly.’

2. **Free subject-verb** (Table 1:2): inflecting, SV/VS word order.

(2) Ο Πέτρος τις άρπαξε
the Peter-nom CL-pl-fem-acc grab-3-sg-past
‘Petros was beaten up.’

3&4. **Impersonal verb-complement**: inflecting, fixed object (Table 1:3) or saturated sentential subject (Table 1:4), intervening XPs between the verb and its object or subject, VO/OV word order (but not VS/SV).

(3) Έριξε καρεκλοπόδαρα χθες.
pour-3-sg-past chair-legs yesterday
‘It rained cats and dogs yesterday.’

(4) Έχει γούστο να βρέξει.
have-3-sg-pres gusto-noun to rain
‘Don’t tell me that it might rain.’

	LFG representation	Sub-WWS	C
1	V: PRED παίρνω_πέντε		Y
2	V: PRED εγώ_**αρπάζω** <SUBJ >		Y
3	V: PRED **ρίχνω** <SUBJ,OBJ>, OBJ PRED= καρεκλοπόδαρο		N
4	V: PRED **έχω**_γούστο<SUBJ>, SUBJ COMPL=να	**έχω**_γούστο	N
5	V: PRED **μένω** <SUBJ,XCOMP>, XCOMP PRED=στήλη_άλας, XCOMP SUBJ=SUBJ	στήλη_άλας	N
6	V: PRED **μένω**< SUBJ,XCOMP>, XCOMP PRED=ταπί-και-**ψύχραιμος**, XCOMP SUBJ=SUBJ	ταπί_και _**ψύχραιμος**	N
7	V: PRED **τρώω/αρπάζω**<SUBJ,OBJ>, OBJ PRED=ο _ξύλο_ο _χρονιά, OBJ POSS PRED= **εγώ**, OBJ POSS TYPE= weak pronoun, OBJ POSS PERSON/NUMBER/GENDER =SUBJ PERSON/NUMBER/GENDER	ο_ξύλο_ο _χρονιά	N
8	V: PRED **ρίχνω** <SUBJ, OBJ, XCOMP>, XCOMP COMPL= να, OBJ PRED=άδειος, XCOMP PRED= **πιάνω**_γεμάτος, XCOMP SUBJ=SUBJ, XCOMP PERF=+, ¬(XCOMP TENSE)	**πιάνω** _γεμάτος	N
9	V: PRED **κάνω** <SUBJ, OBJ, XCOMP>, XCOMP COMPL=να, OBJ PRED= μαύρος_μάτι, XCOMP PRED=**βλέπω** <SUBJ, OBJ>, OBJ PRED=**εγώ,** XCOMP SUBJ=SUBJ, XCOMP PERF=+, ¬(XCOMP TENSE)	μαύρος_μάτι	N
10	V: PRED **τραβώ**<SUBJ, OBJ>, OBJ PRED= ο_λινάρι_ο_πάθος	ο_λινάρι ο_πάθος	N

Table 1. LFG analysis of MG verb MWEs used in this text. Boldfaced words inflect within the MWE. C: compositional. Only lemmatised forms are given.

5&6. **Free subject-copula-complement**: inflecting copula, complement fixed (Table 1:5), intervening XPs between the subject and the verb or between the copula and the complement, constituent permutations.

(5) Μένει η Ρέα στήλη άλατος
be-left-3-sg-pres the Rea-nom stele-of-salt
'Rea was left speechless.'

Alternatively, the complement may inflect (Table 1:6) and agree with the free subject.

(6) Και μένει η Ρέα
and be-left3-sg-pres the Rea-sg-fem-nom
ταπί και ψύχραιμη
penniless and calm-sg-fem-nom
'Rea lost all her money.'

7. **Free subject-verb-fixed object with subject bound possessive** (Table 1:7): inflecting verb, object modified with a subject bound possessive weak pronoun, intervening XPs between the object and the verb, constituent permutations.

(7) έφαγε/άρπαξε η Ρέα$_j$ το
eat/grab-3-sg-past the Rea-nom the
ξύλο της χρονιάς της$_j$
beating the year-gen weak-pron-fem-gen
'Rea was beaten up.'

8&9. **Free subject (controller)-verb-object-subordinated clause with controlled subject**: inflecting verb, object possibly fixed (Table 1: 9), the subordinated clause possibly semi-fixed (Table 1:8), intervening XPs, VSO/OVS word orders.

(8) Έριξαν άδεια να πιάσουν γεμάτα
throw-3-pl-past empty to catch-3-pl full
'They tried to obtain information.'

(9) έκανε η μάνα του
make-3-sg-past the mother-sg-nom his$_j$
μαύρα μάτια να τον δει
black eyes to him$_j$ see-3-sg
'It took his mother a long time to meet him.'

The transitive verb ρίχνω "throw" (8) is used as a control verb only in (8). An alternative analysis that would insure identity of subjects could treat the exemplified MWE as a coordination structure. We opted for the control approach and defined a special entry of the verb ρίχνω "throw" because the particle να typically introduces (probably controlled) subordinated clauses and the constraints on verbal forms are those of να-subordination and not of coordination.

10. **Free subject-verb-object** (Table 1:10): inflecting verb, fixed or non-fixed object, intervening XPs and OVS/VOS word order.

(10) Οι άνθρωποι τράβηξαν τότε
the people-pl-nom pull-3-pl-past then
του λιναριού τα πάθη
the linen the sufferings
'People suffered a lot then.'

3 Conclusions and future research

This is ongoing work but up to this point, natural analyses of the verb MWEs are possible with the standing rule component of our LFG grammar of MG. On the other hand, the entries of the two lexica we have developed, namely the filter and the XLE lexicon, provide a rich resource for studying the features of the idiomaticity that verb MWEs bring into 'normal' MG (indicatively, see discussion of (8)). In the immediate future, we will use the same methodology to parse the remaining types of MWE in our collection and will draw on the accumulated evidence to study the linguistic phenomena observed in verb MWEs against more general semasio-syntactic properties of MG, for instance the role of control constructions and of animacy in this language. We will consider a more sophisticated design of the filter. Last, we plan to investigate the issue of semantic representation of MWEs.

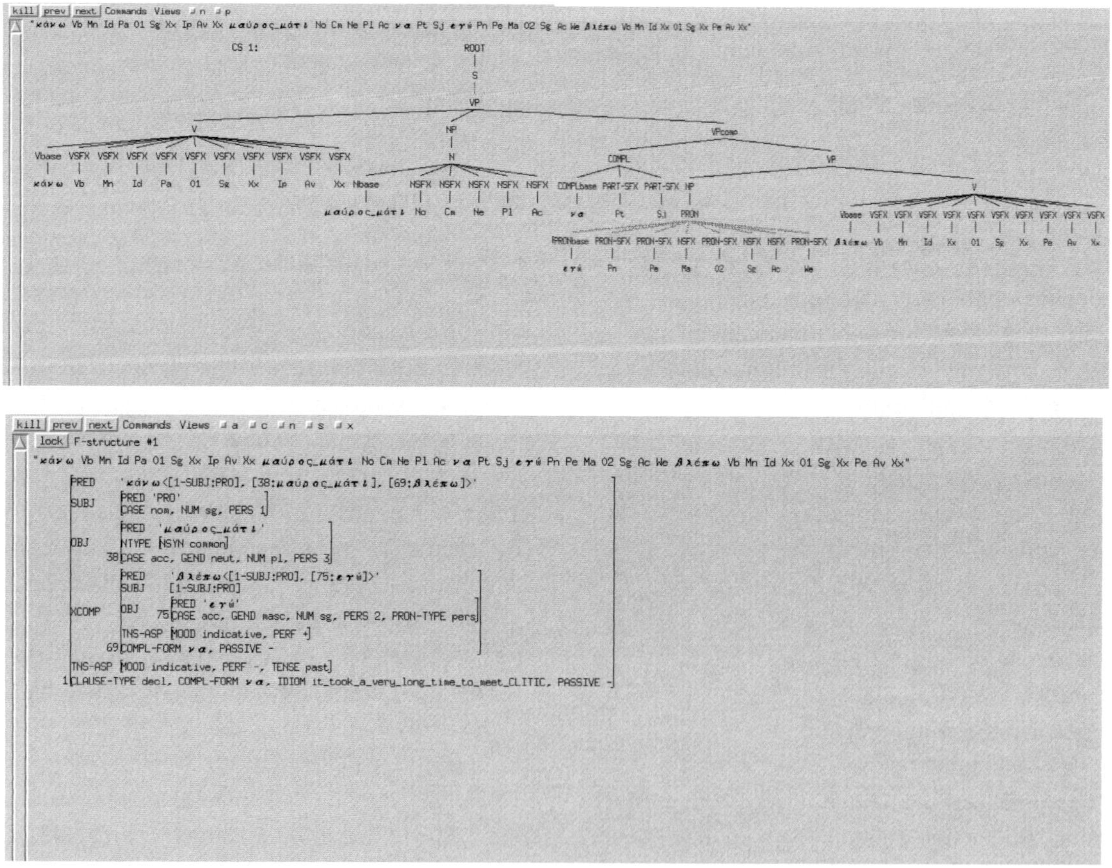

Fig. 1. The XLE output for the flexilbe verb MWE έκανα μαύρα μάτια να σε δω (Table 1: 9).

Acknowledgements

We thank Tracy Holloway-King for her contribution to the development of the sublexical rules.

References

Αναστασιάδη-Συμεωνίδη, Άννα. 1986. *Η Νεολογία στην Κοινή Νεοελληνική*, Θεσσαλονίκη. ΕΕΦΣ του ΑΠΘ, Παράρτημα αρ. 65.

Attia, Mohammed A. 2006. Accommodating Multiword Expressions in an Arabic LFG Grammar. Salakoski, Tapio, Ginter, Filip, Pahikkala, Tapio, Pyysalo, Tampo: *Lecture Notes in Computer Science: Advances in Natural Language Processing, 5th International Conference, FinTAL*. Turku, Finland. Vol. 4139: 87-98. Springer-Verlag Berlin Heidelberg.

Copestake, Ann, Fabre Lambeau, Aline Villavicencio, Francis Bond, Timothy Balwin, Ivan A. Sag, and Dan Flickinger. 2002. Multiword expressions: linguistic precision and reusability. *Proceedings of the 3rd International Conference on Language Resources and Evaluation*. Las Palmas, Canary Islands.

Fotopoulou, Aggeliki. 1993. *Une Classification des Phrases a Complements Figes en Grec Moderne*. Doctoral Thesis, Universite Paris VIII.

Gross, Maurice. 1988a. Les limites de la phrase figée. *Langage* 90: 7-23.

Gross, Maurice. 1988b. Sur les phrases figées complexes du français. *Langue française* 77: 47-70.

Mini, Marianna, Kleopatra Diakogiorgi and Aggeliki Fotopoulou. 2011. What can children tell us about idiomatic phrases' fixedness: the psycholinguistic relevance of a linguistic model. *DISCOURS (Revue de linguistique, psycholinguistique et informatique)(9)*.

Oflazer, Kemal, Ozlem Cetinoglu and Bilge Say. 2004. Integrating Morphology with Mutli-word Expression Processing in Turkish. *Second ACL Workshop on Multiword Expressions: Integrating Processing*: 64-71.

Papageorgiou, Haris, Prokopis Prokopidis, Voula Giouli and Stelios Piperidis. 2000. A Unified POS Tagging Architecture and its Application to Greek. *Proceedings of the 2nd Language Resources and Evaluation Conference*. Athens.

Sag, Ivan A., Timothy Baldwin, Francis Bond, Ann Copestake and Dan Flickinger. 2002. Multiword Expressions: A Pain in the Neck for NLP. LinGO Working Paper No. 2001-03. In Alexander Gelbukh, ed., (2002) *Proceedings of CICLING-2002*. Springer.

ILSP FBT Tagger http://lrt.clarin.eu/tools/ilsp-feature-based-multi-tiered-pos-tagger

XLE documentantion http://www2.parc.com/isl/groups/nltt/xle/doc/xle_toc.html

References used for the development of the filter:

http://interoperating.info/courses/perl4data/node/26
http://stackoverflow.com/questions/2970845/how-to-parse-multi-record-xml-file-ues-xmlsimple-in-perl
http://stackoverflow.com/questions/2039143/how-can-i-access-attributes-and-elements-from-xmllibxml-in-perl
http://stackoverflow.com/questions/7041719/using-perl-xmllibxml-to-parse
http://stackoverflow.com/questions/10404152/perl-script-to-parse-xml-using-xmllibxml
http://www.perlmonks.org/index.pl?node_id=490846
http://lethain.com/xml-simple-for-non-perlers/

Perl:
http://perldoc.perl.org/perlintro.html
http://learn.perl.org/
http://qntm.org/files/perl/perl.html
http://www.perl.org/books/beginning-perl/
http://www.it.uom.gr/project/perl/win32perltut.html

http://www.comp.leeds.ac.uk/Perl/sandtr.html
http://www.troubleshooters.com/codecorn/littperl/perlreg.htm
http://www.cs.tut.fi/~jkorpela/perl/regexp.html
http://www.somacon.com/p127.php
http://perlmaven.com/splice-to-slice-and-dice-arrays-in-perl
http://www.perlmonks.org/?node_id=822947
http://www.perlmonks.org/?node_id=911102

Evaluation of a Substitution Method for Idiom Transformation in Statistical Machine Translation

Giancarlo D. Salton and **Robert J. Ross** and **John D. Kelleher**
Applied Intelligence Research Centre
School of Computing
Dublin Institute of Technology
Ireland
giancarlo.salton@mydit.ie {robert.ross,john.d.kelleher}@dit.ie

Abstract

We evaluate a substitution based technique for improving Statistical Machine Translation performance on idiomatic multiword expressions. The method operates by performing substitution on the original idiom with its literal meaning before translation, with a second substitution step replacing literal meanings with idioms following translation. We detail our approach, outline our implementation and provide an evaluation of the method for the language pair English/Brazilian-Portuguese. Our results show improvements in translation accuracy on sentences containing either morphosyntactically constrained or unconstrained idioms. We discuss the consequences of our results and outline potential extensions to this process.

1 Introduction

Idioms are a form of figurative multiword expressions (MWE) that are ubiquitous in speech and written text across a range of discourse types. Idioms are often characterized in terms of their having non-literal and non-compositional meaning whilst occasionally sharing surface realizations with literal language uses (Garrao and Dias, 2001). For example the multiword expression *s/he took the biscuit* can have both a figurative meaning of being (pejoratively) remarkable, and a literal meaning of removing the cookie.

It is notable that idioms are a compact form of language use which allow large fragments of meaning with relatively complex social nuances to be conveyed in a small number of words, i.e., idioms can be seen as a form of compacted regularized language use. This is one reason why idiom use is challenging to second language learners (see, e.g., Cieslicka(2006)).

Another difficulty for second language learners in handling idioms is that idioms can vary in terms of their morphosyntactic constraints or *fixedness* (Fazly et al., 2008). On one hand some idiomatic expressions such as *popped the question* are highly fixed with syntactic and lexical variations considered unacceptable usage. On the other hand idioms such as *hold fire* are less fixed with variations such as *hold one's fire* and *held fire* considered to be acceptable instances of the idiom type.

For reasons such as those outlined above idioms can be challenging to human speakers; but they also pose a great challenge to a range of Natural Language Processing (NLP) applications (Sag et al., 2002). While idiomatic expressions, and more generally multiword expressions, have been widely studied in a number of NLP domains (Acosta et al., 2011; Moreno-Ortiz et al., 2013), their investigation in the context of machine translation has been more limited (Bouamor et al., 2011; Salton et al., 2014).

The broad goal of our work is to advance machine translation by improving the processing of idiomatic expressions. To that end, in this paper we introduce and evaluate our initial approach to the problem. We begin in the next section by giving a brief review of the problem of idiom processing in a Statistical Machine Translation (SMT) context. Following that we outline our substitution based solution to idiom processing in SMT. We then outline a study that we have conducted to evaluate our initial method. This is followed with results and a brief discussion before we draw conclusions and outline future work.

2 Translation & Idiomatic Expressions

The current state-of-the-art in machine translation is phrase-based SMT (Collins et al., 2005). Phrase-based SMT systems extend basic word-by-word SMT by splitting the translation process into 3 steps: the input source sentence is segmented into "phrases" or multiword units; these phrases are then translated into the target language; and finally the translated phrases are reordered if needed (Koehn, 2010). Although the term phrase-based translation might imply the system works at the semantic or grammatical phrasal level, it is worth noting that the concept of a phrase in SMT is simply a frequently occurring sequence of words. Hence, standard SMT systems do not model idioms explicitly (Bouamor et al., 2011).

Given the above, the question arises as to how SMT systems can best be enhanced to account for idiom usage and other similar multiword expressions. One direct way is to use a translation dictionary to insert the idiomatic MWE along with its appropriate translation into the SMT model phrase table along with an estimated probability. While this approach is conceptually simple, a notable drawback with such a method is that while the MWEs may be translated correctly the word order in the resulting translation is often incorrect (Okuma et al., 2008).

An alternative approach to extending SMT to handle idiomatic and other MWEs is to leave the underlying SMT model alone and instead perform intelligent pre- and post-processing of the translation material. Okuma et al. (2008) is an example of this approach applied to a class of multi- and single word expressions. Specifically, Okuma et al. (2008) proposed a substitution based pre and post processing approach that uses a dictionary of *surrogate words* from the same word class to replace low frequency (or unseen) words in the sentences before the translation with high frequency words from the same word class. Then, following the translation step, the *surrogate words* are replaced with the original terms. Okuma et al.'s direct focus was not on idioms but rather on place names and personal names. For example, given an English sentence containing the relatively infrequent place name ***Cardiff***, Okuma et al.'s approach would: (1) replace this low frequency place name with a high frequency *surrogate* place name, e.g. ***New York***; (2) translate the updated sentence; and (3) replace the *surrogate words* with the correct translation of the original term.

The advantage of this approach is that the word order of the resulting translation has a much higher probability of being correct. While this method was developed for replacing just one word (or a highly fixed name) at a time and those words must be of the same open-class category, we see the basic premise of pre- and post- substitution as also applicable to idiom substitution.

3 Methodology

The hypothesis we base our approach on is that the work-flow that a human translator would have in translating an idiom can be reproduced in an algorithmic fashion. Specifically, we are assuming a work-flow whereby a human translator first identifies an idiomatic expression within a source sentence, then 'mentally' replaces that idiom with its literal meaning. Only after this step would a translator produce the target sentence deciding whether or not to use an idiom on the result. For simplicity we assumed that the human translator should use an idiom in the target language if available. While this work-flow is merely a proposed method, we see it as plausible and have developed a computational method based on this work-flow and the substitution technique employed by (Okuma et al., 2008).

Our idiom translation method can be explained briefly in terms of a reference architecture as depicted in Figure 1. Our method makes use of 3 dictionaries and 2 pieces of software. The first dictionary contains entries for the source language idioms and their literal meaning, and is called the "Source Language Idioms Dictionary". The second dictionary meanwhile contains entries for the target language idioms and their literal meaning, and is called the "Target Language Idioms Dictionary". The third dictionary is a bilingual dictionary containing entries for the idioms in the source language pointing to their translated literal meaning in the target language. This is the "Bilingual Idiom Dictionary".

The two pieces of software are used in the pre- and post-processing steps. The first piece of software analyzes the source sentences, consulting the "Source Language Idioms Dictionary", to identify and replace the source idioms with their literal meaning in the source language. During this first step the partially rewritten source sentences are marked with replacements. Following the subsequent translation step the second piece of software is applied for the post-processing step. The software first looks into the marked sentences to obtain the original idioms. Then, consulting the "Bilingual Idiom Dictionary", the software tries to match a substring with the literal translated mean-

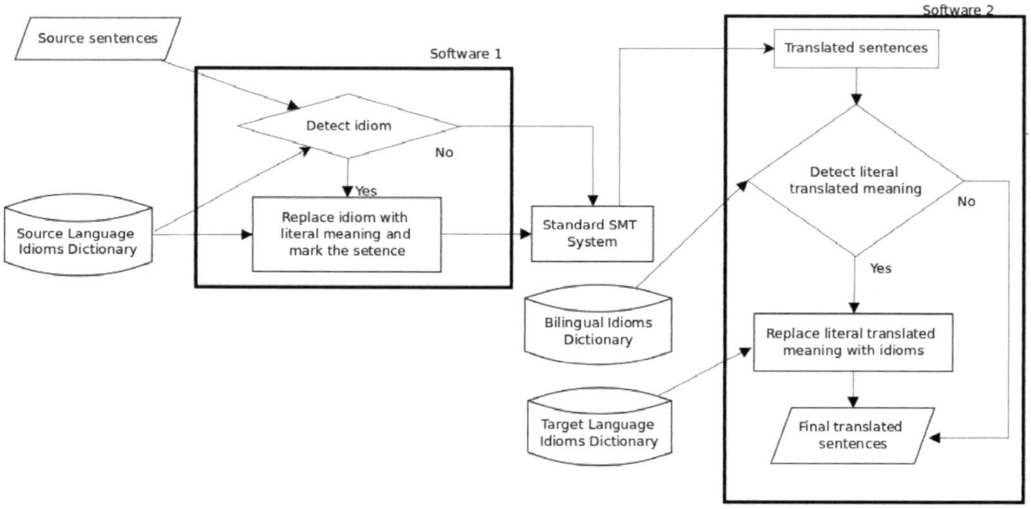

Figure 1: Reference Architecture for Substitution Based Idiom Translation Technique.

ing in the target translation. If the literal meaning is identified, it then checks the "Target Language Idioms Dictionary" for a corresponding idiom for the literal use in the target language. If found, the literal wording in the target translation is then replaced with an idiomatic phrase from the target language. However if in the post-processing step the original idiom substitution is not found, or if there are no corresponding idioms in the target language, then the post-processing software does nothing.

4 Study Design

We have developed an initial implementation of our substitution approach to SMT based idiom translation for the language pair English/Brazillian-Portugese. To evaluate our method we created test corpora where each sentence contained an idiom, and compared the BLEU scores (Papineni et al., 2002) of a baseline SMT system when run on these test corpora with the BLEU scores for the same SMT system when we applied our pre and post processing steps. No sentences with literal uses of the selected idiom form were used in this experiment.

Consequently, three corpora were required for this experiment in addition to the three idiomatic resources introduced in the last section. The first corpus was an initial large sentence-aligned bilingual corpus that was used to build a SMT model for the language pair English/Brazilian-Portuguese. The second corpus was the first of two test corpora. This corpus contained sentences with "highly fixed" idioms and will be referred to as the "High Fixed Corpus". Finally a second test corpus containing sentences with "low fixed" idioms, the "Low Fixed Corpus", was also constructed. In order to make results comparable across test corpora the length of sentences in each of the two test corpora were kept between fifteen and twenty words.

To create the initial large corpus a series of small corpora available on the internet were compiled into one larger corpus which was used to train a SMT system. The resources used in this step were Fapesp-v2 (Aziz and Specia, 2011), the OpenSubtitles2013[1] corpus, the PHP Manual Corpus[2] and the KDE4 localizaton files (v.2)[3]. No special tool was used to clean these corpora and the files were compiled as is.

To create the "High Fixed Corpus" and "Low Fixed Corpus" we built upon the previous work of Fazly et al. (2008) who identified a dataset of 17 "highly fixed" English verb+noun idioms, and 11 "low fixed" English verb+noun idioms. Based on these lists our two test corpora were built by extracting English sentences from the internet which contained instances of each of the high and low fixed idiom types. Each collected sentence was manually translated into Brazilian-Portuguese, before each translations was manually checked and corrected by a second translator. Ten sentences were collected for each idiom type. This resulted in a High Fixed corpus consisting of 170 sentences

[1]http://opus.lingfil.uu.se/OpenSubtitles2013.php
[2]http://opus.lingfil.uu.se/PHP.php
[3]http://opus.lingfil.uu.se/KDE4.php

containing idiomatic usages of those idioms, and a Low-Fixed corpus consisting of 110 sentences containing instances of low-fixed idioms.

As indicated three idiomatic resources were also required for the study. These were: a dictionary of English idioms and their literal meanings; a dictionary of Brazilian-Portuguese idioms and their literal meanings; and a bilingual dictionary from English to Brazilian-Portuguese. The English idioms dictionary contained entries for the idioms pointing to their literal English meanings, along with some morphological variations of those idioms. The Brazilian-Portuguese idioms dictionary similarly contained entries for the idioms pointing to their literal meanings with some morphological variations of those idioms. Finally, the bilingual dictionary contained entries for the same idioms along with morphological variations of the English idioms dictionary but pointing to their literal translated meaning. The Oxford Dictionary of English idioms and the Cambridge Idioms Dictionary were used to collect the literal meanings of the English idioms. Literal meanings were manually translated to Brazilian-Portuguese.

Following resource collection and construction a SMT model for English/Brazilian-Portuguese was trained using the Moses toolkit (Koehn et al., 2007) using its baseline settings. The corpus used for this training consisted of 17,288,109 pairs of sentences (approximately 50% of the initial collected corpus), with another 34,576 pairs of sentences used for the "tuning" process. Following this training and tuning process the baseline translation accuracy, or BLEU scores, were calculated for the two test corpora, i.e., for the "High Fixed Corpus", and the "Low Fixed Corpus".

Having calculated the baseline BLEU scores, the substitution method was then applied to retranslate each of the two test corpora. Specifically both the "High Fixed Corpus" and the "Low Fixed Corpus" were passed through our extended pipeline with new substitution based translations constructed for each of the test corpora. BLEU scores were then calculated for these two output corpora that were built using the substitution method.

5 Results and Discussion

Table 1 presents the results of the evaluation. The BLEU scores presented in the table compare the baseline SMT system against our proposed method for handling English idiomatic MWE of the verb+noun type.

Corpus	Baseline	Substitution
High Idiomatic	23.12	31.72
Low Idiomatic	24.55	26.07

Table 1: Experiment's results.

Overall the results are positive. For both the high and low idiomatic corpora we find that applying the pre- and post-processing substitution approach improves the BLEU score of the SMT system. However, it is notable that the High-Fixed idiomatic corpus showed a considerably larger increase in BLEU score than was the case for the Low-Fixedness idiomatic cases, i.e., a positive increase of 8.6 versus 1.52. To investigate further we applied a paired t-test to test for significance in mean difference between baseline and substitution methods for both the high-fixed and low-fixed test corpora. While the results for the "High Idiomatic Corpus" demonstrated a statistically significant difference in BLEU scores ($p \ll 0.05$), the difference between the baseline and substitution method was not statistically significant for the case of the "Low Idiomatic Corpus" ($p \approx 0.7$). We believe the lack of improvement in the case of low fixed idioms may be caused by a higher morphosyntactic variation in the translations of the low fixed idioms. This higher variation makes the post-processing step of our approach (which requires matching a substring in the translated sentence) more difficult for low fixed idioms with the result that our approach is less effective for these idioms.

It is worth noting that the same SMT system (without the substitution extension) achieved a BLEU score of 62.28 on a corpus of sentences from general language; and, achieved an average BLEU score of 46.48 over a set of 5 corpora of sentences that did not contain idioms and were of simlar length to the idiomatic corpora used in this study (15 to 20 words). Both these BLEU scores are higher than the scores we report in Table 1 for our substitution method. This indicates that although our substitution approach does improve BLEU scores when translating idioms there is still a lot of work to be done to solve the problems posed by idioms to SMT.

6 Conclusion

Our results indicate that this substitution approach does improve the performance of the system. However, we are aware that this method is not the entire solution for the MWE problem in SMT. The effectiveness of the approach is dependent on the fixedness of the idiom being translated.

This approach relies on several language resources, including: idiomatic dictionaries in the source and target languages and a bilingual dictionary containing entries for the idioms in the source language aligned with their translated literal meaning in the target language. In future work we investigate techniques that we can use to (semi)automatically address dictionary construction. We will also work on enabling the system to distinguish between idiomatic vs. literal usages of idioms.

Acknowledgments

Giancarlo D. Salton would like to thank CAPES ("Coordenação de Aperfeiçoamento de Pessoal de Nível Superior") for his Science Without Borders scholarship, proc n. 9050-13-2. We would like to thank Acassia Thabata de Souza Salton for her corrections on the Brazilian-Portuguese translation of sentences containing idioms.

References

Otavio Costa Acosta, Aline Villavicencio, and Viviane P. Moreira. 2011. Identification and Treatment of Multiword Expressions applied to Information Retrieval. In *Proceedings of the Workshop on Multiword Expressions: from Parsing and Generation to the Real World (MWE 2011)*, pages 101–109.

Wilker Aziz and Lucia Specia. 2011. Fully automatic compilation of a portuguese-english and portuguese-spanish parallel corpus for statistical machine translation. In *STIL 2011*.

Dhouha Bouamor, Nasredine Semmar, and Pierre Zweigenbaum. 2011. Improved Statistical Machine Translation Using MultiWord Expressions. In *Proceedings of the International Workshop on Using Linguistic Information for Hybrid Machine Translation)*, pages 15–20.

Anna Cieślicka. 2006. Literal salience in on-line processing of idiomatic expressions by second language learners. 22(2):115–144.

Michael Collins, Philipp Koehn, and Ivona Kučerová. 2005. Clause Restructuring for Statistical Machine Translation. In *Proceedings of the 43rd Annual Meeting of the ACL*, pages 531–540.

Afsanesh Fazly, Paul Cook, and Suzanne Stevenson. 2008. Unsupervised Type and Token Identification of Idiomatic Expressions. In *Computational Linguistics*, volume 35, pages 61–103.

Milena U. Garrao and Maria C. P. Dias. 2001. Um Estudo de Expressões Cristalizadas do Tipo V+Sn e sua Inclusão em um Tradutor Automático Bilíngüe (Português/Inglês). In *Cadernos de Tradução*, volume 2, pages 165–182.

Philipp Koehn, Hieu Hoang, Alexandra Birch, Chris Callison-Burch, Marcello Federico, Nicola Bertoldi, Brooke Cowan, Wade Shen, Christine Moran, Richard Zens, Chris Dyer, Ondrej Bojar, Alexandra Constantin, and Evan Herbst. 2007. Moses: Open Source Toolkit for Statistical Machine Translation. In *45th Annual Meeting of the Association for Computational Linguistics*.

Philipp Koehn. 2010. *Statistical Machine Translation*. Cambridge University Press, New York. 2 Ed.

Antonio Moreno-Ortiz, Chantal Pérez-Hernández, and M. Ángeles Del-Olmo. 2013. Managing Multiword Expressions in a Lexicon-Based Sentiment Analysis System for Spanish. In *Proceedings of the 9th Workshop on Multiword Expressions (MWE 2013)*, pages 1–10.

Hideo Okuma, Hirofumi Yamamoto, and Eiichiro Sumita. 2008. Introducing Translation Dictionary Into Phrase-based SMT. In *IEICE - Transactions on Information and Systems*, number 7, pages 2051–2057.

Kishore Papineni, Salim Roukos, Todd Ward, and Wei-Jing Zhu. 2002. BLEU: a method for automatic evaluation of machine translation. In *Proceedings of the 40th Annual Meeting of the Association for Computational Linguistics (ACL)*, pages 311–318.

Ivan A. Sag, Thimothy Baldwin, Francis Bond, Ann Copestake, and Dan Flickinger. 2002. Multiword Expressions: A Pain in the Neck for NLP. In *Computational Linguistics and Intelligent Text Processing: Third International Conference: CICLing-2002, Lecture Notes in Computer Science*, volume 2276, pages 1–15.

Giancarlo D. Salton, Robert J. Ross, and John D. Kelleher. 2014. An Empirical Study of the Impact of Idioms on Phrase Based Statistical Machine Translation of English to Brazilian-Portuguese. In *Third Workshop on Hybrid Approaches to Translation (HyTra) at 14th Conference of the European Chapter of the Association for Computational Linguistics*.

Encoding MWEs in a conceptual lexicon

Aggeliki Fotopoulou, Stella Markantonatou, Voula Giouli

Institute for Language and Speech Processing, R.C. "Athena'

{afotop;marks;voula}@ilsp.athena-innovation.gr

Abstract

The proposed paper reports on work in progress aimed at the development of a conceptual lexicon of Modern Greek (MG) and the encoding of MWEs in it. Morphosyntactic and semantic properties of these expressions were specified formally and encoded in the lexicon. The resulting resource will be applicable for a number of NLP applications.

1 Introduction

Substantial research in linguistics has been devoted to the analysis and classification of MWEs from different perspectives (Fraser, 1970; Chomsky, 1980; M. Gross 1982, 1988; Ruwet, 1983; der Linden, 1992; Nunberg et al., 1994; Howarth, 1996; Jackendoff, 1997; Moon, 1998; Fellbaum, 2007). Moreover, cognitive and psycholinguistic approaches to MWEs (Lakoff, 1993; Gibbs, 1998; Glucksberg, 1993; Diakogiorgi&Fotopoulou, 2012) have accounted for their interpretation. Within the NLP community, there is a growing interest in the identification of MWEs and their robust treatment, as this seems to improve parsing accuracy (Nivre and Nilsson, 2004; Arun and Keller, 2005). In this respect, the development of large-scale, robust language resources that may be integrated in parsing systems is of paramount importance. Representation, however, of MWEs in lexica poses a number of challenges.

2 Basic Notions

Typically, fixed MWEs are identified and classified on the basis of semantic, lexical and morphosyntactic criteria. (M. Gross, 1982, 1987; Lamiroy, 2003), namely:

- non-compositionality: i.e., the meaning of the expression cannot be computed from the meanings of its constituents and the rules used to combine them. Nevertheless, according to (Nunberg et *al,* 1994), compositionality refers to the fact that the constituents of some idioms "carry identifiable parts of the idiomatic meaning". *Variability* has been further emphasised in (Hamblin and Gibbs 1999) and (Nunberg et al. 1994): fixed expressions appear in a continuum of compositionality, which ranges from expressions that are very analysable to others that are partially analysable or ultimately non-analysable.
- non-substitutability: at least one of the expression constituents does not enter in alternations at the paradigmatic axis
- non-modifiability: MWEs are syntactically rigid structures, in that there are constraints concerning modification, transformations, etc.

These criteria, however, do not apply in all cases in a uniform way. The *variability* attested brings about the notion 'degree of fixedness' (G. Gross 1996). The kind and degree of fixedness result in the classification of these expressions as *fixed, semi-fixed, syntactically flexible* or *collocations* (Sag et al, 2002). It is crucial for a satisfactory MWEs representation in a computational lexicon to provide an accurate and functional formal modelling of *fixedness, variability* and *compositionality.*

In this paper, we will discuss the classification and encoding of compounds and fixed MWEs in a conceptually organised lexicon of MG.

3 The conceptual lexicon

The conceptually organised lexicon that is under development (Markantonatou & Fotopoulou, 2007) capitalises on two basic notions: (a) the notion of lexical fields, along with (b) the Saussurian notion of sign and its two inseparable facets, namely, the *SIGNIFIER* and the *SIGNIFIED* as the building blocks (main classes) of the underlying ontology.

In this sense, the intended language resource is a linguistic ontology in which words are instances in the *SIGNIFIER* class. At this level, morphological, syntactic and functional information about lemmas is encoded. Similarly, word meanings are instances in the *SIGNIFIED* class. Each instance in the *SIGNIFIER* class is mapped onto a concept, the latter represented as an instance in the *SIGNIFIED* class.

The Instances of the class *SIGNIFIER* are specified for (a) features pertaining to lexical semantic relations (i.e, synonymy, antonymy); (b) lexical relations such as word families, allomorphs, syntactic variants etc.; and (c) morphosyntactic properties (PoS, gender, declension, argument structure, word specific information etc.). Values for these features are assigned to both single- and multi-word entries in the lexicon. MWEs are further coupled with rich linguistic information pertaining to the lexical, syntactic and semantic levels.

4 Encoding MWEs in the lexicon

MWEs are encoded as instances in the SIGNIFIER class of our ontology and are also mapped onto the corresponding concepts or word meanings (instances in the SIGNIFIED class).

In the remaining, we focus on the encoding of MWEs as instances in the SIGNIFIER class. We cater for sub-classes corresponding to grammatical categories (verb, noun, adjective, adverb, preposition, etc) under the class SIGNIFIER in our schema. The class MWEs (as opposed to the class Simple Lexical Units) has been defined further under the verb, noun, adjective and adverb sub-classes.

Syntactic configurations pertaining to each class are also represented as distinct sub-classes hierarchically organised under the verb, noun, adjective and adverb classes. Morphosyntactic properties, selectional preferences, and semantic interpretation patterns are provided for each MWE depending on the grammatical category it pertains to; encoding is based on a set of parameters represented as feature-value pairs.

More precisely, a typology of Greek verbal MWEs has been defined in (Fotopoulou, 1993, Mini, 2009) (NP V NP1 NP2…) and of nominal MWEs in (Anastasiadis, 1986) (Adj N, NN…) on the basis of the lexical and syntactic configurations involved. This typology has been mapped onto a hierarchy under classes *verb* and *noun*).

In our approach, the main distinction between *collocations* and *fixed MWEs* is made explicit. The degree and type of fixedness are then encoded as features. Further morphosyntactic information is also encoded depending on the grammatical category of the MWE (i.e., declension of one or more constituents, *only_singular* or *only_plural* for nouns, etc.). In this way, information that may be useful for the automatic identification and interpretation of the MWEs may be retained. Moreover, the standard set of features inherited from the class SIGNIFIER is also retained (PoS, Gender, Number, Tense, synonyms, antonyms, etc.).

4.1. The encoding schema

We have so far implemented an encoding schema for nominal and verbal MWEs. We aimed at encoding rich linguistic knowledge in a formal way that would be exploitable in computer applications. The two types of fixedness (collocations and fixed) are encoded as features: (a) *Lexical_variance*, and (b) *Is_actually*.

The feature *Lexical_variance*[1] has as possible values (yes or no). Collocations (assigned a yes value) are further specified with respect to alternative lemmas; these lemmas are encoded in the appropriate feature *Variants*. For instance, in example (1) the two alternative lemmas are *καταστάσεις* and *περιστάσεις*:

(1) *έκτακτες (καταστάσεις / περιστάσεις)*
(=emergency (situations / circumstances))

The feature *Is_actually* (with possible values yes or no) encodes information about the interpretation pattern: a value *yes* signifies a compositional or partially compositional meaning; on the contrary, a value *no* denotes a non-compositional interpretation (fixed meaning).

Collocations are by default assigned feature values corresponding to a compositional meaning. In these cases, the feature *maintains_meaning* further specifies the constituent(s) that contribute to the non-fixed interpretation of the expression. For example, the meaning of the compound in (2) is retained from the meaning of the first noun *ταξίδι* (=trip), which, in turn, is the value assigned to the *maintains_meaning* feature:

[1]In our MWE classification scheme, a lexical unit is considered 'fixed' at the lemma level. This is because MG is a heavily inflected language.

(2) *ταξίδι αστραπή* (trip - lightning (=very sudden and short trip)

<maintains_meaning = ταξίδι />

Finally, the feature *has_meta_meaning* signifies further the constituent(s) – if any – bearing a figurative meaning. For example, the compound *ταξίδι αστραπή* in (2) assumes the figurative meaning of the second noun *αστραπή* (=very sudden and short-term).

On the contrary, verbal and nominal expressions with a non-compositional meaning are assigned a negative value *(no)* for the *Is_actually* feature since their constituents do not contribute to a compositional meaning; therefore, the features *maintains_meaning* and *has_meta_meaning* are left empty as non-applicable. This is exemplified in (3) below; the constituents *παιδική* (=kids') and χαρά (=joy) of the expression *παιδική χαρά* (=playground) do not contribute to the overall interpretation:

(3) *παιδική χαρά* (=playground*)*

<maintains_meaning/>

<has_meta_meaning/>

This schema that applies to both nominal and verbal MWES, is presented in Table 1 below.

Slot	**Values**
mwe_type	*Fixed; collocation*
Lexical_variance	*Boolean (yes, no)*
Variants	*string*
Is_actually	*Boolean (yes, no)*
maintains_meaning	*String*
has_meta_meaning	*String*

Table 1 The encoding schema for nouns & verbs

4.2. Nominal MWEs

Furthermore, nominal MWEs are also assigned values for features that are specific to the nominal MWEs. Information on inflected constituents - if any – is provided in the declension feature; values for *only_singular* and *only_plural* provide further morphological/usage information; when used in combination with other features (i.e, *is_actually*) this type of information is evidence of fixedness. Frequent co-occurrence patterns with verbs are provided in the *verb_combined* feature; finally, alternative nominalised forms are listed as values of the feature *nominalization*. The schema is presented in the table below:

only singular	*Boolean (yes, no)*
only plural:	*Boolean (yes, no)*
N_declension	*N1, N2, N1_N2, Adj_N*
verb_combined	*string*
Nominalization	*string*

Table 2 The encoding schema for nouns

4.3. Verbal MWEs

In the typology adopted for the verbal idiomatic expressions, fixedness can be limited to only certain constituents of the sentence; a combination of fixed and non-fixed constituents in *Subject* or *Object* position is permitted. For example, in sentences (4) and (5) below, fixedness relies on the relation among the verbs and the nouns that function as *Objects* (direct and indirect) and as *Subject* respectively:

(4) *δίνω τόπο*$_{NP\text{-acc, Obj}}$ *στην οργή*$_{PP}$

to give way to anger (=to swallow one's pride/anger)

(5) *ανάβουν τα λαμπάκια μου*$_{\text{NP-nom, Subj}}$

my lights are switched on (=to become very angry)

Moreover, the typology allows for a restricted alternation of fixed elements of the expression. For example, in the MWE in (6), the two alternative lemmas are *τάζω* and *υπόσχομαι*:

(6) *τάζω / υπόσχομαι τον ουρανό με τ' άστρα*

to undertake to offer / promise the sky with the stars

This information is encoded in verbal MWEs, namely: (a) the syntactic properties of the verb that occurs in the expression (*valency*); and (b) fixed and non-fixed arguments either in *Subject* or *Object* position. Moreover, selectional restrictions applied to the arguments (such as +/-human) are also added.

The encoding schema that applies to verbal MWEs specifically is presented in Table 3. In this schema, *N* signifies a non-fixed noun, whereas C denotes a fixed one; number *0* (in *N0* and *C0*) is used to represent a noun (either fixed or non-fixed in Subject position), and *1, 2, 3,* etc. denote complements in *Object* position (or complements of prepositional phrases). Other features provide rich linguistic information regarding facets of the expression in terms of: (a) selectional restrictions (i.e., the features *N0_type, N1_type,* etc., accept as values the semantic category in which a noun in *Subject* or *Object* position respectively, belongs to), (b) syntactic alternations (i.e., *Poss_Ppv* encodes the alternation among possessive and personal pronoun), grammatical information (i.e., *Ppv_case* encodes the case of the personal pronoun), etc.

Slot	Value
N0_type	*hum, -hum, npc*
C0_variants	*string*
Poss=Ppv	*Boolean (yes or no)*
Ppv_case	*gen, acc*
N1_type	*hum, -hum, npc (Nom de partie du corps/noun of the part of body)*
N2_type	*hum, -hum, npc*
N3_type	*hum, -hum, npc*
C1_variants	*string*
C2_variants	*string*
C3_variants	*string*

Table 3. The encoding schema for verbs

Alternative nouns (in Subject or Object position) that oftern co-occur with the verbal expression are also provided for (C0_variant, C1_variant, etc).

5. Discussion

As it has been shown above, in our lexicon we have opted for an approach to MWE representation that builds on rich linguistic knowledge. The linguistic classifications adopted deal with morphology, syntax, and semantics interface aspects. Thus, a lexicon – grammar representation of MWEs has been constructed by encoding key morphosyntactic and semantic information.The typology of verbal MWEs shares common characteristics with similar efforts for other languages (i.e, DuELME, Gregoire, 2010 Morphosyntactic properties and selectional preferences account better for a number of phenomena, inherent in the Greek language, as for example word order and gaps attested in running text.

More specifically, Greek is a language with a relatively free word order, and idiomatic expressions often occur in texts in various configurations. The encoding of fixed and non-fixed constituents provides, therefore, extra information for the identification of expressions in texts. Moreover, the identification of MWEs as collocations entails a relatively loose fixedness, allowing, thus, for gaps and discontinuities as shown in (7):

(7) *Το κόμμα έχει <u>αριθμό</u> υποψηφίων-<u>ρεκόρ</u>*

The political party has a <u>number</u> of candidates <u>record</u> (=many candidates)

6. Conclusions and Future work

We have given an overview of the conceptual lexicon currently under development and the treatment of MWEs in it. We have so far treated nominal and verbal MWEs (~1000 entries). Future work involves the population of the lexicon with new expressions also pertaining to the grammatical categories adjective and adverb and the definition of a fine-grained typology for the latter. Moreover, a more granular representation of fixedness will be attempted. Compatibility of the resource with diverse syntactic approaches will also be investigated. The evaluation of the final resource will be performed by integrating it in a tool that automatically recognizes MWEs in texts.

References

Αναστασιάδη-Συμεωνίδη Ά. (1986). *Η νεολογία στην Κοινή Νεοελληνική.* Θεσσαλονίκη: Αριστοτέλειο Πανεπιστήμιο Θεσσαλονίκης (Επιστημονική Επετηρίδα Φιλοσοφικής Σχολής).

Arun, A. and F. Keller. 2005. Lexicalisation in crosslinguistic probablisitic parsing: The case of french. In *Proceedings of the 43rd Annual Meeting of the Association for Computational Linguistics*, pp 306–313. Ann Arbor, MI

Chomsky, N. 1980. *Rules and Representations*. New York: Columbia University Press.

Diakogiorgi, K. & Fotopoulou, A. 2012. Interpretation of Idiomatic Expressions by Greek Speaking Children: implications for the Linguistic and Psycholinguistic Research. An interdisciplinary approach. *Lingvisticae Investigationes*, Volume 35:1. 1-27, John Benjamins, Paris, France

Fellbaum, C. 2007. Introduction. Fellbaum, C. (ed). *Idioms and Collocations: Corpus-based Linguistic and Lexicographic Studies*. London: Continuum, 1-

Fotopoulou, A. 1993. *Une Classification des Phrases à Compléments Figés en Grec Moderne*. Doctoral Thesis, Universite Paris VIII.

Fraser, B. 1970. Idioms within a Transformational Grammar. *Foundations of language*, 1, 22-42.

Fritzinger, F., Weller, M., and Heid. U. 2010. A survey of idiomatic preposition-noun-verb tiples on token level. In *Proceedings of LREC-10.*

Grégoire, N. 2010. DuELME: a Dutch electronic lexicon of multiword expressions; *Lang Resources & Evaluation* (2010) 44:23–39

Gibbs R.W. 1998. The Fight over Metaphor in Thought and Language. In A.N. Katz, C. Cacciari, R.W. Gibbs & M. Turner (eds.), *Figurative Language and Thought*. OUP, 88-118.

Glucksberg, S. 1993. Idiom meanings and allusional context. In *Idioms: Processing, structure, and intepretation*. C. Cacciari and P. Tabossi (eds.). Hillsdale, NJ: Erlbaum, 201-225.

Gross, G. 1996. Les expressions figées en français. Noms composés et autres locutions. Paris/Gap: Ophrys.

Gross, M. 1982. Une classification des phrases figées du français. Revue Québécoise de Linguistique 11 (2), 151-185.

Gross, M. 1988a. Les limites de la phrase figée. *Langage* 90: 7-23

Gross, Maurice. 1988b. Sur les phrases figées complexes du français. *Langue française* 77: 4770.

Hamblin, J., and Gibbs, W. R. 1999. Why You Can't Kick the Bucket as You Slowly Die: Verbs in Idiom Comprehension. *Journal of Psycholinguistic Research*. 28 (1): 25-39.

Howarth P.A. 1996. Phraseology in English academic writing. *Lexicographica Series* 75. Tübingen: Max Niemeyer. Jackendoff R. 1997. *The Architecture of the Language Faculty*. MIT Press.

Lakoff G. 1993. The Contemporary Theory of Metaphor. In A. Ortony (ed.), *Metaphor and Thought*, 2nd edition Cambridge University Press, 202-251.

Lamiroy, B. 2003. Les notions linguistiques de figement et de contrainte. *Lingvisticae Investigationes* 26:1, 53-66, Amsterdam/Philadelphia: John Benjamins.

van der Linden E-J. 1992. Incremental processing and the hierarchical lexicon. *Computational Linguistics*, 18, 219-238

Markantonatou, Stella and Fotopoulou, Aggeliki. 2007. The tool "Ekfrasi". In *Proceedings of the 8th International Conference on Greek Linguistics, The Lexicography Workshop*. Ioannina, Greece.

Markantonatou, S., Fotopoulou, A., Mini, M. & Alexopoulou, M. 2010. In search of the right word. In *Proceedings of Cogalex-2: Cognitive Aspects of the Lexicon, 2nd SIGLEX endorsed Workshop*. Beijing.

Mini, M. 2009. *Linguistic and Psycholinguistic Study of Fixed Verbal Expressions with Fixed Subject in Modern Greek: A Morphosyntactic Analysis, Lexicosemantic Gradation and Processing by Elementary School Children*. Unpublished doctoral dissertation. University of Patras.

Moon, R. 1998. *Fixed Expressions and Idioms in English: A Corpus-Based Approach*. Oxford: OUP.

Nivre, J. and Nilsson, J. 2004. Multiword units in syntactic parsing. *Workshop on Methodologies and Evaluation of Multiword Units in Real-World Applications*.

Nunberg ,G., Sag I., Wasow, T. 1994. Idioms. *Language* 70, 491-538.

Ruwet, N. 1983. Du Bon Usage des Expressions Idiomatiques dans l'Argumentation en Syntaxe Générative. *Revue Québecoise de Linguistique* 13 (1): 9-145.

Sag, I.A., Bond, F., Copestake A., Flickinger, D. 2001. Multiword Expressions. LinGO Working PaperNo.2001-01.

Sag, Ivan A., T.Baldwin, F.Bond, A. Copestake and Dan Flickinger.2001.Multiword Expressions: A Pain in the Neck for NLP. LinGO Working Paper No. 2001-03. In Alexander Gelbukh, ed., (2002) Proceedings of COLING-2002.

German Compounds and Statistical Machine Translation. Can they get along?

Carla Parra Escartín
University of Bergen
Bergen, Norway
carla.parra@uib.no

Stephan Peitz
RWTH Aachen University
Aachen, Germany
peitz@cs.rwth-aachen.de

Hermann Ney
RWTH Aachen University
Aachen, Germany
ney@cs.rwth-aachen.de

Abstract

This paper reports different experiments created to study the impact of using linguistics to preprocess German compounds prior to translation in Statistical Machine Translation (SMT). Compounds are a known challenge both in Machine Translation (MT) and Translation in general as well as in other Natural Language Processing (NLP) applications. In the case of SMT, German compounds are split into their constituents to decrease the number of unknown words and improve the results of evaluation measures like the Bleu score. To assess to which extent it is necessary to deal with German compounds as a part of preprocessing in SMT systems, we have tested different compound splitters and strategies, such as adding lists of compounds and their translations to the training set. This paper summarizes the results of our experiments and attempts to yield better translations of German nominal compounds into Spanish and shows how our approach improves by up to 1.4 Bleu points with respect to the baseline.

1 Introduction

The pair of languages German→Spanish is not a widely researched combination in Statistical Machine Translation (SMT) and yet it is a challenging one as both languages belong to different language families (Germanic and Romance) and their characteristics and inner structure differ greatly. As it may happen with other language pair combinations involving a Germanic and a Romance language, when it comes to the translation of German compounds into Spanish, the challenge is greater than when translating into other Germanic languages such as English. The translation of the German compound does not correspond to the translation of its parts, but rather constitutes a phraseological structure which must conform the Spanish grammatical rules. Examples 1 and 2 show the splittings of the German compounds *Warmwasserbereitung* and *Wärmerückgewinnungssysteme* and their translations into English and Spanish.

(1)

Warm	*Wasser*	*Bereitung*
caliente	agua	preparación
warm	water	production

[ES]: 'Preparación de agua caliente'
[EN]: 'Warm water production'

(2)

Wärme	*Rückgewinnung*	*s*	*Systeme*
calor	recuperación	Ø	sistemas
heat	recovery	Ø	Systems

[ES]: 'sistemas de recuperación de calor'
[EN]: 'heat recovery systems'

As may be observed in Examples 1 and 2, in Spanish not only there is word reordering, but also there is usage of other word categories such as prepositions. While the examples above are quite simple, the work done by researchers such as Angele (1992), Gómez Pérez (2001) and Oster (2003) for the pair of languages German→Spanish shows that the translational equivalences in Spanish not only are very varied, but also unpredictable to a certain extent. Thus, while a mere compound splitting strategy may work for English, in the case of Spanish further processing is required to yield the correct translation.

According to Atkins et al. (2001)[1], complex nominals (i.e. nominal compounds and some nominal phrases) are to be considered a special type of MWE because they do have some particular features and to some extent they behave as a single unit because they refer to a single concept. Despite focusing on another language pair

[1]Appendix F of Deliverable D2.2-D3.2 of the ISLE project.

(English→Italian), in the case of our language pair (German→Spanish) a similar claim could be done. Besides, the issue of compounds being translated into phrases in different languages is essentially a MWE problem.

In this paper, we report on the results of our research facing this particular challenge. More concretely, Section 2 briefly discusses the problem of compounds in general and Section 3 describes our case of study. Subsection 3.1 briefly discusses the large presence of German nominal compounds in specialized corpora and presents the results of a preliminary study and Subsection 3.2 summarizes the state-of-the-art strategies to deal with compounds in SMT. Section 4 focuses on the experiments carried out and reported here and the results thereof are presented and discussed in Section 5. Finally, Section 6 summarizes the findings of our research and discusses future work.

2 German Compounds

German compounds may be lexicalized or not. Lexicalized compounds are those which can be found in general dictionaries, such as *Straßenlampe* ("street lamp/light" in German). Non lexicalized compounds are formed in a similar manner to that of phrases and/or sentences and are coined on-the-fly (i.e. *Warmwasserbereitungsanlagen*, see Example 3). Non lexicalized compounds usually appear in technical and formal texts and German shows a great tendency to produce them. In SMT, the translational correspondences are computed from a sentence aligned training corpus and translation dictionaries are not present. Rather, word alignment algorithms are used to produce the phrase tables that will in turn be used to produce the translations. Thus, although non lexicalized compounds pose a greater challenge (they are unpredictable), lexicalized compounds are not distinguished either. As this formal distinction cannot be done when dealing with SMT, here we will refer to compounds irrespectively whether they are lexicalized or not, unless otherwise specified.

Moreover, German compounds may be nouns, adjectives, adverbs and verbs, although the largest group is the one corresponding to nominal compounds. Finally, it is also important to highlight that sometimes more than one compound-forming phenomenon may take place subsequently to form a new, longer, compound. Previous Example 1 is the result of such a process, and as illustrated in Example 3 it can, in turn, be the base for a yet newer compound.

(3) warm (ADJ) + Wasser(N) = **Warmwasser** (N) + Bereitung(N) = **Warmwasserbereitung** (N) + s + Anlagen(N) = **Warmwasserbereitungsanlagen** (N) [*EN: warm water production systems*]

As may also be observed in Example 3, the word class of the compound is determined by the element located in the rightmost position of the compound (i.e. the combination of the adjective *warm* and the noun *Wasser* yields a nominal compound). Finally, it is also important to highlight that besides words, compounds may also include particles to join those words together, as the "*s*" between *Warmwasserbereitung* and *Anlagen* in Example 3 or truncations (part of one of the component words is deleted). Example 4 illustrates the case when one of the component words has been truncated:

(4) abstellen(V) - en + Anlagen(N) = Abstellanlagen (N) [*EN: parking facilities*]

The morphology of German compounds has been widely researched, both within linguistics (Fleischer, 1975; Wellman, 1984; Eichinger, 2000, among others), as in NLP (Langer, 1998; Girju et al., 2005; Marek, 2006; Girju, 2008, among others). Here, we will focus on the impact of preprocessing nominal compounds in SMT.

Baroni et al. (2002) report that 47% of the vocabulary (types) in the APA corpus[2] were compounds. As will be observed in Section 4, the compound splitters we used also detected a high percentage of compounds in the corpora used in our experiments. This fact confirms that it is crucial to find a successful way of processing compounds in NLP applications and in our case in SMT.

3 Case Study

The experiments carried out here have used the texts corresponding to the domain *B00: Construction* of the TRIS corpus (Parra Escartín, 2012), and an internally compiled version of the Europarl Corpus (Koehn, 2005) for the pair of languages German-Spanish[3]. The domain (*B00: Construction*) was selected because it is the biggest one of

[2]Corpus of the Austria Presse Agentur (APA). Recently it has been released as the AMC corpus (Austrian Media Corpus) (Ransmayr et al., 2013).

[3]See Table 2 for an overview of the corpus statistics.

the three domains currently available in the TRIS corpus[4]. Only one domain was used because we aimed at testing in-domain translation. Besides, the TRIS corpus was selected because it is a specialised German-Spanish parallel corpus. As opposed to the Europarl, the TRIS corpus is divided in domains and the source and target languages have been verified (i.e. the texts were originally written in German and translated into Spanish). Moreover, the texts included in the Europarl are transcriptions of the sessions of the European Parliament, and thus the style is rather oral and less technical. As compounds tend to be more frequent in domain specific texts, the TRIS corpus has been used for testing, while the Europarl Corpus has been used in the training set to avoid data scarcity problems and increase the vocabulary coverage of the SMT system.

In the case of Machine Translation (MT), both rule-based MT systems (RBMT systems) and Statistical MT systems (SMT systems) encounter problems when dealing with compounds. For the purposes of this paper, the treatment of compounds in German has been tested within the SMT toolkit *Jane* (Wuebker et al., 2012; Vilar et al., 2010). We have carried out several experiments translating German specialized texts into Spanish to test to which extent incorporating a linguistic analysis of the corpora and compiling compound lists improves the overall SMT results. At this stage, including further linguistic information such as Part-of-Speech tagging (POS tagging) or phrase chunking has been disregarded. Forcing the translation of compounds in the phrase tables produced by *Jane* has also been disregarded. The overall aim was to test how the SMT system performs using different pre-processing strategies of the training data but without altering its mechanism. Since it is a challenge to factor out what is really the translation of the compounds, the overall quality of the translations at document level has been measured as an indirect way of assessing the quality of the compound translations[5]. To evaluate the compound translations into Spanish, these need to be manually validated because we currently do not have access to fully automatic methods. A qualitative analysis of the compound translations will be done in future work.

[4]The domain *C00A: Agriculture, Fishing and Foodstuffs* has 137.354 words and the domain *H00: Domestic Leisure Equipment* has 58328 words).

[5]The results of this evaluation are reported in Section 5.

3.1 Preliminary study

With the purpose of assessing the presence of compounds in the TRIS corpus and evaluating the splittings at a later stage as well as the impact of such splittings in SMT, we analysed manually two short texts of the TRIS corpus. The two files correspond to the subcorpus *B30: Construction - Environment* and account for 261 sentences and 2870 words. For this preliminary study, all German nominal compounds and their corresponding Spanish translations were manually extracted. Adjectival and verbal compounds were not included at this stage. Abbreviated nominal compounds (i.e. "*EKZ*" instead of "*Energiekennzahl*", [energy index]) were not included either. Table 1 offers an overview of the number of running words in each file without punctuation, the number of nominal compounds found (with an indication as to which percentage of the total number of words they account for), the number of unique compounds (i.e. compound types), and the number of lexicalized and non lexicalized compounds in total (with the percentage of the text they account for), and unique. For the purposes of this study, all compounds found in a German monolingual dictionary were considered lexicalized, whereas those not appearing where considered non-lexicalized.

As can be seen in Table 1, compound nominals constitute a relatively high percentage of the total number of words in a text. This is specially the case of domain specific texts such as the ones taken into consideration here. We can thus assume that finding a way to translate compounds appropriately into other languages would improve the overall quality of the translations produced by SMT.

3.2 Related work: compounds in SMT

RBMT systems require that compounds are included in their dictionaries to be able to retrieve the appropriate translation in each case. Alternatively, they should include a special rule for handling compounds which are beyond their lexical coverage. On the other hand, SMT systems encounter problems when dealing with compounds because they rely on the words observed during the training phase. Thus, if the compound did not appear in the training set of the system its translation will subsequently fail. The state-of-the-art strategy to deal with compounds in SMT systems consists on splitting the compounds to reduce the number of unseen words. Previous research (Koehn

	Text A	Text B
Number of words	2431	439
Number of comp.	265 (10.9%)	62 (14.12%)
Number of unique comp.	143	25
Lexicalized comp.	99 (4.07%)	18 (4.1%)
Unique lexicalized comp.	63	4
Not lexicalized comp.	166 (6.8%)	44 (10.06%)
Unique not lexicalized comp.	80	21

Table 1: Compound nominals found in the two texts taken for the preliminary study.

and Knight, 2003; Popović et al., 2006; Stymne, 2008; Fritzinger and Fraser, 2010; Stymne et al., 2013) has shown that splitting the compounds in German results in better Bleu scores (Papineni et al., 2001) and vocabulary coverage (fewer "unknown" words). However, the experiments carried out so far have also claimed that significant changes in error measures were not to be expected because the percentage of running words affected by compound splitting was rather low (Popović et al., 2006; Stymne, 2008). As will be observed in Section 4.1, in our case the percentage of running words affected by compound splitting was higher. This might be due to the kind of texts used in our experiments.

4 Experiments

As mentioned in Section 3, for the experiments reported here two corpora have been used: the TRIS corpus and the Europarl corpus for German→Spanish. In order to focus on in-domain translation, only the largest subcorpus of TRIS has been used.

Table 2 summarizes the number of sentences and words in our experiment setup.

To reduce possible mistakes and mismatches observed in the corpora used in the experiments, the spelling of the German vowels named umlaut ("¨") was simplified. Thus, "*Ä, Ö, Ü, ä, ö, ü*" were transformed into "*Ae, Oe, Ue, ae, oe, ue*" correspondingly. Also the German "ß" was substituted by a double s: "ss". By doing this, words appearing in the corpus and written differently were unified and thus their frequencies were higher.

Additionally, a list of 185 German nominal compounds present in the training set was manually extracted together with their translations into Spanish. If different translations had been found for the same compound, these were included in our list too. This list was used in some of our experiments to determine whether extracting such lists has an impact in the overall translation quality of SMT systems. As the texts belong to the same domain, there was partial overlap with the compounds found in the test set. However, not all compounds in the test set were present in the training corpus and viceversa.

4.1 Training environments

Taking the normalised version of our corpus as a baseline, different training environments have been tested. We designed five possible training environments in which German compounds were preprocessed.

In our first experiment (hereinafter "*compList*"), the list of manually extracted compounds was appended to the end of the training set and no further preprocessing was carried out.

In our second experiment (hereinafter "*RWTH*"), the state-of-the-art compound splitting approach implemented by Popović et al. (2006) was used to split all possible compounds. As also implemented by Koehn and Knight (2003), this approach uses the corpus itself to create a vocabulary that is then subsequently used to calculate the possible splittings in the corpus. It has the advantage of being a stand-alone approach which does not depend on any external resources. A possible drawback of this approach would be that it relies on a large corpus to be able to compute the splittings. Thus, it may not be as efficient with smaller corpora (i.e. if we were to use only the TRIS corpus, for instance).

The third experiment (hereinafter "*RWTH+compList*") used the split corpus prepared in our second experiment ("*RWTH*") but merged with the list of compounds that was also used in the first experiment. In total, 128 of all compounds detected by the splitter were also in our compound list. In order to avoid noise, the compounds present in the list were deleted from

	training	dev	test
Sentences	1.8M	2382	1192
Running words without punctuation (tokens)	40.8M	20K	11K
Vocabulary size (types)	338K	4050	2087

Table 2: Corpus statistics. The training corpus is a concatenation of the complete Europarl Corpus German→Spanish and a greater part of the TRIS corpus, while in `dev` and `test` only texts from the TRIS corpus were used.

the list of splittings to be carried out in the corpus. Thus, after all possible splittings were calculated, those splittings that were present in the manually compiled compound list were deleted to ensure that they were not split in the corpus and remained the same.

In the fourth experiment (hereinafter "*IMS*") we used another compound splitter developed at the *Institut für Maschinelle Sprachverarbeitung* of the University of Stuttgart (Weller and Heid, 2012). This splitter was also developed using a frequency-based approach. However, in this case the training data consists of a list of lemmatized word-forms together with their POS tags. A set of rules to model transitional elements is also used. While this splitter might be used by processing our corpus with available tools such as TreeTagger (Schmid, 1994)[6] and then computing frequencies, in our experiments we used the CELEX[7] database for German (Baayen et al., 1993). This was done so because CELEX is an extensive high quality lexical database which already included all the information we needed to process and did not require any further preprocessing and clean up of our corpus.

In the fifth experiment (hereinafter "*IMS+compList*"), we repeated the same procedure of our third experiment ("*RWTH+compList*"): we added the compound list to our training corpus already split, but this time using the compound splitter developed in Stuttgart. In total, 125 of all compounds detected by the splitter were also in our compound list. The splitting of such compounds was avoided.

4.2 Compounds detected

Table 3 summarizes the number of compounds detected by the two compound splitters and the percentage they account for with respect to the vocabulary and the number of running words.

As can be observed in Table 3, the percentage of compounds in the test set is considerably higher than in the training set. This is due to the fact that in the test set only a subcorpus of the TRIS corpus was used, whereas in the training corpus Europarl was also used and as stated earlier (cf. Subsection 3.1 and table 1), domain specific corpora tend to have more compounds. It is also noticeable that the compound splitter developed in Stuttgart detects and splits fewer compounds. A possible explanation would be that Weller and Heid (2012) only split words into content words and use POS tags to filter out other highly frequent words that do not create compounds. The presence of lexicalized compounds in the CELEX database does not seem to have affected the accuracy of the splitter (i.e. they were not skipped by the splitter). Finally, it is also noticeable that the percentage of compounds detected in the training set is similar to the one reported by Baroni et al. (2002) and referenced to in Section 2. This seems to indicate that both splitting algorithms perform correctly. A thorough analysis of their outputs has been carried out confirming this hypothesis as the accuracies of both splitters were considerably high: 97.19% (RWTH) and 97.49% IMS (Parra Escartín, forthcoming)[8].

As SMT system, we employ the state-of-the-art phrase-based translation approach (Zens and Ney, 2008) implemented in *Jane*. The baseline is trained on the concatination of the TRIS and Europarl corpus. Word alignments are trained with *fastAlign* (Dyer et al., 2013). Further, we apply a 4-gram language model trained with the SRILM toolkit (Stolcke, 2002) on the target side of the training corpus. The log-linear parameter weights are tuned with MERT (Och, 2003) on the development set (`dev`). As optimization criterion we use Bleu. The parameter setting for all experiments was the same to allow for comparisons.

[6] `http://www.ims.uni-stuttgart.de/projekte/corplex/TreeTagger/`

[7] `http://wwwlands2.let.kun.nl/members/software/celex_gug.pdf`

[8] The analysis was done following the method proposed by Koehn and Knight (2003).

	Popovic et al. (2006)	Weller and Heid (2012)
Compounds in `training`	182334	141789
% Vocabulary	54%	42%
% Running words	0.4%	0.3%
Compounds in `test`	924	444
% Vocabulary	44.3%	21.3%
% Running words	8.5%	4%

Table 3: Number of compounds detected by each of the splitters used and the percentages they account for with respect to the vocabulary (types) and the number of running words (tokens) in the corpora used in the experiments.

5 Results

Table 4 reports the results of the five training environments described in Subsection 4.1 and the baseline. We report results in Bleu [%] and Ter [%] (Snover et al., 2006). All reported results are averages over three independent MERT runs, and we evaluate statistical significance with *MultEval* (Clark et al., 2011).

As can be observed in Table 4, adding compound lists to the training set significantly improves the Bleu and Ter scores with respect to the baseline. This is also the case when compounds were preprocessed and split. Moreover, while the Bleu scores for both splitters are the same when processing the entire corpus, adding the compound list to the training corpus yields better scores. In fact, the combination of the compound list and the compound splitter developed by Weller and Heid (2012) improves by 3.8 points in Bleu, while the approach by Popović et al. (2006) improves by 3.4 Bleu points against *Baseline*. When comparing it with *compList*, the improvements are of 3% and 2.4% Bleu respectively. To ensure a fair comparison, *RWTH* is defined as second baseline. Again, we observe significant improvement over this second baseline by adding the compound list to the training corpus. In terms of Bleu we gain an improvement of up to 1.4 points.

These results seem promising as they show significant improvements both in terms of Bleu and Ter scores. As previously mentioned in Section 3.2, one possible explanation to the higher Bleu scores we obtained might be that the number of running words affected by compound splitting was higher than in other experiments like the ones carried out by Popović et al. (2006) and Stymne (2008). Fritzinger and Fraser (2010) used a hybrid splitting algorithm which combined the corpus-based approach and linguistic information and also reported better Bleu scores for German→English translations than splitting algorithms based only in corpus frequencies. They suggested that fewer split compounds but better split could yield better results. However, in our case the two splitters score the same in terms of Bleu. Further experiments with other language pairs should be carried out to test whether this is only the case with German→Spanish translation tasks or not. If this were to be confirmed, a language dependent approach to dealing with compounds in SMT might then be needed. The improvements in terms of Bleu and Ter obtained when adding the manually extracted compound list to our training corpus (particularly in the *IMS+compList* experiment) suggest that further preprocessing than just splitting the compounds in the corpora would result in overall better quality translations. It is particularly noticeable that while the fewest number of unknown words occurs when using a corpus-based splitting algorithm (experiments *RWTH* and *RWTH+compList*), this does not seem to directly correlate with better Bleu and Ter scores. Experiments *IMS* and *IMS+compList* had in fact a larger number of unknown words and yet obtain better scores.

Table 5 reports the number of compounds of the compound list found in the test sets across the different experiments. As the compound list was not preprocessed, the number of compounds found in *RWTH* and *IMS* is smaller than those found in *Baseline* and *compList*. In the case of *RWTH+compList* and *IMS+compList*, however, the productivity of German compounds mentioned earlier in Section 2 may have influenced the number of compounds found. If a compound found in our compound list was present in other compounds and those were split in such a way that it resulted in one of the

Experiment	Splitting Method	Compound List	test Bleu[%]	test Ter[%]	test OOVs
Baseline	-	no	45.9	43.9	181
compList	-	yes	**46.7**	**42.9**	169
RWTH	Popović et al. (2006)	no	48.3	40.8	104
RWTH+compList		yes	**49.1**	40.5	104
IMS	Weller and Heid (2012)	no	48.3	40.5	114
IMS+compList		yes	**49.7**	**39.2**	114

Table 4: Results for the German→Spanish TRIS data. Statistically significant improvements with at least 99% confidence over the respective baselines (*Baseline* and *RWTH*) are printed in boldface.

formants being that compound, its frequency got higher. As can be observed, the highest number of correct translations of compounds corresponds to *RWTH+compList* and *IMS+compList*.

Table 6 shows the results of a sample sentence in our test set including several compounds. As can be observed, in the *IMS+compList* experiment all compounds are correctly translated. This seems to indicate that the manually compiled list of compounds added to the training corpus helped to increase the probabilities of alignment of 1:n correspondences (German compound – Spanish MWE) and thus the compound translations in the phrase tables are better.

6 Conclusion and future work

In this paper, we have reported the results of our experiments processing German compounds and carrying out SMT tasks into Spanish. As has been observed, adding manually handcrafted compound lists to the training set significantly improves the qualitative results of SMT and therefore a way of automating their extraction would be desired. Furthermore, a combination of splitting compounds and adding them already aligned to their translations in the training corpus yields also significant improvements with respect to the baseline. A qualitative analysis is currently being done to assess the kind of improvements that come from the splitting and/or the compound list added to training.

As a follow up of the experiments reported here, the compound splitters used have being evaluated to assess their precision and recall and determine which splitting algorithms could be more promising for SMT tasks and whether or not their quality has a correlation with better translations. From the experiments carried out so far, it seems that it may be the case, but this shall be further explored as our results do not differ greatly between each other.

In future work we will research whether the approach suggested here also yields better results in data used by the MT community. Obtaining better overall results would confirm that our approach is right, in which case we will research how we can combine both strategies (compound splitting and adding compound lists and their translations to training corpora) in a successful and automatic way. We also intend to explore how we can do so minimizing the amount of external resources needed.

Obtaining positive results in these further experiments would suggest that a similar approach may also yield positive results in dealing with other types of MWEs within SMT.

Acknowledgments

The research reported in this paper has received funding from the EU under FP7, Marie Curie Actions, SP3 People ITN, grant agreement n° 238405 (project CLARA[9]). The authors would also like to thank the anonymous reviewers for their valuable comments.

References

Sybille Angele. 1992. *Nominalkomposita des Deutschen und ihre Entsprechungen im Spanischen. Eine kontrastive Untersuchung anhand von Texten aus Wirtschaft und Literatur*. iudicium verlag GmbH, München.

S. Atkins, N. Bel, P. Bouillon, T. Charoenporn, D. Gibbon, R. Grishman, C.-R. Huan, A. Kawtrakul, N. Ide, H.-Y. Lee, P. J. K. Li, J. McNaught, J. Odijk, M. Palmer, V. Quochi, R. Reeves, D. M. Sharma, V. Sornlertlamvanich, T. Tokunaga, G. Thurmair, M. Villegas, A. Zampolli, and E. Zeiton. 2001. Standards and Best Practice for Multiligual Computational Lexicons. MILE (the Multilingual ISLE Lex-

[9]`http://clara.uib.no`

Experiment	Compounds (DE)	Compound translations (ES)
Baseline	154	48
compList	154	54
RWTH	85	61
RWTH+compList	175	**80**
IMS	46	57
IMS+compList	173	**76**

Table 5: Number of compounds present in our compound list found in the test set for each of the experiments both in German and in Spanish. The experiments with the highest number of translations present in our compound list are printed in boldface.

Sentence type	Example
Original (DE)	**Abstellanlagen** fuer *Kraftfahrzeuge* in Tiefgaragen oder in *Parkdecks* mit mindestens zwei Geschossen
Reference (ES)	**instalaciones de estacionamiento** de *automóviles* en garajes subterráneos o en *estacionamientos cubiertos* que tengan como mínimo dos plantas
Baseline (DE)	**Abstellanlagen** fuer *Kraftfahrzeuge* in Tiefgaragen oder in *Parkdecks* mit mindestens zwei Geschossen
Baseline (ES)	**plazas** para *vehículos* en aparcamientos subterráneos o en *plantas* con al menos dos pisos
IMS (DE)	**abstellen Anlagen** fuer *Kraft fahren Zeuge* in tief Garagen oder in *Park Decks* mit mindestens zwei Geschossen
IMS (ES)	**plazas** para *vehículos* en aparcamientos subterráneos o en *plantas* con al menos dos pisos
IMS+compList (DE)	**Abstellanlagen** fuer *Kraftfahrzeuge* in Tiefgaragen oder in *Parkdecks* mit mindestens zwei Geschossen
IMS+compList (ES)	**instalaciones de estacionamiento** para *automóviles* *estacionamientos cubiertos* en garajes subterráneos o en plantas con al menos dos pisos

Table 6: Sample translations for German→Spanish for the baseline and the experiments *IMS* and *IMS+compList*. Each compound and its translation have the same format.

ical Entry) Deliverable D2.2-D3.2. ISLE project: ISLE Computational Lexicon Working Group.

R. H. Baayen, R. Piepenbrock, and H. van Rijn. 1993. *The CELEX Lexical Database (CD-ROM)*. Linguistic Data Consortium, University of Pennsylvania, Philadelphia, PA.

Marco Baroni, Johannes Matiasek, and Harald Trost. 2002. Wordform- and Class-based Prediction of the Components of German Nominal Compounds in an AAC System. In *19th International Conference on Computational Linguistics, COLING 2002*, Taipei, Taiwan, August 24 - September 1, 2002.

Jonathan H. Clark, Chris Dyer, Alon Lavie, and Noah A. Smith. 2011. Better hypothesis testing for statistical machine translation: Controlling for optimizer instability. In *49th Annual Meeting of the Association for Computational Linguistics:shortpapers*, pages 176—181, Portland, Oregon, June.

Chris Dyer, Victor Chahuneau, and Noah A. Smith. 2013. A simple, fast, and effective reparameterization of ibm model 2. In *Proc. of NAACL*.

Ludwig M. Eichinger. 2000. *Deutsche Wortbildung. Eine Einführung*. Gunter Narr Verlag Tübingen.

Wolfgang Fleischer. 1975. *Wortbildung der deutschen Gegenwartssprache*. Max Niemeyer Verlag Tübingen, 4 edition.

Fabienne Fritzinger and Alexander Fraser. 2010. How to Avoid Burning Ducks: Combining Linguistic Analysis and Corpus Statistics for German Compound Processing. In *Proceedings of the Joint Fifth Workshop on Statistical Machine Translation and MetricsMATR*, WMT '10, pages 224–234, Stroudsburg, PA, USA. Association for Computational Linguistics.

Roxana Girju, Dan Moldovan, Marta Tatu, and Daniel Antohe. 2005. On the semantics of noun compounds. *Computer Speech and Language*, (4):479–496.

Roxana Girju. 2008. The Syntax and Semantics of Prepositions in the Task of Automatic Interpretation of Nominal Phrases and Compounds: A Cross-Linguistic Study. *Computational Linguistics*, 35(2):185–228.

Carmen Gómez Pérez. 2001. *La composición nominal alemana desde la perspectiva textual: El compuesto nominal como dificultad de traducción del alemán al español*. Ph.D. thesis, Departamento de Traducción e Interpretación, Universidad de Salamanca, Salamanca.

Philipp Koehn and Kevin Knight. 2003. Empirical Methods for Compound splitting. In *Proceedings of the Tenth Conference of the European Chapter of the Association for Computational Linguistics*, pages 187–193, Stroudsburg, PA, USA. Association for Computational Linguistics.

Philipp Koehn. 2005. Europarl: A Parallel Corpus for Statistical Machine Translation. In *Conference Proceedings: the Tenth Machine Translation Summit*, pages 79–86, Phuket, Thailand.

Stefan Langer. 1998. Zur morphologie und semantik von nominalkomposita. In *Tagungsband der 4. Konferenz zur Verarbeitung natürlicher Sprache (KOVENS)*.

Torsten Marek. 2006. Analysis of German Compounds Using Weighted Finite State Transducers. Technical report, Eberhard-Karls-Universität Tübingen.

Franz Josef Och. 2003. Minimum Error Rate Training in Statistical Machine Translation. pages 160–167, Sapporo, Japan, July.

Ulrike Oster. 2003. *Los términos de la cerámica en alemán y en español. Análisis semántico orientado a la traducción de los compuestos nominales alemanes*. Ph.D. thesis, Departament de Traducció i Comunicació, Universitat Jaume I, Castellón.

Kishore Papineni, Salim Roukos, Todd Ward, and Wei-Jing Zhu. 2001. Bleu: a Method for Automatic Evaluation of Machine Translation. IBM Research Report RC22176 (W0109-022), IBM Research Division, Thomas J. Watson Research Center, P.O. Box 218, Yorktown Heights, NY 10598, September.

Carla Parra Escartín. 2012. Design and compilation of a specialized Spanish-German parallel corpus. In *Proceedings of the Eight International Conference on Language Resources and Evaluation (LREC'12)*, Istanbul, Turkey, May. European Language Resources Association.

Carla Parra Escartín. forthcoming. Chasing the perfect splitter: A comparison of different compound splitting tools. In *Proceedings of the Ninth Conference on International Language Resources and Evaluation (LREC'14)*, Reykjavik, Island, May. European Language Resources Association.

Maja Popović, Daniel Stein, and Hermann Ney. 2006. Statistical machine translation of german compound words. In *Proceedings of the 5th international conference on Advances in Natural Language Processing*, FinTAL'06, pages 616–624, Berlin, Heidelberg. Springer-Verlag.

Jutta Ransmayr, Karlheinz Moerth, and Matej Durco. 2013. Linguistic variation in the austrian media corpus. dealing with the challenges of large amounts of data. In *Proceedings of International Conference on Corpus Linguistics (CILC)*, Alicante. University Alicante, University Alicante.

Helmut Schmid. 1994. Probabilistic Part-of-Speech Tagging Using Decision Trees. In *International Conference on New Methods in Language Processing*, pages 44–49, Manchester, UK.

Matthew Snover, Bonnie Dorr, Richard Schwartz, Linnea Micciulla, and John Makhoul. 2006. A Study of Translation Edit Rate with Targeted Human Annotation. In *Proceedings of the 7th Conference of the Association for Machine Translation in the Americas*, pages 223–231, Cambridge, Massachusetts, USA, August.

Andreas Stolcke. 2002. SRILM – An Extensible Language Modeling Toolkit. In *Proc. of the Int. Conf. on Speech and Language Processing (ICSLP)*, volume 2, pages 901–904, Denver, CO, September.

Sara Stymne, Nicola Cancedda, and Lars Ahrenberg. 2013. Generation of Compound Words in Statistical Machine Translation into Compounding Languages. *Computational Linguistics*, pages 1–42.

Sara Stymne. 2008. German Compounds in Factored Statistical Machine Translation. In *GoTAL'08: Proceedings of the 6th international conference on Advances in Natural Language Processing*, pages 464–475. Springer-Verlag.

David Vilar, Daniel Stein, Matthias Huck, and Hermann Ney. 2010. Jane: open source hierarchical translation, extended with reordering and lexicon models. In *Proceedings of the Joint Fifth Workshop on Statistical Machine Translation and MetricsMATR*, WMT '10, pages 262–270, Stroudsburg, PA, USA. Association for Computational Linguistics.

Marion Weller and Ulrich Heid. 2012. Analyzing and Aligning German compound nouns. In *Proceedings of the Eight International Conference on Language Resources and Evaluation (LREC'12)*, Istanbul, Turkey, May. European Language Resources Association.

Hans Wellman, 1984. *DUDEN. Die Grammatik. Unentbehrlich für richtiges Deutsch*, volume 4, chapter Die Wortbildung. Duden Verlag.

Joern Wuebker, Matthias Huck, Stephan Peitz, Malte Nuhn, Markus Freitag, Jan-Thorsten Peter, Saab Mansour, and Hermann Ney. 2012. Jane 2: Open source phrase-based and hierarchical statistical machine translation. In *International Conference on Computational Linguistics*, pages 483–491, Mumbai, India, December.

Richard Zens and Hermann Ney. 2008. Improvements in Dynamic Programming Beam Search for Phrase-based Statistical Machine Translation. In *International Workshop on Spoken Language Translation*, pages 195–205, Honolulu, Hawaii, October.

Extracting MWEs from Italian corpora: A case study for refining the POS-pattern methodology

Malvina Nissim
FICLIT
University of Bologna
malvina.nissim@unibo.it

Sara Castagnoli
LILEC
University of Bologna
s.castagnoli@unibo.it

Francesca Masini
LILEC
University of Bologna
francesca.masini@unibo.it

Abstract

An established method for MWE extraction is the combined use of previously identified POS-patterns and association measures. However, the selection of such POS-patterns is rarely debated. Focusing on Italian MWEs containing at least one adjective, we set out to explore how candidate POS-patterns listed in relevant literature and lexicographic sources compare with POS sequences exhibited by statistically significant n-grams including an adjective position extracted from a large corpus of Italian. All literature-derived patterns are found—and new meaningful candidate patterns emerge—among the top-ranking trigrams for three association measures. We conclude that a final solid set to be used for MWE extraction will have to be further refined through a combination of association measures as well as manual inspection.

1 Introduction

The CombiNet project[1] has the goal of building an online resource for Word Combinations in Italian, including MWEs of various degrees of fixedness (such as phrasal lexemes, collocations and usual combinations) as well as distributional profiles of Italian lexemes. Within this project, the present paper aims at investigating ways to refine a well-known methodology for MWE-extraction, namely the combined use of previously identified POS-patterns and association measures (Evert and Krenn, 2005). While POS-patterns are widely used to extract MWEs from corpora in order to constrain the array of possible outputs (Krenn and Evert, 2001; Wermter and Hahn, 2006, e.g.), the way in which POS-patterns are created in the first place is much less addressed. This step is however crucial, especially considering that the list of patterns is necessarily language-specific. The goal of this paper is to propose a method to optimize – in terms of both recall and precision – the list of POS patterns to be used for the subsequent extraction of potential MWEs. In order to do this, we compare predetermined patterns, which would be normally used as a first-pass sieve for potential MWEs, with patterns exhibited by statistically significant n-grams extracted from data.

[1]https://sites.google.com/site/enwcin/home

2 Methodology

In this pilot study, we focus on MWEs containing at least one adjective, and we limit the extraction to trigrams (Section 2.1). We make use of the following sets of data: (a) a list of frequently used Italian adjectives; (b) a list of previously identified POS-patterns containing at least one adjective.[2]

The adjectival lemmas were taken from the Senso Comune dictionary,[3] which contains 2,010 fundamental lemmas of the Italian lexicon, 211 of which are adjectives (e.g. *bello* "beautiful", *brutto* "ugly", *ricco* "rich"). These adjectives are used to constrain the extraction procedure, and we refer to this set as $\{SC\}$.

The list of predetermined POS-patterns for MWEs involving one adjective was obtained by merging the following information: (a) patterns of word combinations included in existing combinatory dictionaries for Italian (Piunno et al., 2013), see Table 1a; (b) additional combinatory types mentioned in the relevant theoretical literature (Voghera, 2004; Masini, 2012), summarised in Table 1b; and (c) a few more patterns based on our own intuition, i.e. identified by elaborating on the previous two lists (Table 2). This joint collection contains a total of 19 patterns, most of which are bigrams (11), and fewer are trigrams (8). Note

[2]For information on POS tags see Appendix.

[3]http://www.sensocomune.it/

that trigrams (put together in Table 2) come for the most part from our intuition, indicating that these patterns are rather neglected in the literature and in combinatory dictionaries of Italian, which tend to focus on bigrams. For this reason, and because longer sequences are intrinsically more idiosyncratic, we concentrate on trigrams for this pilot experiment, although in the discussion we take into account bigrams, too (Section 3).

Table 1: Italian POS-patterns with ADJ(s)

POS-pattern	Example	Translation
(a) from lexicographic sources		
ADJ ADJ	stanco morto	dead tired
ADJ CON ADJ	vivo e vegeto	live and kicking
ADJ NOUN	prima classe	first class
ADJ PRE	pronto a	ready to
ADV ADJ	molto malato	very ill
NOUN ADJ	casa editrice	publishing house
VER ADJ	uscire pazzo	to go crazy
(b) from relevant literature		
ADJ PRO	qual esso	which/who
ADJ_i ADJ_i	papale papale	bluntly
ARTPRE ADJ	alla francese	French-style
PRE ADJ	a caldo	on the spot
PRE ADJ NOUN	di bassa lega	vulgar/coarse
PRE NOUN ADJ	a senso unico	one-way
PRO ADJ	tal altro	some other

2.1 Extracting the trigrams

From the corpus La Repubblica (Baroni et al., 2004), which consists of 300M words of newswire contemporary Italian, we extracted all trigrams featuring at least one adjective, deriving this information from the pre-existing POS tags in the corpus. All trigrams were extracted as sequences of lemmas. We created three separate lists according to the adjective's position in the trigram (first, second, or third). All instances containing any punctuation item were discarded.

For each of the three sets, we kept only trigrams occurring more than five times in the whole corpus. As a further step, we selected those instances featuring one of the 211 adjectives in $\{SC\}$, yielding a total of 89,217 different trigrams featuring an adjective as first member (191 adjectives from $\{SC\}$ occur in this position), 100,861 as second (192 adjectives), and 114,672 as third (193).

2.2 Ranking the trigrams

We used the Text-NSP package (Banerjee and Pedersen, 2003) to rank the trigrams in each of the three sets according to three association measures (AMs), namely the Poisson-Stirling measure (PS), the log-likelihood ratio (LL) and pointwise mutual information (PMI). However, on the basis of preliminary inspection and observations in the literature on ranking Italian MWEs extracted from corpora (Nissim and Zaninello, 2013), we discarded PMI as not too accurate for this task. We also considered raw frequencies, as they have proved good indicators for collocations, on a par with AMs (Krenn and Evert, 2001; Bannard, 2007).

The idea is to check which POS sequences are exhibited by the highest instances in the rank, under the rationale that such patterns might be good representations of Italian MWEs containing adjectives, and can be used for further extraction and characterisation of the phenomenon (in dictionaries and resources). Thus, we selected the top 10% instances in each rank, extracted their POS patterns, and ranked such patterns according to the number of times they appeared. Tables 3–5 report the ten most frequent patterns according to each measure, when an adjective is found in first, second, and third position, respectively.

3 Analysis and discussion

By comparing the ranked patterns in Tables 3–5 with the predetermined POS-patterns for trigrams in Table 2, we draw the following observations.

We first consider patterns that are ranked high for *all* measures. Some find a correspondence to those in Table 2, implying that these are likely to be solid, characteristic POS sequences to be used in extraction (ADJ CONJ ADJ (for ADJ in first position), ADJ PRE VER, PRE ADJ NOUN, and VER PRE ADJ). Other found patterns, instead, are *not* among the pre-identified ones, but are definitely typical sequences, as the analysis of some of the extracted trigrams shows. Among these: ADJ PRE NOUN (*ospite d'onore* "special guest"), VER ART ADJ (*essere il solo* "to be the only one"), NOUN PRE ADJ (*agente in borghese* "plain-clothes policeman"), ARTPRE ADJ NOUN (*all'ultimo momento* "at the last moment"). Envisaging an extraction procedure based on POS sequences, such structures should be included to improve recall.

Conversely, the PRE ART ADJ pattern exhibits an incomplete sequence, and is therefore unsuitable for MWE extraction. Since the inclusion of such patterns would possibly affect precision, they need to be filtered out on the grounds of grammatical

Table 2: Trigram POS-patterns containing ADJ(s)

POS-pattern	Example	Translation
from literature and resources		
ADJ CON ADJ	pura e semplice	pure and simple
PRE ADJ NOUN	a breve termine	short-run
PRE NOUN ADJ	in tempo reale	(in) real-time
from our own intuition		
ADJ PRE VER	duro a morire	die-hard
NOUN ADJ ADJ	prodotto interno lordo	gross national product
NOUN NOUN ADJ	dipartimento affari sociali	social affairs division
PRE ADJ VER	per quieto vivere	for the sake of quiet and peace
VER PRE ADJ	dare per scontato	to take for granted

Table 3: Top 10 POS patterns featuring an adjective as word1, extracted from the top 10% trigrams ranked according to LL, PS, and raw frequency.

LL	PS	raw frequency
ADJ PRE VER	ADJ NOUN PRE	ADJ NOUN PRE
ADJ PRE ART	ADJ NOUN ARTPRE	ADJ NOUN ARTPRE
ADJ NOUN PRE	ADJ NOUN ADJ	ADJ ARTPRE NOUN
ADJ PRE NOUN	ADJ ARTPRE NOUN	ADJ PRE ART
ADJ NOUN ARTPRE	ADJ PRE VER	ADJ PRE VER
ADJ ARTPRE NOUN	ADJ PRE NOUN	ADJ NOUN ADJ
ADJ PRE DET	ADJ CON ADJ	ADJ PRE NOUN
ADJ CON ADJ	ADJ NPR NPR	ADJ CON ADJ
ADJ CHE CLI	ADJ NOUN CON	ADJ NOUN CON
ADJ DET NOUN	ADJ PRE ART	ADJ CON ART

constraints, or, ultimately, manual inspection.

Additionally, there are patterns that *contain* or are *portions of* more relevant patterns for MWE-hood. Some capture what are in fact bigrams (Table 6), while others are portions of 4-grams or possibly larger sequences, namely NOUN ADJ PRE (NOUN), (NOUN) ADJ ARTPRE NOUN, and NOUN ARTPRE ADJ (NOUN), where the "missing" POS is given in brackets. Examples are: *concorso esterno in (omicidio)* "external participation in (murder)", *(banca) nazionale del lavoro* "National (Bank) of Labour", and *paese del terzo (mondo)* "third world (country)", respectively. Running a full-scale extraction procedure that accounts for all n-grams should naturally take care of this.

Some of patterns from Table 2 are ranked high only by *some measures*: PRE NOUN ADJ only according to PS and raw frequency (Table 5), and NOUN ADJ ADJ both for second and third position, but only by PS. Overall, with respect to their ability to extract previously identified POS-patterns, AMs perform similarly when the adjective is the first member (Table 3), whereas PS seems to be more indicative when the adjective is second and third (Tables 4-5), together with raw frequency, while LL seems to be generally performing the worst. This point calls for a combination of AMs (Pecina, 2008), but will require further work.

As for predetermined patterns that are *not* found among the top ones, we observe that NOUN NOUN ADJ is basically an adjective modifying a noun-noun compound, and should be best treated as a "complex bigram". Similarly, the PRE ADJ VER pattern can be seen as an extension of the ADJ VER bigram, which is usually not considered (Table 1). Investigating the combination of bigrams, trigrams and n-grams with n>3 is left for future work.

4 Conclusion

In summary, basically all of the literature/intuition-based patterns are retrieved from highly ranked plain trigrams. However, top-ranking trigrams also exhibit other POS sequences which should be included in a set of patterns used for MWE extrac-

Table 4: Top 10 POS patterns featuring an adjective as word2, extracted from the top 10% trigrams ranked according to LL, PS, and raw frequency.

LL	**PS**	**raw frequency**
ART ADJ NOUN	ART ADJ NOUN	ART ADJ NOUN
NOUN ADJ PRE	ARTPRE ADJ NOUN	ARTPRE ADJ NOUN
PRE ADJ NOUN	PRE ADJ NOUN	PRE ADJ NOUN
ARTPRE ADJ NOUN	NOUN ADJ ARTPRE	NOUN ADJ PRE
DET ADJ NOUN	NOUN ADJ PRE	NOUN ADJ ARTPRE
ART ADJ NPR	NOUN ADJ CON	NOUN ADJ CON
ART ADJ CON	DET ADJ NOUN	ADV ADJ PRE
ADV ADJ PRE	VER ADJ NOUN	DET ADJ NOUN
DET ADJ VER	NOUN ADJ ADJ	ADV ADJ ARTPRE
VER ADJ PRE	ADV ADJ PRE	ADV ADJ CON

Table 5: Top 10 POS patterns featuring an adjective as word3, extracted from the top 10% trigrams ranked according to LL, PS, and raw frequency.

LL	**PS**	**raw frequency**
VER ART ADJ	ART NOUN ADJ	ART NOUN ADJ
PRE ART ADJ	ARTPRE NOUN ADJ	ARTPRE NOUN ADJ
NOUN PRE ADJ	PRE NOUN ADJ	VER ART ADJ
NOUN ARTPRE ADJ	NOUN ARTPRE ADJ	PRE ART ADJ
VER ARTPRE ADJ	VER ART ADJ	PRE NOUN ADJ
VER PRE ADJ	NOUN PRE ADJ	NOUN ARTPRE ADJ
NOUN ART ADJ	PRE ART ADJ	NOUN PRE ADJ
ADV ART ADJ	NOUN ADV ADJ	VER PRE ADJ
ADV ADV ADJ	VER PRE ADJ	NOUN ADV ADJ
ART DET ADJ	NOUN ADJ ADJ	VER ARTPRE ADJ

Table 6: Extracted trigram patterns that subsume a bigram pattern (boldfaced).

Pattern	Example	Translation
ADJ PRE ART	**degno di** un	**worthy of** a
ADJ NOUN PRE	**utile netto** di	**net profit** of
ADJ NOUN ARTPRE	**alto funzionario** del	**senrior official** of
ART **ADJ NOUN**	il **pubblico ministero**	the **public prosecutor**
NOUN ADJ PRE	**centro storico** di	**historical centre** of
ARTPRE **ADJ NOUN**	della **pubblica amministrazione**	of the **public administration**
DET **ADJ NOUN**	altro **duro colpo**	another **hard blow**
ADV **ADJ PRE**	sempre **pronto a**	always **ready to**

tion to improve recall. At the same time, several patterns extracted with this technique are to be discarded. Some are just irrelevant (e.g. ADJ CHE CLI, *nero che le* "black that them"): in this respect, combining various AMs or setting grammatical constraints could help refine precision, but human intervention also seems unavoidable. Others are not meaningful trigrams as such, but may be meaningful as parts of larger MWEs or because they contain meaningful bigrams. Here, it would be interesting to explore how to combine n-grams with different n-values.

This pilot experiment shows that trigram ranking is useful to extract new patterns that are not considered in the initial set. The latter can be therefore expanded by following the proposed methodology, as a preliminary step towards the actual extraction of candidate MWEs from corpora. Clearly, the validity of the expanded POS-pattern set can only be evaluated after the extraction step is completed.

Acknowledgments

This research was carried out within the PRIN project 2010-2011 (n. 20105B3HE8_003) *Word Combinations in Italian: theoretical and descriptive analysis, computational models, lexicographic layout and creation of a dictionary*, coordinated by Raffaele Simone (Roma Tre University) and funded by the Italian Ministry of Education, University and Research (MIUR). We are grateful to the anonymous reviewers for their useful comments.

References

Satanjeev Banerjee and Ted Pedersen. 2003. The design, implementation, and use of the ngram statistics package. In A. F. Gelbukh, editor, volume 2588 of *Lecture Notes in Computer Science*, pages 370–381.

Colin Bannard. 2007. A measure of syntactic flexibility for automatically identifying multiword expressions in corpora. In *Proc. of the Workshop on A Broader Perspective on Multiword Expressions*, pages 1–8, Prague, ACL.

Marco Baroni, Silvia Bernardini, Federica Comastri, Lorenzo Piccioni, Alessandra Volpi, Guy Aston, and Marco Mazzoleni. 2004. Introducing the La Repubblica Corpus: A Large, Annotated, TEI(XML)-Compliant Corpus of Newspaper Italian. In *Proc. of LREC 2004*, pages 1771–1774.

Stefan Evert and Brigitte Krenn. 2005. Using small random samples for the manual evaluation of statistical association measures. *Computer Speech & Language*, 19(4):450–466. Special issue on Multiword Expression.

Brigitte Krenn and Stefan Evert. 2001. Can we do better than frequency? A case study on extracting PP-verb collocations. In *Proc. of the ACL-EACL Workshop on Collocations*, pages 39–46, Toulouse.

Francesca Masini. 2012. *Parole sintagmatiche in italiano*. Caissa, Roma.

Malvina Nissim and Andrea Zaninello. 2013. Modeling the internal variability of multiword expressions through a pattern-based method. *ACM Trans. Speech Lang. Process.*, 10(2):7:1–7:26.

Pavel Pecina. 2008. A Machine Learning Approach to Multiword Expression Extraction. In *Proceedings of the LREC 2008 Workshop Towards a Shared Task for Multiword Expressions*, pages 54–57, Marrakech, Morocco. European Language Resources Association.

Valentina Piunno, Francesca Masini and Sara Castagnoli. 2013. Studio comparativo dei dizionari combinatori dell'italiano e di altre lingue europee. *CombiNet Technical Report*. Roma Tre University and University of Bologna.

Miriam Voghera. 2004. Polirematiche. In Grossmann, Maria & Franz Rainer, editors, La formazione delle parole in italiano, Tübingen, Max Niemeyer Verlag, 56-69.

Joachim Wermter and Udo Hahn. 2006. You can't beat frequency (unless you use linguistic knowledge): A qualitative evaluation of association measures for collocation and term extraction. In *Proc. of COLING-ACL '06*, pages 785–792, USA.

Appendix

The tagset for all patterns extracted from the corpus "La Repubblica" is accessible at `http://sslmit.unibo.it/~baroni/collocazioni/itwac.tagset.txt`. In the context of this experiment we collapsed all fine-grained tags into the corresponding coarse-grained tag (e.g. all verbal tags such as VER:fin or VER:ppast were collapsed into VER). The POS tags used in this paper are to be interpreted as in the Table below.

Table 7: POS tags used in this paper.

abbreviation	part of speech
ADJ	adjective
ADV	adverb
ART	article
ARTPRE	prepositional article
CHE	any function of the word "che" (adjective, conjunction, pronoun)
CLI	clitic
DET	determiner
NOUN	noun
PRE	preposition
VER	verb

Mickey Mouse is not a Phrase: Improving Relevance in E-Commerce with Multiword Expressions

Prathyusha Senthil Kumar, Vamsi Salaka, Tracy Holloway King, and **Brian Johnson**
Search Science
eBay, Inc.
San Jose, CA, USA
{ prathykumar, vsalaka, tracyking, bjohnson } @ebay.com

Abstract

We describe a method for detecting phrases in e-commerce queries. The key insight is that previous buyer purchasing behavior as well as the general distribution of phrases in item titles must be used to select phrases. Many multiword expression (mwe) phrases which might be useful in other situations are not suitable for buyer query phrases because relevant items, as measured by purchases, do not contain these terms as phrases.

1 Phrase MWE in e-Commerce Search

Processing buyers' queries is key for successful e-commerce. As with web search queries, e-commerce queries are shorter and have different syntactic patterns than standard written language. For a given query, the system must provide sufficient recall (i.e. return all items relevant to the buyers' query, regardless of the tokens used) and sufficient precision (i.e. exclude items which are token matches but not relevant for the query). This paper looks at how identifying phrases in buyer queries can help with recall and precision in e-commerce at eBay. We focus primarily on precision, which is the harder problem to solve.

Phrases are a sub-type of mwe: one where the tokens of the mwe appear strictly adjacent to one another and in a specified order ((Sag et al., 2002)'s words with spaces).

The eBay product search engine takes buyer queries and retrieves items relevant to the buyer's purchasing intent. The items are listed in categories (e.g. women's dresses) and each item has a title provided by the seller. The buyer can choose to sort the items by most relevant (e.g. similar to web search ranking) or deterministically (e.g. price low to high). There are versions of the e-commerce site for different countries such as US, UK, Germany, France, Poland, etc. and so the query processing is language-specific according to site. Here we report on incorporating phrases into English for the US and German for Germany.

2 Controlling Retrieval via Query Phrases

The query processing system has three core capabilities[1] which expand tokens in the buyer's query into other forms. Both single and multiple tokens can be expanded. Token-to-token expansions (Jammalamadaka and Salaka, 2012) include acronyms, abbreviations, inflectional variants (e.g. *hats* to *hat*), and space synonyms (e.g. *ray ban* to *rayban*). Category expansions expand tokens to all items in a given category (e.g. *womens shoes* retrieves all items in the Womens' Shoes category). Finally, attribute expansions map tokens to structured data (e.g. *red* retrieves any item with Color=Reds in its structured data). These expansions are used to increase the number of relevant items brought back for a specific buyer query.

Precision issues occur when a buyer's query returns an item that is a spurious match. For example, the query *diamond ring size 10* matches all the tokens in the title "10 kt gold, size 7 diamond ring" even though it is not a size 10 ring.

Recall issues occur when relevant items are not returned for a buyer's query. The core capabilities of token-to-token mappings, category mappings, and attribute mapping largely address this. However, some query tokens are not covered by these capabilities. For example, the query *used cars for sale* contains the tokens *for sale* which rarely occur in e-commerce item titles.

[1] Here we ignore tokenization, although the quality of the tokenizer affects the quality of all remaining components (Manning et al., 2008).

2.1 Hypothesis: Phrasing within Queries

To address these precision and recall issues, we provide special treatment for phrases in queries. To address the precision issue where spurious items are returned, we require certain token sequences to be treated as phrases. For example, *size 10* will be phrased and hence only match items whose titles have those tokens in that order. To address the recall issue, we identify queries which contain phrases that can be dropped. For example, in the query *used cars for sale* the tokens *for sale* can be dropped; similarly for German *kaufen* (buy) in the query *waschtrockner kaufen* (washer-dryer buy). For the remainder of the paper we will use the terminology:

- REQUIRED PHRASES: Token sequences required to be phrases when used in queries (e.g. *apple tv*)
- DROPPED PHRASES: Phrases which allow sub-phrase deletion (e.g. *used cars for sale*)

The required-phrases approach must be high confidence since it will block items from being returned for the buyer's query.

We first mined candidate phrases for required phrases and for dropped phrases in queries. From this large set of candidates, we then used past buyer behavior to determine whether the candidate was viable for application to queries (see (Ramisch et al., 2008) on mwe candidate evaluation in general). As we will see, many phrases which seem to be intuitively well-formed mwe cannot be used as e-commerce query phrases because they would block relevant inventory from being returned (see (Diab et al., 2010) on mwe in NLP applications).

The phrases which pass candidate selection are then incorporated into the existing query expansions (i.e. token-to-token mappings, category mappings, attribute mappings). The phrases are a new type of token-to-token mapping which require the query tokens to appear in order and adjacent, i.e. as a mwe phrase, or to be dropped.

2.2 Phrase Candidate Selection

The first stage of the algorithm is candidate selection: from all the possible buyer query n-grams we determine which are potential mwe phrase candidates. We use a straight-forward selection technique in order to gather a large candidate set; at this stage we are concerned with recall, not precision, of the phrases.

First consider required phrases. For a given site (US and Germany here), we consider all the bi- and tri-grams seen in buyer queries. Since e-commerce queries are relatively short, even shorter than web queries, we do not consider longer n-grams. The most frequent of these are then considered candidates. Manual inspection of the candidate set shows a variety of mwe semantic types. As expected in the e-commerce domain, these contain primarily nominal mwe: brand names, product types, and measure phrases (see (Ó Séaghdha and Copestake, 2007) on identifying nominal mwe). Multiword verbs are non-existent in buyer queries and relatively few adjectives are candidates (e.g. *navy blue, brand new*).

Next consider dropped phrases. These are stop words specialized to the e-commerce domain. They are mined from behavioral logs by looking at query-to-query transitions. We consider query transitions where buyers drop a word or phrase in the transition and show increased engagement after the transition. For example, buyers issue the query *used cars for sale* followed by the query *used cars* and subsequently engage with the search results (e.g. view or purchase items). The most frequent n-grams identified by this approach are candidates for dropped phrases and are contextually dropped, i.e. they are dropped when they are parts of specific larger phrases. Query context is important because *for sale* should not be dropped when part of the larger phrase *plastic for sale signs*.

2.3 Phrase Selection: Sorry Mickey

Once we have candidate phrases, we use buyer behavioral data (Carterette et al., 2012) to determine which phrases to require in buyer queries. For each query which contains a given phrase (e.g. for the candidate phrase *apple tv* consider queries such as *apple tv*, *new apple tv*, *apple tv remote*) we see which items were purchased. Item titles from purchased items which contain the phrase are referred to as "phrase bought" while item titles shown in searches are "phrase impressed". We are interested only in high confidence phrases and so focus on purchase behavior: this signal is relatively sparse but is the strongest indicator of buyer interest. To determine the candidates, we want to compute the conditional probability of an item being bought (B(ought)) given a phrase (Ph(rase)).

$$P(B|Ph) = \frac{P(Ph|B) * P(B)}{P(Ph)} \quad (1)$$

However, this is computationally intensive in that all items retrieved for a query must be considered. In equation 1, P(Ph|B) is easy to compute since only bought items are considered; P(Ph) can be approximated by the ratio of phrases to non-phrases for bought items; P(B) is a constant and hence can be ignored. So, we use the following two metrics based on these probabilities:

- SALE EFFICIENCY: Probability of phrases in bought items, P(Ph|B) $> 95\%$. Ensures quality and acts as an upper bound for the expected loss (equation 2).
- LIFT: Ensures phrasing has a positive revenue impact and handles presentation bias (equation 3).

First consider sale efficiency:

$$P(Ph|B) = \frac{P(Ph \bigcap B)}{P(B)} = \frac{n(ph\_bought)}{n(bought)} \quad (2)$$

One drawback of sale efficiency P(Ph|B) is data sparsity. There is a high false positive rate in identifying phrases when the frequency of bought items is low since it is hard to distinguish signal from noise with a strict threshold. We used Beta-Binomial smoothing to avoid this (Schuckers, 2003; Agarwal et al., 2009). Conceptually, by incorporating Beta-Binomial smoothing, we model the number of phrases bought as a binomial process and use the Beta distribution, which is its conjugate prior, for smoothing the sale efficiency.

However the sale efficiency as captured by the conditional probability of being bought as a phrase (equation 2) does not take into account the distribution of the phrases in the retrieved set. For example for the phrase *apple tv*, 80% of the impressed items contained the phrase while 99% of the bought items contained the phrase, which makes it an excellent phrase. However, for *mount rushmore* 99% of the impressed items contained the phrase while only 97% of the bought items contained the phrase. This implies that the probability of being bought as a phrase for *mount rushmore* is high because of presentation bias (i.e. the vast majority of token matches contain phrases) and not because the phrase itself is an indicator of relevance. To address the issue of presentation bias in P(Ph|B), we use the following lift metric:

$$\frac{P(Ph|B) - P(Ph)}{P(Ph)} > 0 \quad (3)$$

Lift (equation 3) measures the buyers' tendency to purchase phrase items. For a good phrase this value should be high. For example, for *apple tv* this value is +23.13% while for *mount rushmore* it is -1.8%. We only consider phrases that have a positive lift.

Examples of English phrases for buyer queries include *apple tv, bubble wrap, playstation 3, 4 x 4, tank top, nexus 4, rose gold, 1 gb, hot pack, 20 v, kindle fire, hard rock* and *new balance* and German phrases include *geflochtene schnur* (braided line) and *energiespar regler* (energy-saving controller). These form a disparate semantic set including brand names (*new balance*), product types (*bubble wrap*), and units of measure (*1 gb*).

Consider the phrases which were not selected because a significant percentage of the buyer demand was for items where the tokens appeared either in a different order or not adjacent. These include *golf balls, hard drive* and *mickey mouse*. You might ask, what could possibly be a stronger phrase in American English than *mickey mouse*? Closer examination of the buyer behavioral data shows that many buyers are using queries with the tokens *mickey mouse* to find and purchase *mickey and minnie mouse* items. The introduction of *and minnie* in the item titles breaks the query phrase.

3 Experiment Results

We selected phrase candidates for two sites: The US and Germany. These sites were selected because there was significant query and purchasing data which alleviates data sparsity issues and because the language differences allowed us to test the general applicability of the approach.[2]

We created query assets which contained the existing production assets and modified them to include the required phrases and the dropped phrases. The relative query frequency of required phrases (blue) vs. dropped phrases (red) in each experiment is shown in Figure 2.

Figure 2: Impacted Query Frequency: red=dropped; blue=required

For US and Germany, 10% of users were ex-

[2]English and German are closely related languages. We plan to apply mwe phrases to Russian and French.

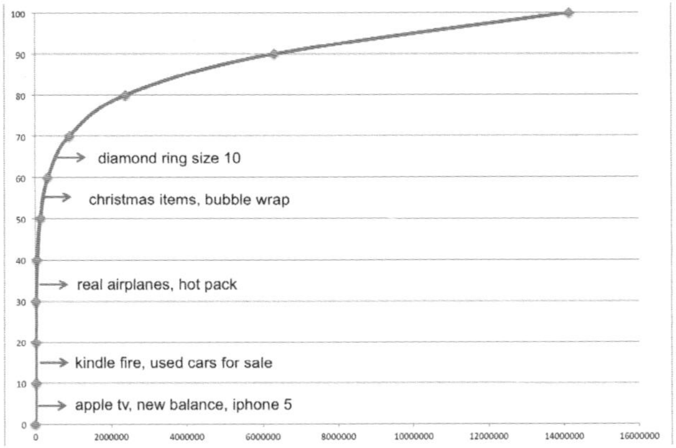

Figure 1: US Phrase Query Impressions: Head-vs.-tail queries

posed to the new phrase assets, while a 10% control[3] were exposed to the existing production assets. The test was run for two weeks. We measured the number of items bought in test vs. control, the revenue, and the behavior of new users. Bought items and revenue are both measured to determine whether changes in purchases are coming from better deals (e.g. bought items might increase while revenue is constant) or improved discovery (e.g. more items are bought at the same price). New user success is measured because new users are generally sensitive to irrelevant items being returned for their queries; the required phrase mwe in this experiment target this use case.

As a result of the phrase experiment, in the US, revenue, bought items, and new user engagement increased statistically significantly ($p<0.1$). The German test showed directionally similar results but was only statistically significant for new buyers. We cannot show proprietary business results, but both experiences are now in production in place of the previous query processing. The graph in Figure 1 shows the distribution of head-vs.-tail queries for the US with some sample affected head queries.

4 Discussion and Conclusion

We described a relatively straight-forward method for detecting phrases in buyer queries. The key insight is that previous buyer purchasing behavior as well as the distribution of phrases in item titles must be used to select which candidate phrases to keep in the final analysis. Many mwe phrases which might be useful in other situations (e.g. our friend *mickey mouse* (§2.3)) are not suitable for buyer queries because many relevant items, as measured by purchases, do not contain these tokens phrases (e.g. *mickey and minnie mouse*).

[3]Technically there were two 5% controls which were compared to determine variability within the control group.

Among the rejected candidate phrases, the higher confidence ones are likely to be suitable for ranking of the results even though they could not be used to filter out results. This is an area of active research: what mwe phrases can improve the ranking of e-commerce results, especially given the presence of the phrase in the buyer query? Another method to increase phrase coverage is to consider contextualized phrases, whereby token sequences may be a phrase in one query but not in another.

The experiments here were conducted on two of our largest sites, thereby avoiding data sparsity issues. We have used the same algorithm on smaller sites such as Australia: the resulting required phrases and dropped phrases look reasonable but have not been tested experimentally. An interesting question is whether phrases from same-language sites (e.g. UK, Australia, Canada, US) can be combined or whether a site with more behavioral data can be used to learn phrases for smaller sites. The later has been done for Canada using US data.

In sum, mwe phrases improved eBay e-commerce, but it was important to use domain-specific data in choosing the relevant phrases. This suggests that the utility of universal vs. domain specific mwe is an area requiring investigation.

References

Deepak Agarwal, Bee-Chung Chen, and Pradheep Elango. 2009. Spatio-temporal models for estimating click-through rate. In *Proceedings of the 18th International Conference on World Wide Web*. ACM.

Ben Carterette, Evangelos Kanoulas, Paul Clough, and Mark Sanderson, editors. 2012. *Information Retrieval Over Query Sessions*. Springer Lecture Notes in Computer Science.

Mona Diab, Valia Kordoni, and Hans Uszkoreit. 2010. Multiword expressions: From theory to applications. Panel at MWE2010.

Ravi Chandra Jammalamadaka and Vamsi Salaka. 2012. Synonym mining and usage in e-commerce. Presented at ECIR.

Christopher D. Manning, Prabhakar Raghavan, and Hinrich Schütze. 2008. *Introduction to Information Retrieval*. Cambridge University Press.

Diarmuid Ó Séaghdha and Ann Copestake. 2007. Co-occurrence contexts for noun compound interpretation. In *Proceedings of the Workshop on A Broader Perspective on Multiword Expressions*, pages 57–64. Association for Computational Linguistics.

Carlos Ramisch, Paulo Schreiner, Marco Idiart, and Aline Villavicencio. 2008. An evaluation of methods for the extraction of multiword expressions. In *Towards a Shared Task for Multiword Expressions*, pages 50–53.

Ivan A. Sag, Timothy Baldwin, Francis Bond, Ann A. Copestake, and Dan Flickinger. 2002. Multiword expressions: A pain in the neck for NLP. In *Proceedings of the Third International Conference on Computational Linguistics and Intelligent Text Processing*, CICLing '02, pages 1–15. Springer-Verlag.

Michael E. Schuckers. 2003. Using the beta-binomial distribution to assess performance of a biometric identification device. *International Journal of Image and Graphics*, pages 523–529.

Encoding of Compounds in Swedish FrameNet

Karin Friberg Heppin
Språkbanken
University of Gothenburg
karin.heppin@svenska.gu.se

Miriam R L Petruck
International Computer Science Institute
Berkeley, CA
miriamp@icsi.berkeley.edu

Abstract

Constructing a lexical resource for Swedish, where compounding is highly productive, requires a well-structured policy of encoding. This paper presents the treatment and encoding of a certain class of compounds in Swedish FrameNet, and proposes a new approach for the automatic analysis of Swedish compounds, i.e. one that leverages existing FrameNet (Ruppenhofer et al., 2010) and Swedish FrameNet (Borin et al. 2010), as well as proven techniques for automatic semantic role labeling (Johansson et al., 2012).

1 Introduction

Like other Germanic languages (e.g. Dutch, German), compounding is a very productive word formation process in Swedish. Swedish FrameNet,[1] which is part of the larger Swedish FrameNet++ effort to create Swedish resources for language technology purposes, analyzes Swedish compositional compounds in a way that reflects the language's grammatical structure, records information about the internal structure of these compounds in Frame Semantic terms, and proposes using that information to automate the analysis.

2 Swedish FrameNet

Swedish FrameNet (SweFN), which began in 2011, is part of Swedish FrameNet++ (Borin et al., 2010), a larger project whose main goal is building a panchronic lexical macro-resource for use in Swedish language technology. Basing its work on the original FrameNet developed in Berkeley (BFN) (Fonetenelle, 2003), SweFN is creating a lexical resource of at least 50,000 lexical units (LUs) with the express goal of automating as much of the process as possible.

Swedish FrameNet bases its contents on three resources: (1) BFN's frames, frame definitions and frame-to-frame relations, for efficiency and compatibility with other FrameNet-like resources; (2) lexical entries from the SALDO lexicon; and (3) example sentences from the KORP corpus collection (Ahlberg et al., 2013).

Building SweFN frames includes several steps. The SweFN researcher chooses a BFN frame with a Swedish analogue, and populates that frame with appropriate LUs. LU selection involves determining which of the BFN LUs have equivalents in Swedish, or searching SALDO for LUs of the frame. Using the KORP corpora, the researcher finds example sentences that illustrate the LU's meaning and annotates each sentence with the frame's FEs. SweFN draws all examples from corpus data; this paper also provides the larger context in which compounds occur.

SweFN LUs, be they single words or multiword expressions (MWEs), evoke frames, i.e. cognitive structuring constituting the basic building blocks of any framenet knowledge base. LUs are pairings of lemmas and frames, the latter schematic representations of events, objects, situations or states of affairs. Frame elements (FEs) identify the semantic roles of the participants of the scenario characterized in a frame, e.g. AGENT, THEME, or TIME. For each frame, example sentences illustrate the linguistic realization of LUs together with the frame's FEs for the Frame Semantic annotation of the sentence's constituents (Borin et al., 2013a; Borin et al., 2013b).

3 Multiword expressions in SALDO

As mentioned above, the SALDO lexicon serves as the primary resource for LUs in SweFN++ and consequently also for LUs in SweFN. SALDO contains almost 6,000 MWEs of three types, dis-

[1] SweFN, <http://spraakbanken.gu.se/eng/swefn>, a free resource (CC-BY-SA 3.0, LGPL 3.0) funded by Vetenskapsrådet under contract 2010-6013.

tinguished as follows (Borin et al., 2013a):

- **Continuous MWEs** corresponding to fixed and semi-fixed expressions[2], which may have internal inflection, but no intervening words, e.g. *enarmad bandit* (one-armed bandit) - 'slot machine'.

- **Discontinuous MWEs** corresponding to syntactically flexible expressions[2], which may have intervening words, such as particle or phrasal verbs, e.g. *ge ut* (give out) - 'publish'.

- **Constructions** partially schematic constructions or syntactic templates with one or more slots filled with items of specific types, those described in construction grammars, e.g. *ju X desto Y* - 'The Xer the Yer' (Fillmore et al., 1988).

SALDO treats solid compounds, i.e. single orthographic words, just as it treats single-word items, and does not normally define their formal structure explicitly. In most cases, Swedish compounds are written without space between its constituents, as in *korvgubbe* (sausage+man) - 'hot dog seller'. However, different possible forms yield different meanings. The adjective + noun NP *varm korv* literally means 'hot sausage' (in the temperature sense); the continuous MWE *varm korv* means 'hot dog'; and the solid compound *varmkorv* refers to not necessarily prepared sausage for making hot dogs. As LUs in a SweFN frame, the solid compounds, when compositional or partially transparent, have constituents which manifest FEs or other LUs in the same frame. The next section discusses these compounds and their annotation in SweFN.

4 MWEs and compounds as LUs

SALDO's continuous MWEs, discontinuous MWEs, and solid compounds are candidates for SweFN LUs, much like simplex words. Solid endocentric compounds, which identify a more specific instance of the compound's head, constitute a large group of words in Swedish. SweFN provides an analysis for these, even though BFN does not (Friberg Heppin and Toporowska Gronostaj, 2012). In frames where solid endocentric compounds are LUs, SweFN records the pattern FE+LU, where the compound's modifier is a FE of the given frame and the head is another LU in the same frame. Thus, among others, `Observable_body_parts` has ATTACHMENT, and DESCRIPTOR, and POSSESSOR FEs. SweFN records the analysis shown below with segmentation points between compound parts marked with '|'.

- ATTACHMENT+LU stortå|nagel (big+toe+nail) - 'big toe nail', pekfinger|nagel (point+finger+nail) - 'index finger nail'

- DESCRIPTOR+LU ring|finger - 'ring finger', pek|finger (point+finger) - 'index finger', stor|tå 'big toe'

- POSSESSOR+LU häst|hov 'horse hoof'

Generally, compounds with more than two constituents consist of one or more constituents that are themselves compounds. SweFN treats such compounds in the same way as it treats other compounds. For example, stortå|nagel (big+toe+nail) - 'big toe nail' instantiates ATTACHMENT+LU , where stortå (big+toe) - 'big toe' itself is analyzed as DESCRIPTOR+LU.

SweFN analyzes example sentences that include compounds of different types with FE and LU annotation tags. The next section describes this encoding.

5 Encoding of compounds

Ruppenhofer et al. (2010) describes two ways that BFN treats noun compounds. Conventionalized two-part words are treated as single LUs with no internal analysis, e.g., *firing squad*, *sugar daddy*, and *wine bottle*. When a frame-evoking compound has a modifier that happens to be a noun or relational adjective e.g., *restoration costs*, *military supremacy*, the compound's head is annotated as a LU of the frame in question and the modifier instantiates a FE of the same frame. Ruppenhofer et al. (2010) point out that the division between the two groups is not always clear.

SweFN relies on degree of compositionality to determine the extent to which compound analysis is encoded in a frame's example sentences, not the compound's degree of lexicalization. Thus far, the analysis has been produced manually. Section 6 presents a proposal for the automatic Frame Semantic analysis of compounds.

[2] As described by Sag et al. (2001)

5.1 Non-compositional compounds

Typically, non-compositional compounds are lexicalized. Otherwise, understanding them is not possible, since the sense of the compound is not apparent from its parts. SALDO lists lexicalized non-compositional compounds as individual entries, like simplex words. Taking its lead from SALDO, and because constituents of non-compositional compounds do not instantiate FEs, SweFN does not analyze such compounds further, as in (1), where *hästhov* (horse+hoof) - 'coltsfoot' (`Plants`) is annotated only as a whole.

(1) och [hästhovarna]$_{\text{LU}}$ lyser som solar
and coltsfeet+DEF shine like suns
...and the coltsfeet are shining like suns.

5.2 Compositional compounds

SALDO also treats solid compositional compounds as simplex words. In contrast, SweFN treats compositional compounds as LUs, analyzing them as FE+LU, as described above in section 4. Furthermore, SweFN annotates compositional compounds in example sentences both as wholes and with respect to their constituent parts, as in (2).

(2) ...klappret från [snabba]$_{\text{Descriptor}}$
...clatter+DEF from fast
[[häst]$_{\text{Possessor}}$[hovar]$_{\text{LU}}$]$_{\text{LU}}$
horse+hooves
...the clatter from fast horse hooves.

Rather than serving as a modifier, the first element of some compounds is the semantic head of that compound. In such cases, the syntactic head can be semantically transparent, as in *bakterietyp* (bacteria+type) - 'type of bacteria' and *kaffesort* (coffee+kind) - 'kind of coffee', or show the speaker's attitude toward the entity identified in the semantic head of the compound as in *gubbslem* (old man+mucus) - 'dirty old man' or *hästkrake* (horse+wretch) - 'wretched horse'. For this type of compound the modifier and the whole compound are annotated as LUs in the given frame, as illustrated in (3); the syntactic head of the compound does not realize any frame element in the frame.

(3) Han fick syn på en [gammal]$_{\text{Age}}$
He got sight of an old
[vit]$_{\text{Persistent\_characteristics}}$ [[häst]$_{\text{LU}}$krake]$_{\text{LU}}$
white horse+wretch
He caught sight of an old wretched white horse.

5.3 Partially transparent compounds

For some non-compositional compounds, one constituent clearly instantiates a FE or LU of the frame that the compound evokes, but the other is opaque, as in *ryggskott* (back+shot) - 'lumbago' from `Medical_disorders`. The modifier *rygg* - 'back' is the body part location of the disorder; the head *skott* - 'shot' is interpreted as something that appears suddenly, as a gunshot, but its meaning is not transparent. Example (4) shows that SweFN treats the compound as a LU, and the modifier as instantiating the FE BODY_PART; SweFN does not treat the head separately.

(4) [Han]$_{\text{Patient}}$ fick [[rygg]$_{\text{Body_Part}}$skott]$_{\text{LU}}$
He got back+shot
[under uppvärmningen]$_{\text{Time}}$ och
during up+warming+DEF and
tvingades vila
forced+PASS rest+INF
He got lumbago during the warm-up and had to rest.

Naming different types or species of a class of entities often results in groups of compounds whose heads are the name of the class, e.g. *blåbär* (blue+berry) - 'blueberry', where the compound names a type of berry. In these compounds, the modifier may not have an independent meaning, e.g. *körsbär* (?+berry) - 'cherry', where *körs* is a cran morph, i.e. it has no meaning outside of its use as a modifier in the compound. SweFN annotates the modifiers of these compounds with the FE TYPE, as in (5), since they have no meaning except to discern one type (cherry) of the LU in question (berry) from other types.

(5) Ska vi plocka [[körs]$_{\text{Type}}$[bär]$_{\text{LU}}$]$_{\text{LU}}$
Shall we pick cherries
Do you want to pick cherries?

5.4 Modifier as lexical unit

SweFN also chooses to analyze sentences (that illustrate the use of a LU) where a compound's modifier evokes the frame under consideration. For example, the compound *gasdetektor* - 'gas detector' is analyzed with respect to the `Devices` frame, given the head *detektor* - 'detector'. However, the modifier *gas* - 'gas' is analyzed with respect to `Substances`. Typically, SweFN does not choose sentences for annotation where only the modifier of a compound evokes the frame in question. Still, doing so is possible, as in (6).

(6) En vätesensor är en
A hydrogen+sensor is a
[gas]$_{LU}$detektor som visar
gas+detector which shows
närvaron av väte
presence+DEF of hydrogen
A hydrogen sensor is a gas detector showing the presence of hydrogen.

If analyzing a sentence where the LU under consideration is a modifier of a compound, SweFN does not annotate the compound's head. This practice reflects that of BFN (Ruppenhofer et al., 2010, 42).

> [W]e never annotate the head noun as a frame element of a frame that may be evoked by the non-head...While the non-head must figure in some frame evoked by the head, the reverse is not true in the same way....

6 Future Research

With a well-designed encoding for compounds, SweFN is positioned to develop ways to automate its heretofore manual annotation of compounds. Here, we sketch out plans to pursue the automatic Frame Semantic annotation of modifiers of compounds.

Johansson and Nugues (2006) demonstrated the effective use of FN annotation for automatic semantic role labeling (ASRL) of Swedish text to produce annotation (comparable to Padó and Lapata (2005)). More recently, Johansson et al. (2012) investigated the feasibility of using Swedish FrameNet annotation as a resource in constructing an automatic semantic role analyzer for Swedish. We suggest the possibility of using comparable techniques for the analysis of Swedish compound forms, also including FN data for developing and testing the efficacy of the algorithms.

This proposal involves the following: (1) manually add solid compounds from SALDO to appropriate frames based on the head of the compound; (2) use Kokkinakis's (2001) compound analysis technique to identify the component parts of the compound, by finding n-grams of characters which do not occur in simplex words; (3) exploit existing SweFN annotation for adjacent non-compounded words to develop an ASRL system to annotate modifiers of Swedish compounds and test the system; (4) exploit existing SweFN annotation of full sentences to determine if a system trained on that data would improve ASRL of modifiers in compounds; (5) using the same basic techniques for developing training data, determine if BFN data would benefit ASRL of modifiers, as Johansson and Nugues (2006) demonstrated for Swedish text in general.

Initially, the proposed plan for ASRL of modifiers of compounds addresses compounds with (only) two elements. In principle, the same approach can be expanded to annotate multiple modifiers of head nouns, i.e. compounds with more than two elements. These compounds consist at least one constituent that is itself a compound, i.e. the compounding process has occurred more than once as described in section 4.

As more language technology and NLP researchers develop FrameNet knowledge bases for languages other than English, the need for automatic processes to produce annotation that suits the grammatical requirements of the particular language will increase, as will the importance of using existing resources efficiently and effectively. The research proposed here offers the possibility of providing an automatic process that would be useful for the Frame Semantic analysis of Swedish in particular and for other compounding languages (e.g. Dutch, German). Additionally, the technique may prove useful for the processing of compounds more generally.

7 Conclusion

Given the highly productive nature of Swedish compounding, lexical resources such as Swedish FrameNet must attend to the representation and analysis of compounds. This paper has presented a new feature in SweFN, the explicit recording of the FE+LU pattern for the analysis of compositional compounds, and suggests a research plan to analyze Swedish compounds automatically.

Acknowledgments

The authors thank the anonymous reviewers for their helpful comments. The Swedish Research Council (grant agreement 2010-6013) and the University of Gothenburg via its support of the Centre for Language Technology and Språkbanken have supported this work.

References

Malin Ahlberg, Lars Borin, Markus Forsberg, Martin Hammarstedt, Leif Jöran Olsson, Olof Olsson, Johan Roxendal, and Jonatan Uppström. 2013. Korp and Karp – a bestiary of language resources: the research infrastructure of Språkbanken. In *Proceedings of the 19th Nordic Conference of Computational Linguistics, NODALIDA*.

Lars Borin, Dana Dannélls, Markus Forsberg, Maria Toporowska Gronostaj, and Dimitrios Kokkinakis. 2010. The past meets the present in Swedish Framenet++. In *Proceedings of the 14th EURALEX International Congress*.

Lars Borin, Markus Forsberg, and Lennart Lönngren. 2013a. SALDO: a touch of yin to WordNet's yang. *Language Resources and Evaluation*, 47(4).

Lars Borin, Markus Forsberg, and Benjamin Lyngfelt. 2013b. Close encounters of the fifth kind: Some linguistic and computational aspects of the Swedish FrameNet++ project. *Veredas: Frame Semantics and Its Technological Applications*, 17(1).

Charles J. Fillmore, Paul Kay, and Mary Catherine O'Connor. 1988. Regularity and idiomaticity in grammatical constructions: The case of let alone. *Language*, 64.

Thierry Fonetenelle, editor. 2003. *FrameNet and frame semantics*. Number 16.3: 231–385 in International Journal of Lexicography. Oxford University Press.

Karin Friberg Heppin and Maria Toporowska Gronostaj. 2012. The rocky road towards a Swedish FrameNet. In *Proceedings of the 8th Conference on International Language Resources and Evaluation*, Istanbul.

Richard Johansson and Pierre Nugues. 2006. A FrameNet-based semantic role labeler for Swedish. Sydney.

Richard Johansson, Karin Friberg Heppin, and Dimitrios Kokkinakis. 2012. Semantic role labeling with the swedish framenet,. In *Proceedings of the 8th Conference on International Language Resources and Evaluation (LREC-2012);*, Istanbul, Turkey.

Dimitrios Kokkinakis. 2001. *A framework for the aquisition of lexical knowledge; Description and applications*. Ph.D. thesis, Department of Swedish, University of Gothenburg.

Sebastian Padó and Mirella Lapata. 2005. Cross-lingual bootstrapping of semantic lexicons: The case of framenet. In *Proceedings of the American Association of Artificial Intelligence Conference*.

Josef Ruppenhofer, Michael Ellsworth, Miriam R.L. Petruck, Christopher R. Johnson, and Jan Scheffczyk. 2010. *FrameNet II: Extended theory and practice*. <https://framenet2.icsi. berkeley.edu/ ocs/r1.5/book.pdf>.

Ivan A. Sag, Timothy Baldwin, Francis Bond, Ann Copestake, and Dan Flickinger. 2001. Multiword expressions: A pain in the neck for NLP. In *Proceedings of the 3rd International Conference on Intelligent Text Processingand Computational Linguistics (CICLing-2002*. Berlin: Springer.

Extraction of Nominal Multiword Expressions in French

Marie Dubremetz and **Joakim Nivre**
Uppsala university
Department of Linguistics and Philology
Uppsala, Sweden

Abstract

Multiword expressions (MWEs) can be extracted automatically from large corpora using association measures, and tools like mwetoolkit allow researchers to generate training data for MWE extraction given a tagged corpus and a lexicon. We use mwetoolkit on a sample of the French Europarl corpus together with the French lexicon Dela, and use Weka to train classifiers for MWE extraction on the generated training data. A manual evaluation shows that the classifiers achieve 60–75% precision and that about half of the MWEs found are novel and not listed in the lexicon. We also investigate the impact of the patterns used to generate the training data and find that this can affect the trade-off between precision and novelty.

1 Introduction

In alphabetic languages, words are delimited by spaces. Some words can combine to create a new unit of meaning that we call a multiword expression (MWE). However, MWEs such as *kick the bucket* must be distinguished from free combinations of words such as *kick the ball*. A sequence of several words is an MWE if "at least one of its syntactic, distributional or semantic properties cannot be deduced from the properties of its component" (Silberztein and L.A.D.L., 1990). So how can we extract them?

Statistical association measures have long been used for MWE extraction (Pecina, 2010), and by training supervised classifiers that use association measures as features we can further improve the quality of the extraction process. However, supervised machine learning requires annotated data, which creates a bottleneck in the absence of large corpora annotated for MWEs. In order to circumvent this bottleneck, mwetoolkit (Ramisch et al., 2010b) generates training instances by first extracting candidates that fit a certain part-of-speech pattern, such as Noun-Noun or Noun-Adjective, and then marking the candidates as positive or negative instances depending on whether they can be found in a given lexicon or not. Such a training set will presumably not contain any false positives (that is, candidates marked as positive instances that are not real MWEs), but depending on the coverage of the lexicon there will be a smaller or larger proportion of false negatives. The question is what quality can be obtained using such a noisy training set. To the best of our knowledge, we cannot find the answer for French in literature. Indeed, Ramisch et al. (2012) compares the performance of mwetoolkit with another toolkit on English and French corpora, but they never use the data generated by mwetoolkit to train a model. In contrast, Zilio et al. (2011) make a study involving training a model but use it only on English and use extra lexical resources to complement the machine learning method, so their study does not focus just on classifier evaluation.

This paper presents the first evaluation of mwetoolkit on French together with two resources very commonly used by the French NLP community: the tagger TreeTagger (Schmid, 1994) and the dictionary Dela.[1] Training and test data are taken from the French Europarl corpus (Koehn, 2005) and classifiers are trained using the Weka machine learning toolkit (Hall et al., 2009). The primary goal is to evaluate what level of precision can be achieved for nominal MWEs, using a manual evaluation of MWEs extracted, and to what extent the MWEs extracted are novel and can be used to enrich the lexicon. In addition, we will investigate what effect the choice of part-of-speech patterns used to generate the training data has on precision and novelty. Our results indicate that classifiers

[1] http://www-igm.univ-mlv.fr/~unitex/index.php?page=5&html=bibliography.html

achieve precision in the 60–75% range and that about half of the MWEs found are novel ones. In addition, it seems that the choice of patterns used to generate the training data can affect the trade-off between precision and novelty.

2 Related Work

2.1 Extraction Techniques

There is no unique definition of MWEs (Ramisch, 2012). In the literature on the subject, we notice that manual MWE extraction often requires several annotators native of the studied language. Nevertheless, some techniques exist for selecting automatically candidates that are more likely to be the true ones. Candidates can be validated against an external resource, such as a lexicon. It is possible also to check the frequency of candidates in another corpus like the web. Villaviciencio (2005), for example, uses number of hits on Google for validating the likelihood of particle verbs.

However, as Ramisch (2012) states in his introduction, MWE is an institutionalised phenomenon. This means that an MWE is frequently used and is part of the vocabulary of a speaker as well as the simple words. It means also that MWEs have specific statistical properties that have been studied. The results of those studies are statistical measures such as dice score, maximum likelihood estimate, pointwise mutual information, T-score. As Islam et al. (2012) remark in a study of Google Ngram, those measures of association are language independent. And it is demonstrated by Pecina (2008) that combining different collocation measures using standard statistical classification methods improves over using a single collocation measure. However, nowadays, using only lexical association measures for extraction and validation of MWE is not considered the most effective method. The tendency these last years is to combine association measures with linguistic features (Ramisch et al., 2010a; Pecina, 2008; Tsvetkov and Wintner, 2011).

2.2 Mwetoolkit

Among the tools developed for extracting MWEs, mwetoolkit is one of the most recent. Developed by Ramisch et al. (2010b) it aims not only at extracting candidates for potential MWEs, but also at extracting their association measures. Provided that a lexicon of MWEs is available and provided a preprocessed corpus, mwetoolkit makes it possible to train a machine learning system with the association measures as features with a minimum of implementation.

Ramisch et al. (2010b) provide experiments on Portuguese, English and Greek. Zilio et al. (2011) provide experiments with this tool as well. In the latter study, after having trained a machine on bigram MWEs, they try to extract full n-gram expressions from the Europarl corpus. They then reuse the model obtained on bigrams for extraction of full n-gram MWEs. Finally, they apply a second filter for getting back the false negatives by checking every MWE annotated as False by the algorithm against a online dictionary. This method gets a very good precision (over 87%) and recall (over 84%). However, we do not really know if this result is mostly due to the coverage of the dictionary online. What is the contribution of machine learning in itself? Another question raised by this study is the ability of a machine trained on one kind of pattern (e.g., Noun-Adjective) to extract correctly another kind of MWE pattern (e.g., Noun-Noun). That is the reason why we will run three experiments close to the one of Zilio et al. (2011) but were the only changing parameter is the pattern that we train our classifiers on.

3 Generating Training Data

3.1 Choice of Patterns

In contrast to Zilio et al. (2011) we run our experiment on French. The choice of a different language requires an adaptation of the patterns. French indeed, as a latin language, does not show the same characteristic patterns as English. We know that there is a strong recurrence of the pattern Noun-Adjective in bigram MWEs in our lexicon (Silberztein and L.A.D.L., 1990, p.82), and the next most frequent pattern is Noun-Noun. Therefore we extract only candidates that correspond to these patterns. And, since we have two patterns, we will run two extra experiments where our models will be trained only on one of the patterns. In this way, we will discover how sensitive the method is to the choice of pattern.

3.2 Corpus

As Ramisch et al. (2012) we work on the French Europarl corpus. We took the three first million words of Europarl and divided it into three equal parts (one million words each) for running our experiments. The first part will be devoted at 80% to training and 20% to development test set, when training classifiers on Noun-Adjective or Noun-Noun patterns, or both. We use the second million as a secondary development set that is not used in this study. The third million is used as a final test set and we will present results on this set.

3.3 Preprocessing

For preprocessing we used the same processes as described in Zilio et al. (2011). First we ran the sentence splitter and the tokenizer provided with the Europarl corpus. Then we ran TreeTagger (Schmid, 1994) to obtain the tags and the lemmas.

3.4 Extracting Data and Features

The mwetoolkit takes as input a preprocessed corpus plus a lexicon and gives two main outputs: an arff file which is a format adapted to the machine learning framework Weka, and an XML file. At the end of the process we obtain, for each candidate, a binary classification as an MWE (True) or not (False) depending on whether it is contained in the lexicon. For each candidate, we also obtain the following features: maximum likelihood estimate, pointwise mutual information, T-score, dice coefficient, log-likelihood ratio. The machine learning task is then to predict the class (True or False) given the features of a candidate.

3.5 Choice of a Lexicon in French

The evaluation part of mwetoolkit is furnished with an internal English lexicon as a gold standard for evaluating bigram MWEs, but for French it is necessary to provide an external resource. We used as our gold standard the French dictionary Dela (Silberztein and L.A.D.L., 1990), the MWE part of which is called Delac. It is a general purpose dictionary for NLP and it includes 100,000 MWE expressions, which is a reasonable size for leading an experiment on the Europarl corpus. Also the technical documentation of the Delac (Silberztein and L.A.D.L., 1990, p.72) says that this dictionary has been constructed by linguists with reference to several dictionaries. So it is a manually built resource that contains MWEs only referenced in official lexicographical books.

3.6 Processing

Thanks to mwetoolkit we extracted all the bigrams that correspond to the patterns Noun-Adjective (NA), Noun-Noun (NN) and to both Noun-Adjective and Noun-Noun (NANN) in our three data sets and let mwetoolkit make an automatic annotation by checking the presence of the MWE candidates in the Delac. Note that the automatic annotation was used only for training. The final evaluation was done manually.

4 Training Classifiers

For finding the best model we think that we have to favour the recall of the positive candidates. Indeed, when an MWE candidate is annotated as True, it means that it is listed in the Dela, which means that it is an officially listed MWE. However, if an MWE is not in the Dela, it does not mean that the candidate does not fulfil all the criteria for being an MWE. For this reason, obtaining a good recall is much more difficult than getting a good precision, but it is also the most important if we stay on a lexicographical purpose.

4.1 Training on NA

We tested several algorithms offered by Weka as well as the training options suggested by Zilio et al. (2011). We also tried to remove some features and to keep only the most informative ones (MLE, T-score and log-likelihood according to information gain ratio) but we noticed each time a loss in the recall. At the end with all the features kept and for the purpose of evaluating NA MWE candidates the best classification algorithm was the Bayesian network.

4.2 Training on NN

When training a model on NN MWEs, our aim was to keep as much as possible the same condition for our three experiments. However, the NN training set has definitely not the same properties as the NA and NANN ones. The NN training set is twenty-four times smaller than NA training set. Most of the algorithms offered by Weka therefore ended up with a dummy systematic classification to the majority class False. The only exceptions were ibk, ib1, hyperpipes, random trees and random forest. We kept random forest because it gave the best recall with a very good precision. We tried several options and obtained the optimum results with 8 trees each constructed while considering 3 random features, one seed, and unlimited depth of trees. As well as for NA we kept all features.

4.3 Training on NA+NN

For the training on NANN candidates we tried the same models as for NN and for NA candidates.

The best result was obtained with the same algorithm as for NA: Bayesian network.

5 Evaluation

The data automatically annotated by mwetoolkit could be used for training, but to properly evaluate the precision of MWE extraction on new data and not penalize the system for 'false positives' that are due to lack of coverage of the lexicon, we needed to perform a manual annotation. To do so, we randomly picked 100 candidates annotated as True by each model (regardless if they were in the Delac or not). We then annotated all such candidates as True if they were found in Delac (without further inspection) and otherwise classified them manually following the definition of Silberztein and L.A.D.L. (1990) and the intuition of a native French speaker. The results are in Table 1.

Extracting NANN	NA model	NN model	NANN model
In Delac	40 ±9.4	18 ±7.2	28 ±8.6
Not in Delac	34 ±9.0	41 ±9.2	38 ±9.3
Precision	74 ±8.4	59 ±9.2	66 ±9.0

Table 1: Performance of three different models on the same corpus of Noun-Adjective and Noun-Noun candidates. Percentages with 95% confidence intervals, sample size = 100.

As we see in Table 1, the experiment reveals a precision ranging from almost 60% up to 74%. The results of our comparative manual annotation indicate that the model trained on NN candidates has the capacity to find more MWEs not listed in our lexicon (41 out of 59) even if it is the least precise model. On the other hand, we notice that the model based on Noun-Adjective patterns is more precise but at the same time extracts fewer MWEs that are not already in the lexicon (34 out of 74). Our mixed model confirms these two tendencies with a performance in between (38 new MWEs out of 66). Thus, the method appears to be sensitive to the patterns used for training.

We notice during evaluation different kinds of MWEs that are successfully extracted by models but that are not listed in the Delac. Most of them are the MWEs specific to Europarl (e.g., 'dimension communautaire', 'législation européenne'[2]). Another category are those MWEs that became popular in the French language after the years 2000's and therefore could not be included in the Delac, released in 1997. Indeed by reading the first paragraph of the French version of Europarl we notice that the texts have been written after 1999. Of course, they are not the majority of the successfully extracted MWEs but we still manage to find up to 3 of them in a sample of 100 that we checked ('développement durable', 'radiophonie numérique', 'site internet'[3]). Furthermore the corpus in itself is already more than ten years old, so in a text of 2014 we can expect to find even more of them. Finally, there are MWEs that are not in French (e.g., 'Partido popular'), these, however, did not appear systematically in our samples.

It is tricky to learn statistical properties of MWEs when, actually, we do not have all the information necessary for extracting the MWEs in the corpus. Indeed, for this purpose the corpus should ideally be read and annotated by humans. However, we still managed to train models with decent performance, even if it is likely that a lot of candidates pre-annotated as False in the training data were probably perfect MWEs. This means that the Delac has covered enough MWEs for the features to not appear as completely meaningless and arbitrary. The final precision would never be as good as it is, if the coverage had been not sufficient enough. This shows that the method of automatic annotation offered by mwetoolkit is reliable given a lexicon as large as Delac.

6 Conclusion

We wanted to know if the method of automatic extraction and evaluation offered by mwetoolkit could have a decent precision in French. We annotated automatically part of the Europarl corpus given the lexical resource Dela as a gold standard and generated in this way annotated training sets. Classifiers trained on this data using Weka achieved a maximum precision of 74%, with about half of the extracted MWEs being novel compared to the lexicon. In addition, we found that the final precision and novelty scores were sensitive to the choice of patterns used to generate the training data.

[2]'community scale', 'European legislation'

[3]'sustainable development', 'digital radio', 'website'

References

Mark Hall, Eibe Frank, Geoffrey Holmes, Bernhard Pfahringer, Peter Reutemann, and Ian H Witten. 2009. The WEKA data mining software: an update. *SIGKDD Exploration Newsletter*, 11(1):10–18.

Aminul Islam, Evangelos E Milios, and Vlado Keselj. 2012. Comparing Word Relatedness Measures Based on Google n-grams. In *COLING, International Conference on Computational Linguistics (Posters)*, pages 495–506, Mumbai, India.

Philipp Koehn. 2005. Europarl: A Parallel Corpus for Statistical Machine Translation. In *The Tenth Machine Translation Summit*, pages 79–86, Phuket, Thailand.

Pavel Pecina. 2008. A Machine Learning Approach to Multiword Expression Extraction. In *Proceedings of the LREC 2008 Workshop Towards a Shared Task for Multiword Expressions*, pages 54–57, Marrakech, Morocco.

Pavel Pecina. 2010. Lexical association measures and collocation extraction. *Language Resources and Evaluation*, 44(1-2):137–158.

Carlos Ramisch, Helena de Medeiros Caseli, Aline Villavicencio, André Machado, and Maria José Finatto. 2010a. A Hybrid Approach for Multiword Expression Identification. In *Proceedings of the 9th International Conference on Computational Processing of Portuguese Language (PROPOR)*, pages 65–74.

Carlos Ramisch, Aline Villavicencio, and Christian Boitet. 2010b. Multiword Expressions in the wild? The mwetoolkit comes in handy. In *COLING, International Conference on Computational Linguistics (Demos)*, pages 57–60.

Carlos Ramisch, Vitor De Araujo, and Aline Villavicencio. 2012. A Broad Evaluation of Techniques for Automatic Acquisition of Multiword Expressions. In *Proceedings of ACL 2012 Student Research Workshop*, pages 1–6, Jeju Island, Korea. Association for Computational Linguistics.

Carlos Ramisch. 2012. Une plate-forme générique et ouverte pour l'acquisition des expressions polylexicales. In *Actes de la 14e Rencontres des Étudiants Chercheurs en Informatique pour le Traitement Automatique des Langues*, pages 137–149, Grenoble, France.

Helmut Schmid. 1994. Probabilistic Part-of-Speech Tagging Using Decision Trees. In *Proceedings of International Conference on New Methods in Language Processing*, pages 44–49, Manchester, Great Britain.

Max Silberztein and L.A.D.L. 1990. Le dictionnaire électronique des mots composés. *Langue française*, 87(1):71–83.

Yulia Tsvetkov and Shuly Wintner. 2011. Identification of Multi-word Expressions by Combining Multiple Linguistic Information Sources. In *Empirical Methods in Natural Language Processing*, pages 836–845.

Aline Villavicencio. 2005. The availability of verb–particle constructions in lexical resources: How much is enough? *Computer Speech & Language*, 19(4):415–432.

Leonardo Zilio, Luiz Svoboda, Luiz Henrique Longhi Rossi, and Rafael Martins Feitosa. 2011. Automatic extraction and evaluation of MWE. In *8th Brazilian Symposium in Information and Human Language Technology*, pages 214–218, Cuiabá, Brazil.

Towards an Empirical Subcategorization of Multiword Expressions

Luigi Squillante
Dipartimento di Scienze Documentarie, Linguistico-filologiche e Geografiche
"Sapienza" - Università di Roma
Roma, Italy
luigi.squillante@uniroma1.it

Abstract

The subcategorization of multiword expressions (MWEs) is still problematic because of the great variability of their phenomenology. This article presents an attempt to categorize Italian nominal MWEs on the basis of their syntactic and semantic behaviour by considering features that can be tested on corpora. Our analysis shows how these features can lead to a differentiation of the expressions in two groups which correspond to the intuitive notions of multiword units and lexical collocations.

1 Introduction

In contemporary linguistics the definition of those entities which are referred to as multiword expressions (MWEs) remain controversial. It is intuitively clear that some words, when appearing together, have some "special bond" in terms of meaning (e.g. *black hole, mountain chain*), or lexical choice (e.g. *strong tea, to fill a form*), contrary to free combinations. Nevertheless, the great variety of features and anomalous behaviours that these expressions exhibit makes it difficult to organize them into categories and gave rise to a great amount of different and sometimes overlapping terminology.[1] In fact, MWEs can show non-grammatical constructions, syntactic fixedness, morphological frozeness, semantic restrictions, non-compositionality, strong pragmatic connotation, etc. These features are not necessary and sufficient conditions for each expression, but represent only possible behaviours that can be exhibited together or individually and to a different extent.

Traditionally MWEs are seen as entities lying on a *continuum* between two poles that go from a maximum of semantic opacity (*green thumb*) to compositional expressions that show only lexical restrictions (*to catch a cold*). However the "compositional criterion" is a problematic concept in semantics, since it has been shown how difficult it is, in language, to define component parts, rules or functions involved in compositionality (Casadei, 1996) and, above all, that it is impossible to give words an absolute meaning independently from their context (Firth, 1957; Hanks, 2013). Because of this, the problem of subcategorizing the heterogeneous set of MWEs must be based on more reliable and testable criteria.

This work presents a study conducted on the Italian language that aims at dividing MWEs in subcategories on the basis of empirical syntactic and semantic criteria different from compositionality. We show how these features are able to separate two poles of entities which approximately correspond to what is intuitively known as multiword units (*polirematiche* in the Italian lexicographic tradition)[2] as opposed to (lexical) collocations.

2 The need to go beyond statistics

In recent years, the fact that MWE components tend to cooccur more frequently than expected led to the development of several statistical association measures[3] (AMs) in order to identify and automatically extract MWEs. However, as pointed out in Evert (2008), it is important not to confuse the empirical concept of recurrent or statistically relevant word combination in a corpus (*empirical collocation*) with the theoretical concept of MWE (which assumes phraseological implications), although the two sets overlap. In fact, it is common

[1] See Bartsch (2004) or Masini (2007) for an overview on the historical development of MWE terminology.

[2] cf. De Mauro (2007).

[3] See Evert (2004) for a general overview.

that AMs can extract expressions such as *leggere un libro* 'to read a book' or *storcere il naso* 'to stick up [one's] nose' just because the components tend to cooccur often in corpora. However, while the first one seems not to need its own categorical status (Bosque, 2004), the latter is usually denoted as a metaphoric MWE or *idiom*. AMs are not able to distinguish between the two or even differentiate subtypes of true MWEs on the basis of phraseological relevance (e.g. AMs are not able to assign a higher score to more opaque MWEs in opposition to lexical collocations). It is possible, however, to integrate statistical information with the results of syntactic and semantic tests performed on corpora in order to identify subgroups of MWEs.[4]

3 Methodology

As a first approach, in this work only Italian nominal MWE of the form [*noun* + *adjective*][5] are chosen. The corpus used in our study is PAISÀ[6], a freely available large Italian corpus, composed of ca. 250 million tokens and morpho-syntactically annotated. By means of mwetoolkit (Ramisch et al., 2010) the 400 most frequent [*noun* + *adjective*] bigrams are extracted from the corpus and assigned the pointwise mutual information (PMI) association score (Church and Hanks, 1990). Then the bigrams are ordered according to PMI and only the first 300 are retained.[7] The number of occurrences of the expressions contained in this set varies between 20.748 and 641.

Then, we implemented a computational tool that performs empirical tests on modifiability. We chose to study three features, which are a) interruptibility, b) inflection and c) substitutability[8] and for each of them an index is calculated.

Given the expression, the index of interruptibility (I_i) compares the occurrences of the sequence in its basic form [noun + adjective] (n_{bf}), with the occurrences of the same sequence with one word occurring between the two components (n_i). The queries are made over lemmas and its value is given by the ratio: $I_i = n_i/(n_{bf} + n_i)$.

The index of inflection (I_f) compares the number of occurrences of the prevalent (most frequent) inflected form (n_{pf}) with those of the basic lemmatized form[9] (n_{bf}) and its value is given by the ratio: $I_f = (n_{bf} - n_{pf})/n_{bf}$.

Finally, the index of substitutability (I_s) compares the number of occurrences of the basic form (n_{bf}), regardless of inflection, with the occurrences n_s of all the sequences in which one of the two components is replaced by one of its synonyms (if present). If $n_{s_1,i}$ is the number of occurrences of the i-th synonym of the first component word and $n_{s_2,i}$ is an analogous quantity for the second component word, then $n_s = \sum_i n_{s_1,i} + \sum_i n_{s_2,i}$ and $I_s = n_s/(n_{bf} + n_s)$. In order to calculate I_s the tool needs an external synonym list; we chose the GNU-OpenOffice Italian Thesaurus[10] because of its immediate availability, open-source nature and ease of management.[11]

Then the three indices are calculated for each of the 300 MWEs of the candidate list.

4 Results

Figure 1 shows the distribution of the expressions in the planes defined by I_i, I_f,I_s. It is evident that there is a tendency for the expressions to gather more along the axes rather than in the planes, i.e. where one of the indices has low values.

[4]The idea is not new, since already Fazly and Stevenson (2007) showed how lexical and syntactic fixedness is relevant in subcategorizing MWEs. However, their work focused only on a set of English verbal MWEs and subclasses were determined initially and not at the end of the analysis.

[5]This is the unmarked Italian noun phrase.

[6]www.corpusitaliano.it

[7]The first frequency threshold is necessary since PMI tends to overestimate expressions with very low numbers of occurrences (Evert, 2008). Then, considering only the 300 best candidates increases the chances to have a majority of MWEs. In a later stage of our analysis also the top-300 candidates extracted by the log-likelihood (LL) AM (Dunning, 1993) have been considered, in order to check if the initial choice of PMI could affect somehow our results. The LL set was 66% coincident with the PMI set. However, the new expressions seem to show the same tendencies of distributions (cf. Section 4) as those in the PMI set.

[8]In fact, in Italian: a) some nominal MWEs do not allow for the insertion of other words between the components (e.g. *carro armato* 'tank'; cfr. **carro grande armato*) while others do (e.g. *punto debole* 'weak point'; cf. *punto più debole*); b) some nominal MWEs exhibit inflection frozeness (e.g. *diritti umani* 'human rights'; cf. **diritto umano*), while others can be freely inflected (e.g. *cartone animato* 'cartoon'; cfr. *cartoni animati*); c) some nominal MWEs do not allow for the substitution of one of their components with a synonym (e.g. *colonna sonora* 'soundtrack'; cf. **pilastro sonoro*) while others do (e.g. *guerra mondiale* 'world war'; cf. *conflitto mondiale*).

[9]Although Nissim and Zaninello (2011) show how Italian nominal MWEs can exhibit several distinct morphological variations, we chose to consider only the proportion between the prevalent form and the total number of expressions since our pattern generally admits only singular and plural forms, with noun and adjective coherently coupled.

[10]http://linguistico.sourceforge.net/pages/thesaurus_italiano.html

[11]However, other more specific and complete resources could be attached instead in the future, in order to improve the quality of the results.

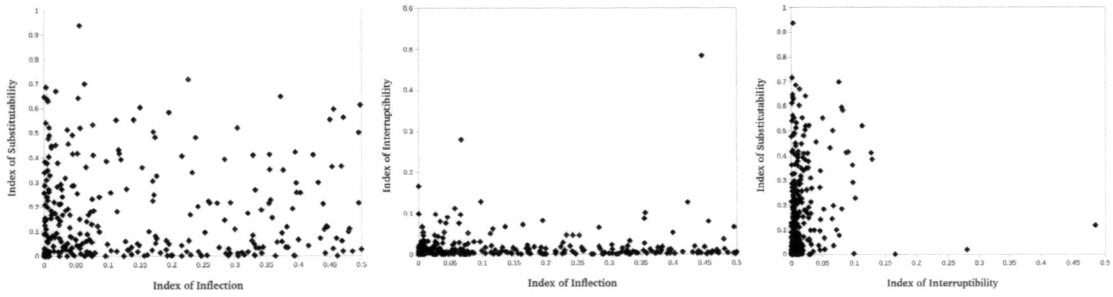

Figure 1: Distribution of MWE candidates according to the values of their indices of inflection (I_f), substitutability (I_s) and interruptibility (I_i).

Since the plane $I_f I_s$ shows the highest dispersion of points, we chose to consider in this plane 4 polarities defined by the intersection of high/low values for both I_f and I_s. We consider a value *high* (and indicate I^+) when $I > 0.33$ and *low* (I^-) when $I < 0.1$. In this way we obtain 4 sets of expressions lying at the extreme corners of the plane and denote them $I_f^+ I_s^+$, $I_f^+ I_s^-$, $I_f^- I_s^+$, $I_f^- I_s^-$.

I_i has a small range of variation (97% of the candidates have $I_i < 0.1$), nevertheless it can differentiate, as a third dimension, the expressions in the 4 groups defined above from a minimum to a maximum of interruptibility.

As one could presume, the expressions appearing in the group $I_f^- I_s^-$ with the lowest score of I_i are examples of opaque, crystallized or terminological expressions, such as *testamento biologico* 'living will' (I_f = 0.066, I_s = 0.004, I_i = 0), *valor militare* 'military valour' (I_f = 0, I_s = 0, I_i = 0), *anidride carbonica* 'carbon dioxide' (I_f = 0, I_s = 0, I_i = 0.001). However expressions in the same group with the highest values of interruptibility[12] seem to be compositional and just lexically restricted: *carriera solista* 'solo career' (I_f = 0.067, I_s = 0.018, I_i = 0.280), *sito ufficiale* 'official website' (I_f = 0.043, I_s = 0.077, I_i = 0.076).

Similar results come out for the group $I_f^+ I_s^-$, where expressions like *cartone animato* 'cartoon' (I_f = 0.333, I_s = 0.033, I_i = 0.0004), *macchina fotografica* 'camera' (I_f = 0.374, I_s = 0.058, I_i = 0.004), appear with low scores of interruptibility, while *punto debole* 'weak point' (I_f = 0.4, I_s = 0.066, I_i = 0.052), *figlio maschio* 'male son' (I_f = 0.479, I_s = 0.098, I_i = 0.037), have the highest values of interruptibility.

[12] Recall that here, due to the high frequency of the expressions and to I_i's range of variation, values of I_i close to 0.1 represent expressions that are sufficiently interrupted.

For $I_f^- I_s^+$, we have free combinations for higher I_i, such as *colore bianco* 'white colour' (I_f = 0.097, I_s = 0.385, I_i = 0.129) or *colore rosso* 'red colour' (I_f = 0.066, I_s = 0.362, I_i = 0.097), and more lexically restricted expressions for lower values, such as *corpo umano* 'human body' (I_f = 0.077, I_s = 0.534, I_i = 0.008), *fama internazionale* 'international fame' (I_f = 0.011, I_s = 0.441, I_i = 0.007).

Finally the group $I_f^+ I_s^+$ presents only expressions with very low values of I_i depending on the fact that expressions with high interruptibility, high substitutability and free inflection have been presumably excluded from the list because of their low AM scores. The remaining expressions in the group are of the kind of *spettacolo teatrale* 'theatre performance' (I_f = 0.468, I_s = 0.365, I_i = 0.006), *partito politico* 'political party' (I_f = 0.471, I_s = 0.562, I_i = 0.003), thus mainly compositional.

5 Discussion and Interpretation

By analysing the distribution of MWE candidates, it is possible to consider the scheme of Table 1 in which the following three categories appear: free combinations, multiword units and lexical collocations. As one can note, inflection variability does not play a role in discriminating between the categories.

It must be underlined that the three indices group the expressions into sets that appear to be more or less homogeneous with respect to the intuitive distinction between semantic units and compositional, lexically restricted expressions.

Free combinations represent the "false positives" of the list, i.e. expressions that do not need a special categorical status in phraseology.

Multiword units (*polirematiche*) represent here a subcategory of MWEs which exhibit the fol-

			Inflection variability	
			low	*high*
Substitutability	*high*	*more* **Interruption**	Free Combinations	//
		less **Interruption**	Lexical Collocations	Lexical Collocations
	low	*more* **Interruption**	Lexical Collocations	Lexical Collocations
		less **Interruption**	Multiword Units	Multiword Units

Table 1: Definition of MWE subcategories with respect to their syntactic and semantic empirical behaviour shown in our experiment. The upper right cell is empty since all the expressions in the group $I_f^+ I_s^+$ have $I_i \ll 0.1$.

lowing features: they can be metaphoric (*catena montuosa* 'mountain chain'), completely crystallized (*quartier generale* 'headquarter'), terminological (*amministratore delegato* 'managing director'), they can present an unpredictable semantic addition (*gas naturale*, 'natural gas', meaning the gas provided in houses for domestic uses), or one of the components assumes a specific and unusual meaning (*casa automobilistica* 'car company', lit. 'car house'). Despite their variability, the entities in this group are all perceived as "units" of meaning because the lack of one of the components makes the expressions lose their overall meaning.

Finally, lexical collocations represent here those entities that are generally perceived as fully compositional, being "not fixed but recognizable phraseological units" (Tiberii, 2012). They exhibit the following possible features: one of the component is used only in combination with the other one (*acqua potabile* 'drinking water', where *potabile* only refers to water), or although other synonymous words are available and could give the expression the same meaning, just one specific component word is preferred (*sito ufficiale* 'official site'; cf. **sito autorizzato*).

6 Further considerations and limits

Although not reported here, expressions with values for $I_f, I_s \in [0.1, 0.33]$ show continuity between the categories of Table 1.[13] Moreover, since our thesaurus does not deal with sense disambiguation, a manual check on concordances was performed. For very few metaphorical expressions, I_s produced non-reliable values, since it can happen that, once a synonym of one component has been substituted for the original word, the new expression is still highly attested in the corpus, although it has lost the original metaphorical meaning.[14] In order to correct this bias in the future, the criterion of substitutability should check, for example, not only the number of attested replaced expressions, but also if they share the same context words of the basic expression.

7 Conclusion and future work

Our analysis shows that the intuitive distinction between two main subcategories of MWEs (multiword units vs. lexical collocations) can be empirically reproduced by testing the syntactic and semantic behaviour of the expressions on corpora. In this way we provide an empirical criterion, related to the intuitive and hardly definable notion of compositionality, able to attest how expressions exhibit different restrictions depending on their subcategory. Multiword units are characterized by low values of interruptibility and low values of substitutability. Lexical collocations can be more easily interrupted if they have low values of substitutability, while they do not allow for interruptibility if they have high substitutability. Since also a subgroup of free combinations is identified when intersecting the values of the indices, our methodology can be useful as well for automatic removal of false positives from MWE candidate lists.[15]

Future work must include the extension of the analysis to other forms of nominal MWEs as well as other grammatical categories by the development of tools which can deal with verbal or adverbial MWEs, as well as tests on different corpora.

[13] E.g. *intervento chirurgico* 'surgery' has $I_f = 0.27$, $I_s = 0.22$ and $I_i = 0$ and moves between multiword unit and lexical collocation; *stile barocco* 'baroque style', with $I_f = 0.005$, $I_s = 0.20$ and $I_i = 0.07$, moves between lexical collocation and free combination.

[14] This is the case of *braccio destro* 'right-hand man', lit. 'right arm', that could be substituted by *ala destra* (*right wing*) since both *braccio* and *ala* can refer to a part of a building.

[15] This consideration relates our work to that of Baldwin et al. (2003), Bannard (2007), Weller and Fritzinger (2010), Cap et al. (2013), whose goal is to implement the identification of true positive candidates by using both syntactic or semantic features and AMs.

References

Timothy Baldwin, Colin Bannard, Takaaki Tanaka, and Dominic Widdows. 2003. An empirical model of multiword expression decomposability. In *Proceedings of the Workshop on Multiword Expressions: Analysis, Acquisition and Treatment (ACL 2003)*, pages 89–96.

Colin Bannard. 2007. A measure of syntactic flexibility for automatically identifying multiword expressions in corpora. In *Proceedings of the Workshop on a Broader Perspective on Multiword Expressions*, pages 1–8.

Sabine Bartsch. 2004. *Structural and Functional Properties of Collocations in English*. Narr, Tübingen.

Ignacio Bosque. 2004. Combinatoria y significación. Algunas reflexiones. In *REDES, Diccionario Combinatorio del Español Contemporaneo*. Hoepli.

Fabienne Cap, Marion Weller, and Ulrich Heid. 2013. Using a Rich Feature Set for the Identification of German MWEs. In *Proceedings of Machine Translation Summit XIV*, Nice, France.

Federica Casadei. 1996. *Metafore ed Espressioni Idiomatiche. Uno studio semantico sull'italiano*. Bulzoni Editore, Roma.

Kenneth W. Church and Patrick Hanks. 1990. Word association norms, mutual information, and lexicography. *Computational Linguistics*, 16(1):22–29.

Tullio De Mauro. 2007. *GRADIT, Grande Dizionario Italiano dell'Uso*. UTET.

Ted Dunning. 1993. Accurate methods for the statistics of surprise and coincidence. *Computational Linguistics*, 19(1):61–74.

Stefan Evert. 2004. *The Statistics of Word Cooccurrences: Word Pairs and Collocations*. Ph.D. thesis, University of Stuttgart.

Stefan Evert. 2008. Corpora and Collocations. In A. Lüdeling and M. Kytö, editors, *Corpus Linguistics. An International Handbook*. Mouton de Gruyter, Berlin.

Afsaneh Fazly and Suzanne Stevenson. 2007. Distinguishing subtypes of multiword expressions using linguistically-motivated statistical measures. In *Proceedings of the Workshop on A Broader Perspective on Multiword Expressions. ACL*, pages 9–16.

J. R. Firth. 1957. *Papers in Linguistics*. Oxford University Press, Oxford.

Patrick Hanks. 2013. *Lexical Analysis*. MIT Press, Cambridge, MA.

Francesca Masini. 2007. *Parole sintagmatiche in italiano*. Ph.D. thesis, Università degli Studi di Roma Tre.

Malvina Nissim and Andrea Zaninello. 2011. A quantitative study on the morphology of italian multiword expressions. *Lingue e linguaggio*, (2):283–300.

Carlos Ramisch, Aline Villavicencio, and Christian Boitet. 2010. mwetoolkit: a Framework for Multiword Expression Identification. In *Proceedings of the Seventh International Conference on Language Resources and Evaluation (LREC 2010)*, Valletta, Malta.

Paola Tiberii. 2012. *Dizionario delle collocazioni. Le combinazioni delle parole in italiano*. Zanichelli.

Marion Weller and Fabienne Fritzinger. 2010. A hybrid approach for the identification of multiword expressions. In *Proceedings of the SLTC 2010 Workshop on Compounds and Multiword Expressions*.

Contexts, Patterns, Interrelations - New Ways of Presenting Multi-word Expressions

Kathrin Steyer
Institute for the German Language
R 5, 6-13
D-68161 Mannheim, Germany
steyer@ids-mannheim.de

Annelen Brunner
Institute for the German Language
R 5, 6-13
D-68161 Mannheim, Germany
brunner@ids-mannheim.de

Abstract

This contribution presents the newest version of our 'Wortverbindungsfelder' (fields of multi-word expressions), an experimental lexicographic resource that focusses on aspects of MWEs that are rarely addressed in traditional descriptions: Contexts, patterns and interrelations. The MWE fields use data from a very large corpus of written German (over 6 billion word forms) and are created in a strictly corpus-based way. In addition to traditional lexicographic descriptions, they include quantitative corpus data which is structured in new ways in order to show the usage specifics. This way of looking at MWEs gives insight in the structure of language and is especially interesting for foreign language learners.

1 Our concept of MWEs

We study MWEs from a linguistic perspective and are mainly interested in two questions: What can we learn about the nature of MWEs and their status in language by studying large corpora? And how can we present MWEs in novel lexicographic ways that reflect our findings? The MWE field presented in this contribution is a prototype that reflects our current ideas regarding these questions. It can be explored online free of charge at `http://wvonline.ids-mannheim.de/wvfelder-v3/index.html`.

Our approach is based on the concept 'Usuelle Wortverbindungen' (UWV, Steyer 2000; Steyer 2004; Steyer 2013), which defines MWEs as conventionalized patterns of language use that manifest themselves in recurrent syntagmatic structures. This includes not only idioms and idiosyncratic structures, but all multi-word units which have acquired a distinct function in communication. Our focus is on real-life usage, pragmatics and context. We work bottom-up in detecting and describing MWE units in a strongly corpus-driven way (Sinclair 1991; Tognini-Bonelli 2001; Hanks 2013), taking iterative steps to arrive at conclusions about language use. Methologically, our approach bears some similarities to Stefanowitsch/Gries' 'collostructions' (Stefanowitsch/Gries 2003) though we are less interested in syntactic and grammatical structures - as it is common in construction grammar approaches - but see MWEs primarily as parts of the lexicon and feel closer to phraseology.

The basis of our research is DeReKo (Deutsches Referenzkorpus, Institut für Deutsche Sprache 2012), the largest collection of written German available today which has over six billion word tokens and is located at the Institute for the German Language (IDS). In the current stage of our work, which is mainly explorative, we use DeReKo as it is. This means our text basis is dominated by newspaper texts from the last 10-15 years. Though this is surely not a 'balanced' corpus, we argue that it still reflects much of contemporary written language use, as newspaper texts are a medium that is widely disseminated.

Though the interpretation and main analysis is done manually, automatic methods form an important basis to our work. We use a sophisticated method of collocation analysis developed at the IDS (Belica 1995) to get indications which word combinations constitute MWEs and to explore contexts in which an MWE is commonly used. In addition to that, we use a pattern matching tool developed in our project to explore and structure corpus evidence and gain further insight into the behavior and variations of MWE candidates.

Our special interest lies in the fact that MWEs are not as fixed as is often assumed, but often behave as patterns and show multiple interrelations. Therefore, we also describe MWE patterns - a

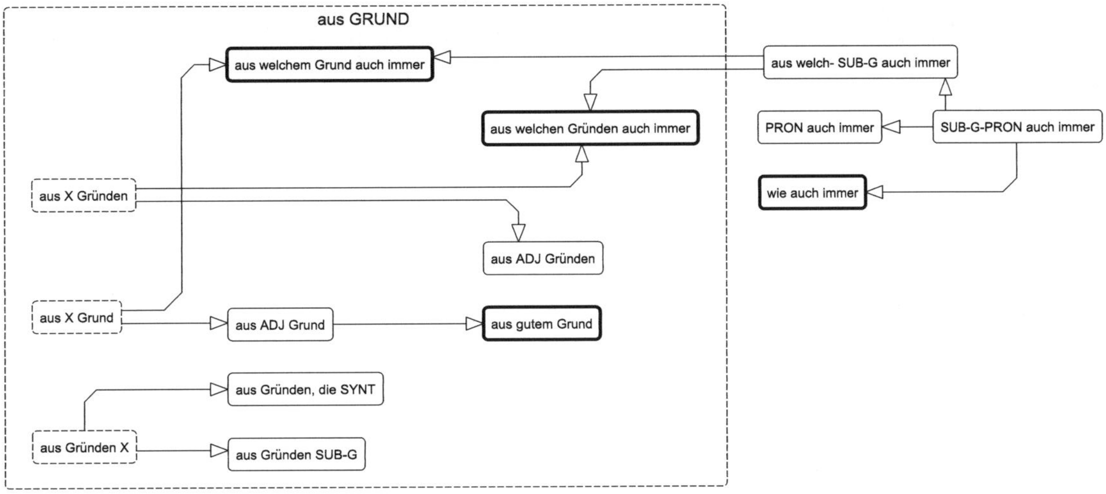

Figure 1: Part of the MWE field centered around *Grund* and preposition *aus*.

more abstract form of MWEs which are only partially fixed. An example for a fixed MWE is *Pi mal Daumen* (*pi times thumb* - 'approximately'), a multi-word expression that is always used in exactly this form. MWE patterns on the other hand consist of fixed lexical components as well as slots that can be filled in different ways. In spite of this variability, the whole pattern has a holistic meaning and function. An example is the expression *wie NOUN in jemandes Ohren klingen* (*to sound like NOUN in someone's ears* - 'to be perceived in a certain way' (specified by NOUN)). The NOUN slot can be filled with different words in order to specify the general meaning of the pattern. In section 2.3 we will go into further detail about how a slot in an MWE pattern can be filled.

The MWE field presented in this contribution centers around the word *Grund* (*reason/basis/foundation*) combined with several prepositions. It is the newest of several versions of MWE fields which have been described elsewhere (cf. Brunner/Steyer 2009; Brunner/Steyer 2010) and are available at our website `http://wvonline.ids-mannheim.de` as well. This newest version focusses more on hierarchies of MWEs and MWE patterns and incorporates additional resources like collocation analyses in its descriptive texts. In the following, we will highlight some features of the MWE field which illustrate our focus on interrelations, contexts and patterns.

2 MWE field *Grund*

2.1 Interrelations

Figure 1 shows a part of the MWE field, centered on the word *Grund* and preposition *aus*. Each node is linked to a lexicographic description. Figure 2 presents a screenshot of one of those articles. In addition to narrative descriptions and manually selected usage examples from our corpus, the articles also include components that are derived from quantitative corpus data. Specifically, these are collocation analyses as well as filler tables for MWE patterns. The function of these components will be explained in more detail in sections 2.2 and 2.3.

In Figure 1, you can observe the relations between MWEs (thick border) and MWE patterns (regular border). The nodes with the dashed border represent repeating surface structures which themselves have no common holistic meaning but show the lexical interconnectedness between the MWEs and MWE patterns.

All nodes enclosed in the square field contain the elements *Grund* and *auf*. The nodes on the far right are extensions which do not belong to the core of the MWE field as it was defined, but are connected lexically and functionally to MWEs that do. We decided to include those 'external nodes' to give a glimpse of how the building blocks of language connect even beyond the artificial borders that where necessary when defining the MWE field.

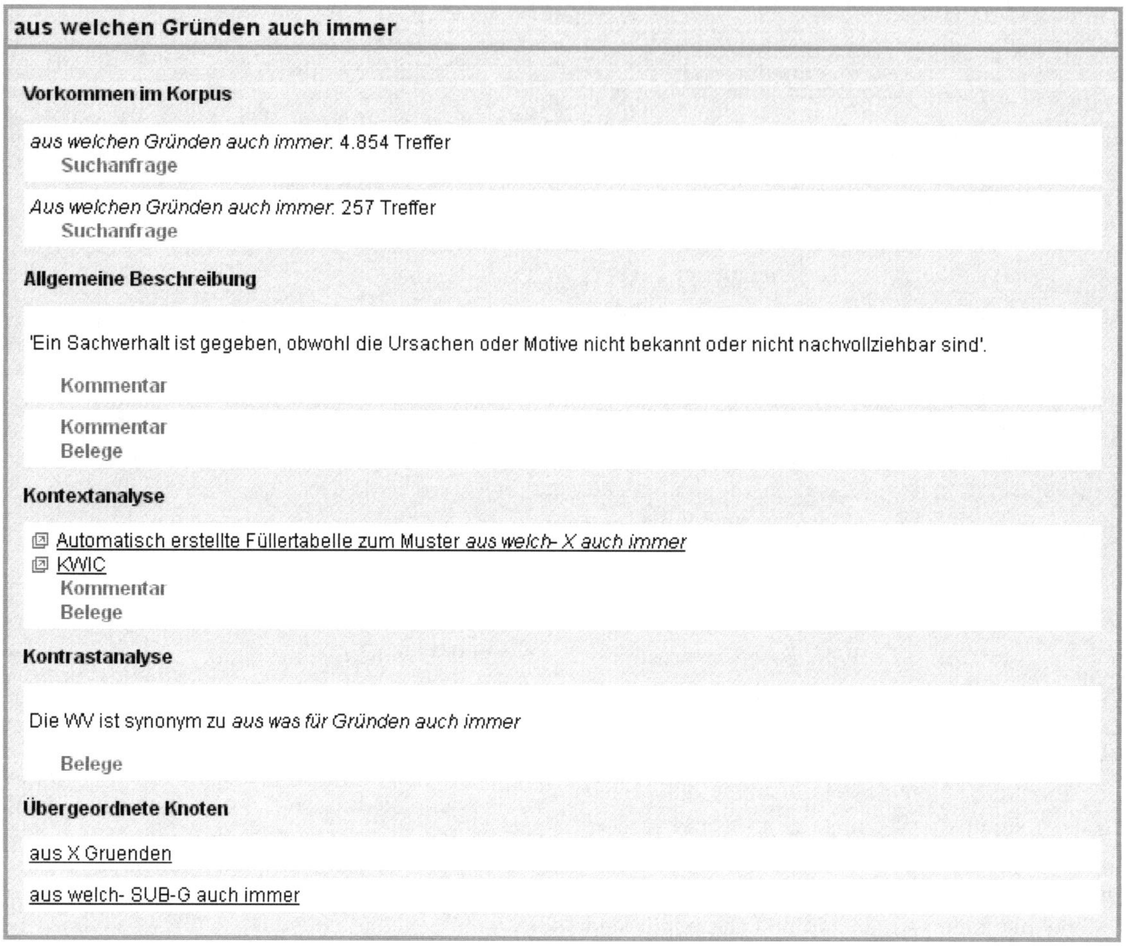
aus welchen Gründen auch immer

Vorkommen im Korpus

aus welchen Gründen auch immer: 4.854 Treffer
Suchanfrage

Aus welchen Gründen auch immer: 257 Treffer
Suchanfrage

Allgemeine Beschreibung

'Ein Sachverhalt ist gegeben, obwohl die Ursachen oder Motive nicht bekannt oder nicht nachvollziehbar sind'.

Kommentar

Kommentar
Belege

Kontextanalyse

Automatisch erstellte Füllertabelle zum Muster *aus welch- X auch immer*
KWIC
Kommentar
Belege

Kontrastanalyse

Die WV ist synonym zu *aus was für Gründen auch immer*

Belege

Übergeordnete Knoten

aus X Gruenden

aus welch- SUB-G auch immer

Figure 2: MWE article *Aus welchen Gründen auch immer* from the MWE field *Grund*. The article parts are 'Frequency in the Corpus', 'General description', 'Context Analysis', 'Contrast Analysis' and 'Superordinated Nodes'. The part 'Context Analysis' contains links to a filler table and to the corresponding KWIC lines.

In this example the core field contains the MWEs *aus welchem Grund auch immer* and *aus welchen Gründen auch immer* ('for whatever reason/s'). However, the lexical components *auch immer* are part of more general patterns as well. The word form *Grund* can be substituted by different nouns in the MWE pattern *aus welch- SUB-G auch immer* (e.g. *Motiv (motive), Richtung (direction)*). In the MWE pattern *PRON auch immer* the place is taken by an interrogative pronoun (e.g. *was (what), wo (where), wer (who), warum (why)*). One of those pronoun fillers, *wie (how)*, is much more frequent than the others, which justifies the definition of a separate MWE *wie auch immer*, which can be translated as 'howsoever' or 'to whatever extent' (see section 2.3 for more details).

The basic structure of the MWE field thus highlights the different degrees of abstraction of MWEs and the functional use of lexical clusters like *auch immer*. The lexicographic descriptions linked to the nodes explain the interrelations and the differences in usage and meaning.

2.2 Contexts

Another important aspect of our approach to MWEs is that we pay close attention to the contexts in which they are commonly used. A good tool to explore this empirically is collocation analysis. In addition to narrative descriptions and manually selected corpus examples we therefore include the results of collocation analysis in our articles.

One interesting aspect is the difference between

Total	Anzahl	LLR	Kookurrenzen	syntagmatische Muster
36400	36400	44956	Was	99% Was [ist ...] eigentlich
51283	14883	29960	Warum	99% Warum [...] eigentlich
102957	51674	28059	was	99% was [...] eigentlich
113896	10939	24436	müsste	99% müsste [...] eigentlich
123499	9603	11569	obwohl	99% obwohl [...] eigentlich
125982	2483	10271	worum	100% worum [es ...] eigentlich
129066	3084	8837	Wieso	100% Wieso [...] eigentlich
132056	2990	8058	Schade	100% Schade [...] eigentlich
138601	6545	7501	Wo	100% Wo [ist ...] eigentlich
138613	12	6969	müßte Humptata-Musik	100% die unvermeindliche |unvermeidliche Humptata-Musik müßte eigentlich
149934	7750	6891	warum	99% warum [...] eigentlich
163416	13482	6513	wollte	99% Ich wollte [...] eigentlich
168752	5336	4620	müssten	99% müssten [...] eigentlich
168769	17	3625	Woher nimmst	100% Woher nimmst [du |Du] eigentlich
177773	7413	3589	wer	99% wer [...] eigentlich
178666	893	3317	Worum	100% Worum [geht es ...] eigentlich
196190	17524	3296	denn	99% denn [...] eigentlich
198747	2557	3229	Gibt	100% Gibt [es] eigentlich
199781	1034	2754	Wozu	100% Wozu [...] eigentlich

Figure 3: Highest ranking results of the collocation analysis for *eigentlich* (scope: 5 words in front).

MWEs and their single-lexeme quasi-synonyms. For example the meaning of the MWE *im Grunde* is very close to the lexeme *eigentlich* (*actually*). Figures 3 and 4 show the highest ranking results of a collocation analysis that focusses on a window of five words in front of the units *eigentlich* and *im Grunde* respectively and calculates the log likelihood ratio.[1] When comparing the results for these two units you can see that there are some contexts that are strongly preferred by *eigentlich* but are not highly ranked for *im Grunde*. Notable are the combination *schade eigentlich* (*sad actually*) as well as combinations with interrogative adverbs like *wie (how), was (what), warum (why)*. The MWE *im Grunde*, on the other hand, has strong collocation partners that are capitalized conjunctions like *aber (but)* or *denn (because)*. This indicates a clear tendency to appear near the beginning of a sentence in contexts where an argument is made, which is not prominent for *eigentlich*. So even if a quasi-synonymous single lexeme exists, the MWE shows differences in usage which become apparent when studying large quantities of data.

2.3 Patterns

As mentioned before, MWE patterns are of special interest to us. When exploring MWEs, we use a pattern matching tool that allows us to search large quantities of keyword in context lines (KWICs) for combinations of fixed strings and slots. The lexical fillers of these slots can also be counted and presented in the form of frequency tables. This allows us to explore which kinds of variations are possible and typical for an MWE. The filler tables can show quite different 'profiles' for a slot. In the following, we will give some examples.

For the MWE *aus welchen Gründen auch immer* (*for whatever reasons*) we checked whether the element *Gründen* can be modified by searching for the pattern `aus welchen #* Gründen auch immer` (`#*` stands for a slot that can be filled by any number of words). Table 1 shows the absolute and relative frequencies that where calculated from KWIC lines of our corpus. In the vast majority of cases, the slot is empty, which means that the MWE is used exactly in the form cited above: *aus welchen Gründen auch immer*. It is thus very stable, though not completely inflexible, as there is also evidence of adjectives that are used to further specify the reasons in question, e.g. *persönlichen Gründen (personal reasons)*.

A different example of filler behavior can be observed when studying the pattern `# auch immer` (# marks a slot that has to be filled with exactly one word). Table 2 shows that this slot

[1] For details on the collocation analysis used here see Perkuhn/Belica 2004. The settings were: *Korpus: W-gesamt - alle Korpora des Archivs W (mit Neuakquisitionen); Archiv-Release: Deutsches Referenzkorpus (DeReKo-2013-II); Analyse-Kontext : 5. Wort links bis 0. Wort rechts; Granularität: grob; Zuverlässigkeit: analytisch; Clusterzuordnung: mehrfach; Auf 1 Satz beschränkt: ja; Lemmatisierung: nein; Funktionswörter: zugelassen; Autofokus: aus*

Total	Anzahl	LLR	Kookurrenzen	syntagmatische Muster
1580	1580	396	Aber	100% Aber [...] im
2783	1203	278	ja	99% ja [...] im
3644	861	251	Denn	100% Denn [...] im
3667	23	147	einchecken	100% einchecken müssen dann starten Sie im
3697	30	121	Dr	100% Herr Dr ... im
3704	7	100	Besitzverteidigung	100% und Besitzverteidigung eingesetzt wird - im
3721	17	96	&	100% & [...] im
3757	36	87	bzw	100% bzw [...] im
3781	24	86	usw	100% usw [... ist] im
3791	10	73	Whishaw Dustin	100% Whishaw Dustin Hoffman"Das Parfüm ist im
4080	279	63	obwohl	100% obwohl [sie] im
4083	3	48	produktionsethischer	100% Sache produktionsethischer Bravheit des Eigensinns im
4086	3	43	Undelicatesse	100% Undelicatesse gegen uns Denker , im
4098	12	43	Kriminalkomödie	100% eine makabre Kriminalkomödie im
4101	3	41	Akku-Beleuchtung	100% heute mit Akku-Beleuchtung unterwegs - im
4106	5	40	Netanjahu-Regierung	100% etwas schwächere Netanjahu-Regierung die aber im
4126	20	40	hinwegtäuschen	100% darüber hinwegtäuschen daß |dass Jodie Foster im
4129	3	40	Bio-Mischung	100% Bio-Mischung seien im
4132	3	38	Zivi-Jobs	100% die Zivi-Jobs bei denen es im

Figure 4: Highest ranking results of the collocation analysis for *im Grunde* (scope: 5 words in front).

Filler	Freq	Rel Freq
	1239	98.33
unerfindlichen	3	0.24
persönlichen	2	0.16
legitimen	1	0.08
durchsichtigen	1	0.08
politischen	1	0.08
rätselhaften	1	0.08
psychologisch-persönlichen	1	0.08
mir nicht verständlichen	1	0.08
besagten	1	0.08
(PR-)	1	0.08
psychologischen	1	0.08
(un)berechtigten	1	0.08
"	1	0.08
(oft ökonomischen)	1	0.08
...	...	...

Table 1: Fillers of the pattern `aus welchen #* Gründen auch immer`.

Filler	Freq	Rel Freq
Wie	9611	10.08
wie	7389	7.75
was	5289	5.55
aber	3397	3.56
Gründen	3157	3.31
es	2288	2.40
Was	1953	2.05
Wer	1825	1.91
sich	1677	1.76
warum	1529	1.60
wo	1486	1.56
wer	1446	1.52
ja	1333	1.40
wem	1292	1.35
ist	1276	1.34
...	...	...

Table 2: Fillers of the pattern `# auch immer`.

is filled by *wie* (capitalized or non-capitalized) in nearly 18 percent of the matches. In this case, a single lexical filler is very dominant. This was a strong indication for us that the pattern *wie auch immer* functions as an MWE while at the same time being a prototypical realization of the pattern *PRON auch immer*. Also quite frequent is the filler *Gründen*, which indicates the pattern *[aus welchen] Gründen auch immer*, and other interrogative pronouns and adverbs like *was (what), wer (who), wem (whom)* etc. This lead us to define the MWE hierarchies as shown in figure 1 and explained in section 2.1.

A different filler profile (Table 3) can be observed for the pattern `aus # Gründen` (*for # reasons*). This is a true MWE pattern, as it has a specific communicative function tied to the plural form of Grund: reasons are mentioned, but left intentionally vague. Table 3 shows that there is a large number of adjectives that can fill the gap. In contrast to the example `X auch immer` above,

Label		Aus|aus	#	Gründen	
SOZ07_10	weshalb das Oratorium	aus	akustischen	Gründen	auch nicht in einer Kirche aufgeführt
WPD11_4133	werden, deren Ausbau	aus	unerfindlichen	Gründen	gestoppt wurde, die Brutalität
BRZ11_258	dem sie sich bisher	aus	finanziellen	Gründen	immer zurückhielten. Um sich auch
M07_208	Oliver Kahn	aus	disziplinarischen	Gründen	für das Hertha-Spiel an Schärfe
E98_409	möglicherweise	aus	wirtschaftlichen	Gründen	zurückgehalten. Schliesslich ist Epo
WDD11_305	schlage diesen Artikel	aus	folgenden	Gründen	als lesenswert vor: fachlich
NUN11_144	die Polizei	aus	ermittlungstaktischen	Gründen	nicht mitteilen.
...	...	...	...	...	...

Table 4: KWIC lines of the pattern `aus # Gründen`.

Filler	Freq	Rel Freq
gesundheitlichen	7355	10.03
beruflichen	6311	8.60
finanziellen	4708	6.42
persönlichen	2660	3.63
organisatorischen	2585	3.52
politischen	2499	3.41
wirtschaftlichen	2180	2.97
privaten	1941	2.65
welchen	1849	2.52
verschiedenen	1779	2.43
diesen	1494	2.04
anderen	1381	1.88
technischen	1260	1.72
zwei	1237	1.69
familiären	1219	1.66
...	...	...

Table 3: Fillers of the pattern `aus # Gründen`.

none of these is so dominant and striking that a separate MWE needs to be considered. However, the fillers can be grouped into functional groups, like type of the reasons (e.g. *politisch (political), persönlich (personal), finanziell (financial)*), validity of the reasons (e.g. *nachvollziehbar (understandable), gut (good), triftig (valid)*) or relevance of the reasons (e.g. *wichtig (important), zwingend (imperative)*).

You can see that filler tables are very useful for different purposes: To confirm the fixedness of an MWE and explore occasional variations, to conceptualize lexical units in order to build up hierarchies, and to further describe and understand the behavior of MWE patterns. Not only do we work with such patterns and filler tables when building the MWE field, we also include them in our descriptions - another way to give a user access to original corpus data structured in an informative way.

Additionally, we provide access to the KWIC lines that were used to calculate the filler tables. Table 4 shows some of the lines that match the pattern `aus # Gründen`. These lines are structured in fields according to the search pattern and the different columns can be sorted. In this way, you can explore the use of specific MWE structures yourself.

3 Conclusion

We believe that our MWE fields allow a different way to look at MWEs which is very useful to understand the structure of language. As they are strictly based on data from a large modern language corpus, our findings also reflect real, contemporary language use. This is especially useful for foreign language learners who struggle to navigate the complexities of fixedness and variability in the German language. In continuing our MWE research, we strive to refine our strategies for description and visualization and also plan to add contrastive studies in the future.

References

Belica, Cyril: Statistische Kollokationsanalyse und Clustering. Korpusanalytische Analysemethode, 1995 ⟨URL: `http://www1.ids-mannheim.de/kl/projekte/methoden/ur.html`⟩ – visited on 28.01.2014.

Brunner, Annelen/Steyer, Kathrin: A Model for Corpus-Driven Exploration and Presentation of Multi-Word Expressions, in:

Levická, Jana/Garabík, Radovan, editors: NLP, Corpus Linguistics, Corpus Based Grammar Research (= Proceedings of SLOVKO 2009, held 25-27.11.2009 in Smolenice, Slovakia), 2009, pp. 54–64.

Brunner, Annelen/Steyer, Kathrin: Wortverbindungsfelder: Fields of Multi-Word Expressions, in: **Granger, Silviane/ Paquot, Magali, editors:** eLexicography in the 21st century: New challenges, new applications. Proceedings of the eLex 2009. Louvaine-la-Neuve: Presses universitaires de Louvain, 2010, Cahiers du CENTAL, pp. 23–31.

Hanks, Patrick: Lexical Analysis: norms and exploitations, Cambridge [u.a.]: MIT Press, 2013.

Institut für Deutsche Sprache: Deutsches Referenzkorpus/Archiv der Korpora geschriebener Gegenwartssprache (DeReKo 2012-II), Webseite, 2012 ⟨URL: `http://www.ids-mannheim.de/DeReKo`⟩ – visited on 28.01.2014.

Perkuhn, Rainer/Belica, Cyril: Eine kurze Einführung in die Kookkurrenzanalyse und syntagmatische Muster. Institut für Deutsche Sprache, Mannheim, 2004 ⟨URL: `http://www1.ids-mannheim.de/kl/misc/tutorial.html`⟩ – visited on 28.01.2014.

Sinclair, John: Corpus, Concordance, Collocation, Oxford: Oxford University Press, 1991.

Stefanowitsch, Anatol/Gries, Stephan Th.: Collostructions: Investigating the interaction of words and constructions, in: International Journal of Corpus Linguistics, 8 2003, Nr. 2, pp. 209–243.

Steyer, Kathrin: Usuelle Wortverbindungen des Deutschen. Linguistisches Konzept und lexikografische Möglichkeiten, in: Deutsche Sprache, 28 2000, Nr. 2, pp. 101–125.

Steyer, Kathrin: Kookkurenz. Korpusmethodik, linguistisches Modell, lexikographische Persepektiven, in: **Steyer, Kathrin, editor:** Wortverbindungen - mehr oder weniger fest, Berlin/New York: de Gruyter, 2004, Jahrbuch des Instituts für Deutsche Sprache, pp. 87–116.

Steyer, Kathrin: Usuelle Wortverbindungen. Zentrale Muster des Sprachgebrauchs aus korpusanalytischer Sicht, Tübingen: Narr, 2013.

Tognini-Bonelli, Elena: Corpus Linguistics at Work, Amsterdam/Philadelphia: J. Benjamins, 2001.

Detecting change and emergence for multiword expressions

Martin Emms
Department of Computer Science
Trinity College, Dublin
Ireland
Martin.Emms@tcd.ie

Arun Jayapal
Department of Computer Science
Trinity College, Dublin
Ireland
jayapala@tcd.ie

Abstract

This work looks at a temporal aspect of multiword expressions (MWEs), namely that the behaviour of a given n-gram and its status as a MWE change over time. We propose a model in which context words have particular probabilities given a usage choice for an n-gram, and those usage choices have time dependent probabilities, and we put forward an expectation-maximisation technique for estimating the parameters from data with no annotation of usage choice. For a range of MWE usages of recent coinage, we evaluate whether the technique is able to detect the emerging usage.

1 Introduction

When an n-gram is designated a 'multiword expression', or MWE, its because it possesses properties which are not straightforwardly predictable given the component words of the n-gram – that *red tape* can refer to bureaucratic regulation would be a simple example. A further aspect is that while some *tokens* of the n-gram *type* may be examples of the irregular MWE usage, others may not be – so *red tape* can certainly also be used in a fashion which is transparent relative to its parts. A further aspect is temporal: that tokens of the n-gram can be sought in language samples from different *times*. It seems reasonable to assume that the irregular MWE usage of *red tape* at some time emerged, and was predated by the more transparent usage. This paper concerns the possibility of finding automatic, unsupervised means to detect the emergence of a MWE usage of a given n-gram.

To illustrate further, consider the following examples (these are all taken from the data set on which we worked)

(1)
(a) *the wind lifted his three-car garage and* **smashed it** *to the ground.* (1995)
(a′) *sensational group CEO, totally* **smashed it** *in the BGT (Britain Got Talent)* (2013)
(b) *my schedule gave* **me time** *to get adjusted* (1990)
(b′) *it's important to set time out and enjoy some* **me time** (2013)

(a) and (a′) feature the n-gram *smashed it*. (a) uses the standard destructive sense of *smashed*, and *it* refers to an object undergoing the destructive transformation. In (a′) the n-gram is used differently and is roughly replaceable by 'excelled', a usage not via the standard sense of *smashed*, nor one where *it* refers to any object at all. Where in both (a) and (a′) the n-gram would be regarded as a phrase, (b) and (b′) involving the n-gram *me time* show another possibility. In (b), *me* and *time* are straightforward dependants of *gave*. In (b′), the two words form a noun-phrase, meaning something like 'personal time'. The usage is arguably more acceptable than would be the case with other object pronouns, and if addressed to a particular person, the *me* would refer to the addressee, which is not the usual function of a first-person pronoun.

For *smashed it* and *me time*, the second (primed) example illustrates an irregular usage-variant of the n-gram, whilst the first illustrates a regular usage-variant, and the irregular example is drawn from a later time than the regular usage. Language is a dynamic phenomenon, with the range of ways a given n-gram might contribute subject to change over time, and for these n-grams, it would seem to be the case that the availability of the *'me time' = 'personal time'* and *'smashed it = 'excelled'* usage-variants is a relatively recent innovation[1], predated by the regular usage-variants. It seems that in work on multiword ex-

[1]That is to say, recent in British English according to the

pressions, there has been little attention paid to this dynamic aspect, whereby a particular multi-word usage starts to play a role in a language at a particular point in time. Building on earlier work (Emms, 2013), we present some work concerning unsupervised means to detect this. Section 2 describes our data, section 3 our EM-based method and section 4 discusses the results obtained.

2 Data

To investigate such emergence phenomena some kind of time-stamped corpus is required. The approach we took to this was to exploit a search facility that Google has offered for some time – *custom date range* – whereby it is possible to specify a time period for text matching the searched item. To obtain data for a given n-gram, we repeatedly set different year-long time spans and saved the first 100 returned 'hits' as potential examples of the n-gram's use. Each 'hit' has a text snippet and an anchor text for a link to the online source from which the snippet comes. If the text snippet or anchor string contains the n-gram it can furnish an example of its use, and the longer of the two is taken if both feature the n-gram.

A number of n-grams were chosen having the properties that they have an irregular, MWE usage alongside a regular one, with the MWE usage a recent innovation. These were *smashed it*, *me time* (illustrated in (1)) and *going forward*, and *biological clock*, illustrated below.

(2)
- (c) **Going forward** *from the entrance, you'll come to a large room.* (1995)
- (c′) **Going forward** *BJP should engage in people's movements* (2009)
- (d) *A* **biological clock** *present in most eukaryotes imposes daily rhythms* (1995)
- (d′) *How To Stop Worrying About Your* **Biological Clock** *... Pressure to have a baby before 35* (2009)

Alongside the plain movement usage-variant seen in (c), *going forward* has the more opaque usage-variant in which it is roughly replaceable by 'in the future', seen in (c′). Alongside a technical use in biology seen in (d), *biological clock* has come to be used in a wider context to refer to a sense of expiring time within which people may be able to have a child, seen in (d′).

first author's intuitions. It is not easy to find sources to corroborate such intuitions

For each n-gram data was downloaded for successive year-long time-spans from 1990 to 2013, retaining the first 100 hits for each year. For some of the earlier years there are less than 100 hits, but mostly there are more than 100. This gives on the order of 2000 examples for each n-gram, each with a date stamp, but otherwise with no other annotation. See Section 4 for some discussion of this method of obtaining data.

3 Algorithm

For an n-gram with usage variants (as illustrated by (1) and (2)), we take the Bayesian approach that each variant gives different probabilities to the words in its immediate vicinity, as has been done in unsupervised word-sense disambiguation (Manning and Schütze, 2003; de Marneffe and Dupont, 2004). In those approaches, which ignore any temporal dimension, it is also assumed that there are *prior* probabilities on the usage-variants. We bring in language change by having a succession of priors, one for each time period.

To make this more precise, where T is an occurrence of a particular n-gram, with $\boldsymbol{W}$ the sequence of words around T, let Y represent its time-stamp. If we suppose there are k different usage-variants of the n-gram, we simply model this with a discrete variable S which can take on k values. So S can be thought of as ranging over positions in an enumeration of the different ways that the n-gram can contribute to the semantics. With these variables we can say that we are considering a probability model for $p(Y, S, \boldsymbol{W})$. Applying the chain-rule this may be re-expresssed without loss of generality as $p(Y)p(S|Y)p(\boldsymbol{W}|S, Y)$. We then make some assumptions: (i) that $\boldsymbol{W}$ is conditionally independent of Y given S, so $p(\boldsymbol{W}|S, Y) = p(\boldsymbol{W}|S)$, (ii) that $p(\boldsymbol{W}|S)$ may be treated as $\prod_i (p(\boldsymbol{W}_i|S)$, and (iii) that $p(Y)$ is uniform. This then gives

$$p(Y, S, \boldsymbol{W}) = p(Y)p(S|Y) \prod_i (p(\boldsymbol{W}_i|S) \quad (3)$$

The term $p(S|Y)$ directly models the fact that a usage variant can vary its likelihood over time, possibly having zero probability on some early range of times. While (i) make context words and times indepedent *given* a usage variant, context words are still time-dependent: the sum $\sum_S [p(S|Y)p(\boldsymbol{W}|S)]$ varies with time Y due to

$p(S|Y)$. Assumption (i) reflects a plausibile idea that given a concept being conveyed, the expected accompanying vocabulary is substantially time-independent. Moreover (i) drastically reduces the number of parameters to be estimated: with 20 time spans and a 2-way usage choice, the word probabilities are conditioned on 2 settings rather than 40.

The parameters of the model in (3) have to be estimated from data which is labelled only for time – the usage-variant variable is a *hidden* variable – and we tackle this with an EM procedure (Dempster et al., 1977). Space precludes giving the derivations of the update formulae but in outline there is an iteration of an E and an M step, as follows:

(**E** step) *based on current parameters, a table, γ, is populated, such that for each data point d, and possible S value s, $\gamma[d][s]$ stores $P(S = s|Y = y^d, \boldsymbol{W} = \boldsymbol{w}^d)$.*

(**M** step) *based on γ, fresh parameter values are re-estimated according to:*

$$P(S = s|Y = y) = \frac{\sum_d(\text{if } Y^d{=}y \text{ then } \gamma[d][s] \text{ else } 0)}{\sum_d(\text{if } Y^d{=}y \text{ then } 1 \text{ else } 0)}$$

$$P(w|S = s) = \frac{\sum_d(\gamma[d][s] \times freq(w \in \boldsymbol{W}^d))}{\sum_d(\gamma[d][s] \times length(\boldsymbol{W}^d))}$$

These updates can be shown to increase the data probability, where the usage variable S is summed-out.

4 Results and Discussion

Running the above-outlined EM procedure on the downloaded data for a particular n-gram generates unsupervised estimates for $p(S|Y)$ – inferred usage distributions for each time span. To obtain a reference with which to compare these inferred distributions, approximately 10% of the data per time-span was manually annotated and used to give simple relative-frequency estimates of $p(S|Y)$ – which we will call empirical estimates. Although the data was downloaded for year-long time spans, it was decided to group the data into successive spans of 3 year duration. This was to make the empirical $p(S|Y)$ less brittle as they are otherwise based on too small a quantity of data.

Figure 1 shows the outcomes, as usage-variant probabilities in a succession of time spans, both the empirical estimates obtained on a subset, and the unsupervised estimates obtained on all the data. The EM method can seek any number of usage variants, and the results show the case where 2 variants were sought. Where the manually annotated subset used more variants these were grouped to facilitate a comparison.

For *smashed it*, *biological clock* and *going forward*, the ○ line in the empirical plot is for the MWE usage, and for *me time* it is the △ line, and it has an upward trend. In the unsupervised case, there is inevitable indeterminacy about which S values may come to be associated with any objectively real usage. Modulo this the unsupervised and supervised graphs broadly concur.

One can also inspect the context-words which come to have high probability in one semantic variant relative to their probability in another. For example, for *smashed it*, for the semantic usage which is inferred to have an increasing probability in recent years, a selection from the most favoured tokens includes *!!, guys, really, completely, They, !*, whilst for the other usage they include *smithereens, bits, bottle, onto, phone*. For *biological clock*, a similar exercise gives for the apparently increasing usage, tokens such as *Ticks, Ticking?, Health, Fertility* and for the other usage *running, 24-hour, controlled, mammalian, mechanisms*. These associations would seem to be consistent with the inferred semantic-usages being in broad correspondence with the annotated usages.

As noted in section 2, as a means to obtain data on relatively recent n-gram usages, we used the *custom date range* search facility of Google. One of the issues with such data is the potential for the time-stamping (inferred by Google) to be innaccurate. Though its not possible to exhaustively verify the time-stamping, some inspection was done, which revealed that although there are some cases of documents which were incorrectly stamped, this was tolerably infrequent. Then there is the question of the representativeness of the sample obtained. The mechanism we used gives the first 100 from the at most 1000 'hits' which Google will return from amongst all index documents which match the n-gram and the date range, so an uncontrollable factor is the ranking mechanism according to which these hits are selected and ordered. The fact that the empirical usage distributions accord reasonably well with prior intuition is a modest indicator that the data is not unusably unrepresentative. One could also argue that for an initial test of the algorithms it suffices for the methods to recover an apparent trend

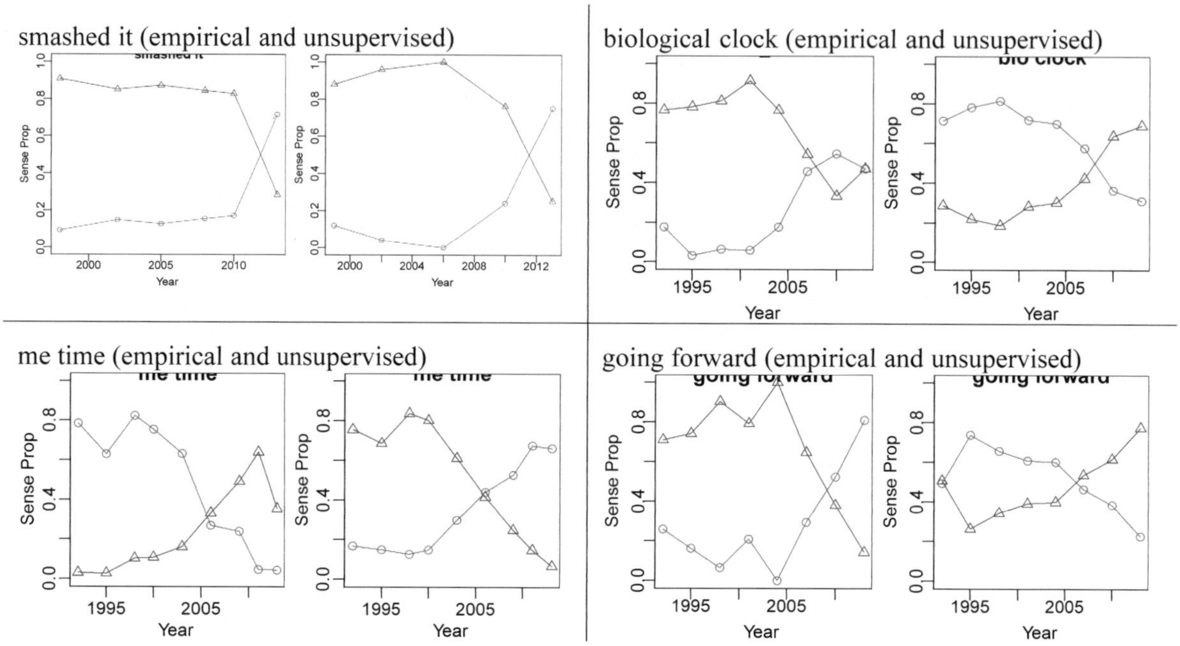

Figure 1: For each n-gram the plots show the empirical usage-variant distributions per time-period in the labelled subset and unsupervised usage-varaint distributions per time-period in the entire data set

in the downloaded data, even if the data is unrepresentative. This being said, one direction for further work will be to consider other sources of time-stamped language use, such as the Google n-grams corpus (Brants and Franz, 2012), or various newswire corpora (Graff et al., 2007).

There does not seem to have been that much work on unsupervised means to identify emergence of new usage of a given expression – there is more work which groups all tokens of a type together and uses change of context words to indicate an evolving single meaning (Sagi et al., 2008; Gulordava and Baroni, 2011). Lau et al. (2012) though they do not address MWEs do look at the emergence of new word senses, applying a word-sense induction technique. Their testing was between two corpora taken to represent two different time periods, the BNC and ukWac corpus, taken to represent the late 20th century and 2007, respectively, and they reported promising results on 5 words. The unsupervised method they used is based on a Hierarchical Dirichlet Process model (Yao and Van Durme, 2011), and a direction for future work will be a closer comparison of the algorithm presented here to that algorithm and other related LDA-based methods in word sense induction (Brody and Lapata, 2009). Also the bag-of-tokens model of the context words which we adopted is a very simple one, and we wish to consider more sophisticated models involving for example part-of-tagging or syntactic structures.

The results are indicative at least that MWE usage of an n-gram can be detected by unsupervised means to be preceded by the other usages of the n-gram. There has been some work on algorithms which seek to quantify the degree of compositionality of particular n-grams (Maldonado-Guerra and Emms, 2011; Biemann and Giesbrecht, 2011) and it is hoped in future work to consider the possible integration of some of these techniques with those reported here. For a given n-gram, it would be interesting to know if the collection of its occurrences which the techniques of the current paper suggest to belong to a more recently emerging usage, are also a corpus of occurrences relative to which a compositionality measure would report the n-gram as being of low compositionality, and conversely for the apparently less recent usage.

Acknowledgements

This research is supported by the Science Foundation Ireland (Grant 12/CE/I2267) as part of the Centre for Next Generation Localisation (www.cngl.ie) at Trinity College Dublin.

References

Chris Biemann and Eugenie Giesbrecht, editors. 2011. *Proceedings of the Workshop on Distributional Semantics and Compositionality.*

Thorsten Brants and Alex Franz. 2012. Google books n-grams. ngrams.googlelabs.com.

Samuel Brody and Mirella Lapata. 2009. Bayesian word sense induction. In *EACL 09: Proceedings of the 12th Conference of the European Chapter of the Association for Computational Linguistics*, pages 103–111, Stroudsburg, PA, USA. Association for Computational Linguistics.

Marie-Catharine de Marneffe and Pierre Dupont. 2004. Comparative study of statistical word sense discrimination. In Gérald Purnelle, Cédric Fairon, and Anne Dister, editors, *Proceedings of JADT 2004 7th International Conference on the Statistical Analysis of Textual Data*, pages 270–281. UCL Presses Universitaire de Louvain.

A.P. Dempster, N.M. Laird, and D.B. Rubin. 1977. Maximum likelihood from incomplete data via the em algorithm. *J. Royal Statistical Society*, B 39:1–38.

Martin Emms. 2013. Dynamic EM in neologism evolution. In Hujun Yin, Ke Tang, Yang Gao, Frank Klawonn, Minho Lee, Thomas Weise, Bin Li, and Xin Yao, editors, *Proceedings of IDEAL 2013*, volume 8206 of *Lecture Notes in Computer Science*, pages 286–293. Springer.

David Graff, Junbo Kong, Ke Chen, and Kazuaki Maeda. 2007. English gigaword corpus. Linguistic Data Consortium.

Kristina Gulordava and Marco Baroni. 2011. A distributional similarity approach to the detection of semantic change in the google books ngram corpus. In *Proceedings of the GEMS 2011 Workshop on GEometrical Models of Natural Language Semantics*, pages 67–71, Edinburgh, UK, July. Association for Computational Linguistics.

Jey Han Lau, Paul Cook, Diana McCarthy, David Newman, and Timothy Baldwin. 2012. Word sense induction for novel sense detection. In *Proceedings of the 13th Conference of the European Chapter of the Association for Computational Linguistics*, EACL '12, pages 591–601, Stroudsburg, PA, USA. Association for Computational Linguistics.

Alfredo Maldonado-Guerra and Martin Emms. 2011. Measuring the compositionality of collocations via word co-occurrence vectors: Shared task system description. In *Proceedings of the Workshop on Distributional Semantics and Compositionality*, pages 48–53, Portland, Oregon, USA, June. Association for Computational Linguistics.

Christopher Manning and Hinrich Schütze, 2003. *Foundations of Statistical Language Processing*, chapter Word Sense Disambiguation, pages 229–264. MIT Press, 6 edition.

Eyal Sagi, Stefan Kaufmann, and Brady Clark. 2008. Tracing semantic change with latent semantic analysis. In *Proceedings of ICEHL 2008*.

Xuchen Yao and Benjamin Van Durme. 2011. Nonparametric bayesian word sense induction. In *Proceedings of TextGraphs-6: Graph-based Methods for Natural Language Processing*, pages 10–14. Association for Computational Linguistics.

An Approach to *Take* Multi-Word Expressions

Claire Bonial* **Meredith Green**** **Jenette Preciado**** **Martha Palmer***
*Department of Linguistics, University of Colorado at Boulder
**Institute of Cognitive Science, University of Colorado at Boulder
{Claire.Bonial,Laura.Green,Jenette.Preciado,Martha.Palmer}@colorado.edu

Abstract

This research discusses preliminary efforts to expand the coverage of the PropBank lexicon to multi-word and idiomatic expressions, such as *take one for the team*. Given overwhelming numbers of such expressions, an efficient way for increasing coverage is needed. This research discusses an approach to adding multi-word expressions to the PropBank lexicon in an effective yet semantically rich fashion. The pilot discussed here uses double annotation of *take* multi-word expressions, where annotations provide information on the best strategy for adding the multi-word expression to the lexicon. This work represents an important step for enriching the semantic information included in the PropBank corpus, which is a valuable and comprehensive resource for the field of Natural Language Processing.

1 Introduction

The PropBank (PB) corpus provides information associating semantic roles with certain syntactic structures, thereby contributing valuable training data for Natural Language Processing (NLP) applications (Palmer et al., 2005). For example, recent research shows that using semantic role information in machine translation systems improves performance (Lo, Beloucif & Wu, 2013). Despite these successes, PB could be improved with greater coverage of multi-word expressions (MWEs). The PB lexicon (http://verbs.colorado.edu/PB/framesets-english) is comprised of senses of verb, noun and adjective relations, with a listing of their semantic roles (thus a sense is referred to as a 'roleset'). Although the lexicon encompasses nearly 12,000 rolesets, relatively few of these apply to instances of MWEs. PB has previously treated language as if it were purely compositional, and has therefore lumped the majority of MWEs in with lexical verb usages. For example, annotations of the single PB sense of *take* meaning *acquire, come to have, choose, bring with you from somewhere* include MWEs such as *take measures, take comfort* and *take advantage*, and likely others. Although PB senses typically, and this sense especially, are quite coarse-grained, valuable semantic information is lost when these distinct MWEs are lumped together with other lexical senses.

The importance of coverage for MWEs is underscored by their prevalence. Jackendoff (1997:156) estimates that the number of MWEs in a speaker's lexicon is approximately equal to the number of single words, and in WordNet 1.7 (Fellbaum, 1998), 41% of the entries were MWEs (cited in Sag et al., 2002). Furthermore, Sag (2002) estimates the vocabularies of specialized domains will continue to contribute more MWEs than simplex words. For systems like PB to continue to provide adequate training data for NLP systems, coverage must extend to MWEs. The lack of coverage in this area has already become problematic for the recently developed Abstract Meaning Representation (AMR) project (Banarescu et al., 2013), which relies upon the PB lexicon, or 'frame files' as the groundwork for its annotations. As AMR and PB have extended into more informal domains, such as online discussion forums and SMS texts, the gaps in coverage of MWEs have become more and more problematic. To address this issue, this research discusses a pilot approach to increasing the coverage of the PB lexicon to a variety of MWEs involving the verb *take*, demonstrating a methodology for efficiently augmenting the lexicon with MWEs.

2 PB Background

PB annotation was developed to provide training data for supervised machine learning classifiers. It provides semantic information, including the basic "who is doing what to whom," in the form of predicate-by-predicate semantic role assignments. The annotation firstly consists of the selection of a roleset, or a coarse-grained sense of the predicate, which includes a listing of the roles, expressed as generic argument numbers, associated with that sense. Here, for example, is the roleset for Take.01, mentioned previously:

Take.01: *acquire, come to have, choose, bring*
Arg0: Taker
Arg1: Thing taken
Arg2: Taken-from, source of thing taken
Arg3: Destination

These argument numbers, along with a variety of modifier tags, such as temporal and locative, are assigned to natural language sentences drawn from a variety of corpora. The roleset and example sentences serve as a guide to annotators on how to assign argument numbers to annotation instances. The goal is to assign these simple, general-purpose labels consistently across the many possible syntactic realizations of the same event participant or semantic role.

PB has recently undertaken efforts to expand the types of predicates that are annotated. Previously, annotation efforts focused on verbs, but events generally, and even the same event, can often be expressed with a variety of different parts of speech, or with MWEs. For example,

1. He fears bears.
2. His fear of bears...
3. He is afraid of bears.
4. He has a fear of bears.

Thus, it has been necessary to expand PB annotations to provide coverage for noun, adjective and complex predicates. While this greatly enriches the semantics that PB is able to capture, it has also forced the creation of an overwhelming number of new rolesets, as generally each new predicate type receives its own set of rolesets. To alleviate this, PB has opted to begin unifying frame files through a process of 'aliasing'(Bonial et al., 2014). In this process, etymologically related concepts are aliased to each other, and aliased rolesets are unified, so that there is a single roleset representing, for example the concept of 'fear,' and this roleset is used for all syntactic instantiations of that concept.

This methodology is suited to complex predicates, such as light verb constructions (LVCs), wherein the eventive noun, carrying the bulk of the event semantics, may have an etymologically related verb that is identical in its participants or semantic roles (for a description of LVC annotation, see (Hwang et al., 2010). Thus, *have a fear* above is aliased to *fear*, as *take a bath* would be aliased to *bathe*. In this research, the possibility of extending aliasing to a variety of MWEs is explored, such that *take it easy*, as in "I'm just going to take it easy on Saturday," would be aliased to the existing lexical verb roleset for *relax*. In many cases, the semantics of MWEs are quite complex, adding shades of meaning that no lexical verb quite captures. Thus, additional strategies beyond aliasing are developed; each strategy is discussed in the following sections.

3 *Take* Pilot

For the purposes of this pilot, the *take* MWEs were gathered from WordNet's MWE and phrasal verb entries (Fellbaum, 1998), the Prague Czech-English Dependency Treebank (Hajič-2012), and Afsaneh Fazly's dissertation work (Fazly, 2007). Graduate student annotators were trained to use WordNet, Sketch Engine (Kilgarriff et al., 2004) and PB to complete double-blind annotation of these MWEs as a candidate for one of the three following strategies for increasing roleset coverage: 1) Aliasing the MWE to a lexically-similar verb or noun roleset from PB, 2) proposing the creation of groups of expressions for which one or several rolesets will be created, or 3) simply designating the MWE as an idiomatic expression. First, annotators were to try to choose a verb or noun roleset from PB that most closely resembled the syntax and semantics of the MWE. Annotators also made comments as necessary for difficult cases. The annotators were considered to have agreed if the proposed lexical verb or noun alias was the same. Strategies (2) and (3) were pursued during adjudication if the annotators were unable to agree upon an appropriate alias. Each of the possible strategies for increasing coverage is discussed in turn in the following sections.

3.1 Aliasing

Aliasing involves proposing an existing roleset from PB as a suitable roleset for future MWE annotation. LVCs were the simplest of these to alias since the eventive or stative noun predicate (e.g.: *take a **look***) may already have an existing roleset, or there is likely an existing, etymologically related verb roleset (e.g. verb roleset Look.01). Some other MWEs were not so straightforward. For instance, *take time off* does not include an etymologically related predicate that would easily encompass the semantics of the MWE, so the annotators proposed a roleset that is not as intuitive, but captures the semantics nonetheless: the roleset for the noun *vacation*. This frame allows for an Agent to take time off, and importantly, what time is taken off from: *take time off from work, school* etc. Selecting an appropriate alias is the ideal strategy for increasing coverage, because it does not require the time and effort of manually creating a new roleset or rolesets.

Both of the instances discussed above are rather simple cases, where their coverage can be addressed efficiently through aliasing. However, many MWE instances were considerably more difficult to assign to an equivalent roleset. One such example includes *take shape*, for which the annotators decided that *shape* was an appropriate roleset. Yet, *shape* does not quite cover the unique semantics of *take shape*, which lacks the possibility of an Agent. In these cases, the MWEs may still be aliased, but they should also include an semantic constraint to convey the semantic difference, such as "-Agent" Thus, in some cases, these types of semantic constraints were used for aliases that were almost adequate, but lacked some shade of meaning conveyed by the MWE. In other cases, the semantic difference between an MWE and existing lexical verb or noun roleset was too great to be captured by the addition of such constraints, thus a new roleset or group of rolesets was created to address coverage of such MWEs, as described in the next section.

3.2 Groups of Syntactically/Lexically Similar Rolesets

In cases in which it was not possible to find a single adequate alias for an MWE, a group of rolesets representing different senses of the same MWE was created. For example, *take down* can mean *to write something down, to defeat something*, or *to deconstruct something*. Thus, a group of *take_down* rolesets were added, with each roleset reflecting one of these senses.

Similarly, some of the proposed rolesets for *take* MWEs were easily subsumed under a more coarse-grained, new frame in PB. For instance, *take one's lumps* and *take it on the chin* both more or less mean *to endure or atone for*, so combining these in a coarser-grained MWE frame is both efficient and allows for valuable distinctions in terms of semantic role labeling. Namely, the Agent choosing to atone for something, and what the entity is atoning for. However, such situations in which it's possible to create new coarse-grained MWE rolesets seem to be rare. Some MWEs initially seem similar enough to combine into a single roleset, but further exploration of usages shows that they are semantically different. *Take comfort* and *take heart in* both involve improving mood, but *take heart in* might be more closely-related to *hope* in meaning, while *take comfort in* might simply mean *to cheer up*.

3.3 Idiomatic Expression Designation

In cases in which PB annotation would be very difficult for annotators, due to polysemy or semantics that cannot be conveyed by aliasing to an existing roleset, MWEs will be listed for future annotation as Idiomatic Expressions (IE), which get special treatment. This designation indicates that the MWE is so unique that it would require its own new roleset(s) in PB, and even with these rolesets, annotators may still have difficulty determining the appropriate roleset choice or sense of the MWE. As mentioned previously, creating multiple rolesets for each expression is inefficient, especially so if the rolesets manually created will be difficult to distinguish; thus, currently such cases are simply marked with the generic IE roleset.

The MWE *take the count* is an illustrative example of this type of case. Undergraduate and graduate annotators trained in linguistics tend to have difficulty with detailed sports references in annotation instances, regardless of how much context is provided. This MWE applies to several sports scenarios: one can *take the count* in boxing or *take the (full) count* in baseball, and some usages were even found for football, where many speakers would use *run down the clock*. Annotators unfamiliar with the somewhat esoteric meanings of these phrases would undoubtedly have trouble distinguishing the rolesets and arguments of the rolesets, thus *take the count* in sports contexts (as opposed to the LVC *take the count*, meaning *to count*) will simply be designated IE.

Currently, IE instances are simply set aside from the rest of the PB corpus, so as to avoid these instances adding noise to the data. In the future, these IE expressions will need to be treated individually to determine the best way to capture their unique semantics.

4 Results & Conclusions

One way of analyzing the validity of this methodology is to examine the Inter-Annotator Agreement (IAA) on the proposed alias. After the training period (in which about 60 MWEs were investigated as a group), annotators worked on double-blind annotation of 100 additional MWEs. Of these, 17 were found to be repeats of earlier MWEs. Of the remaining 83, annotators agreed on the exact alias in 32 cases, giving a rather poor, simple IAA of about 39%. However, the standards used to calculate IAA were rigid, as only instances in which the annotators aliased the multiword expressions to exactly the same lexical verb or noun roleset were counted as an agreement. Annotators often disagreed on lexical verbs, but still chose verbs that were extraordinarily similar. Take, for example, the MWE *take back*. One annotator chose to alias this MWE to *retract* while the other annotator chose *reclaim*. It is safe to say that both of these lexical verbs are equally logical choices for *take back* and have similar semantic and syntactic qualities. In other cases, annotators had discovered different senses in their research of usages, and therefore the aliases reflect different senses of the MWE. Instances like these were marked as disagreements, resulting in a misleadingly low IAA. After discussion of disagreements, IAA for these 83 MWEs rose to 78%, leaving 18 MWEs for which the annotators were unable to agree on a strategy. Annotation proceeded with an additional 76 MWEs, and for this set annotators disagreed on only 6 MWEs. This process demonstrates that although annotators may not agree on the first alias that comes to mind, they tend to agree on similar verbs that can capture the semantics of an MWE appropriately. In a final adjudication pass, adjudicators discussed the cases of disagreement with the annotators and made a final decision on the strategy to be pursued.

In all, 159 unique MWEs were examined in double-blind annotation. Of these, 21 were discarded either because annotators felt they were not truly MWEs, and could be treated compositionally, or because they were very slight variants of other MWEs. The following table shows how many of the remaining 138 MWEs were agreed upon for aliasing (and how many of these were thought to be LVCs), how many cases led to the addition of new rolesets, how many will be labeled IE in future annotation, and how many will remain classed with the existing Take senses (note that 4 MWEs were classed as having both a potential alias for LVC usages, and requiring rolesets or another strategy for other usages; for example, *take the count* discussed above). Overall, this pilot demonstrated that the approach is promising, considering that it requires only about 20 new rolesets to be created, as opposed to over 138 (given that some MWEs have multiple senses, requiring multiple rolesets). As annotations move on to additional MWEs involving other verbs, a similar reduction in the roleset workload will be invaluable to expanding PB.

MWE Example	Strategy	Count
take_tumble	Alias-LVC	45
take_it_easy	Alias-nonLVC	55
take_ down	Roleset(s) Created	20
take_count	IE	4
take_home	Take.XX	18

Table 1: MWE cases addressed by each strategy.

5 Future Work

The next step in this research is to complete the roleset unification, which allows the aliasing to take effect. This process is currently underway. Once this is complete, an investigation of *take* annotations using the unified rolesets will be undertaken, with special focus on whether IAA for *take* instances is improved, and whether performance of automatic Semantic Role Labeling and Word Sense Disambiguation applications trained on this data is improved. If results in these areas are promising, this research will shift to analyzing *make, get,* and *have* MWEs with this methodology.

Acknowledgments

We gratefully acknowledge the support of the National Science Foundation Grant NSF-IIS-1116782, A Bayesian Approach to Dynamic Lexical Resources for Flexible Language Processing, and funding under the BOLT and Machine

Reading programs, HR0011-11-C-0145 (BOLT) FA8750-09-C-0179 (M.R.). Any opinions, findings, and conclusions or recommendations expressed in this material are those of the authors and do not necessarily reflect the views of the National Science Foundation.

References

L. Banarescu, C. Bonial, S. Cai, M. Georgescu, K. Griffitt, U. Hermjakob, K. Knight, P. Koehn, M. Palmer, and N. Schneider 2013. Abstract Meaning Representation for Sembanking. *Proceedings of the Linguistic Annotation Workshop.*

Claire Bonial, Julia Bonn, Kathryn Conger, Jena D. Hwang and Martha Palmer. In preparation. PropBank: Semantics of New Predicate Types. *Proceedings of the Language Resources and Evaluation Conference - LREC-2014.* Reykjavik, Iceland.

Jan Hajič, Eva Hajičov, Jarmila Panevov, Petr Sgall, Silvie Cinkov, Eva Fučkov, Marie Mikulov, Petr Pajas, Jan Popelka, Jiř Semecký, Jana Šindlerov, Jan Štěpnek, Josef Toman, Zdeňka Urešov, Zdeněk Žabokrtský. 2012. *Prague Czech-English Dependency Treebank 2.0.* Linguistic Data Consortium, Philadelphia.

Afsaneh Fazly. 2007. *Automatic Acquisition of Lexical Knowledge about Multiword Predicates.* PhD Thesis, Department of Computer Science, University of Toronto.

Christiane Fellbaum (Ed.) 1998. *Wordnet: An Electronic Lexical Database.* MIT press, Cambridge.

Jena D. Hwang, Archna Bhatia, Claire Bonial, Aous Mansouri, Ashwini Vaidya, Nianwen Xue and Martha Palmer. 2010. PropBank Annotation of Multilingual Light Verb Constructions *Proceedings of the Linguistic Annotation Workshop held in conjunction with ACL-2010.* Uppsala, Sweden.

Adam Kilgarriff, Pavel Rychly, Pavel Smrz, and David Tugwell. 2004. The Sketch Engine. *Proceedings of EURALEX.* Lorient, France.

Chi-kiu Lo, Meriem Beloucif, and Dekai Wu. 2013. Improving machine translation into Chinese by tuning against Chinese MEANT. *Proceedings of 10th International Workshop on Spoken Language Translation (IWSLT 2013).* Heidelberg, Germany.

Martha Palmer, Daniel Gildea, and Paul Kingsbury. 2005. The Proposition Bank: An annotated corpus of semantic roles. *Computational Linguistics* 31(1):71–106.

Ivan Sag, Timothy Baldwin, Francis Bond, Ann Copestake and Dan Flickinger. 2002. Multiword Expressions: A Pain in the Neck for NLP. *In Proceedings of the Third International Conference on Intelligent Text processing and Computational Linguistics (CICLING 2002)* 1–15. Mexico City, Mexico

Paraphrasing Swedish Compound Nouns in Machine Translation

Edvin Ullman and **Joakim Nivre**
Department of Linguistics and Philology, Uppsala University
edvinu@stp.lingfil.uu.se joakim.nivre@lingfil.uu.se

Abstract

This paper examines the effect of paraphrasing noun-noun compounds in statistical machine translation from Swedish to English. The paraphrases are meant to elicit the underlying relationship that holds between the compounding nouns, with the use of prepositional and verb phrases. Though some types of noun-noun compounds are too lexicalized, or have some other qualities that make them unsuitable for paraphrasing, a set of roughly two hundred noun-noun compounds are identified, split and paraphrased to be used in experiments on statistical machine translation. The results indicate a slight improvement in translation of the paraphrased compound nouns, with a minor loss in overall BLEU score.

1 Introduction

Swedish is a highly productive language, new words can be constructed fairly easily by concatenating one word with another. This is done across word classes, although, as can be expected, predominantly with content words. Due to this high productivity, an exhaustive dictionary of noun compounds in Swedish does not, and can not exist. Instead, in this project, noun compounds are extracted from the Swedish Europarl corpus (Koehn, 2005) and a subset of Swedish Wikipedia,[1] using a slight modification of the splitting method described in Stymne and Holmqvist (2008), based on previous work by Koehn and Knight (2003).

The assumption that paraphrases of noun compounds can help in machine translation is supported in Nakov and Hearst (2013). Although this study was conducted with English compound nouns, a similar methodology is applied to the Swedish data. The split compound nouns are paraphrased using prepositional and verb phrases, relying on native speaker intuition for the quality and correctness of the paraphrases. A corpus is then paraphrased using the generated paraphrases and used to train a statistical machine translation system to test whether or not an improvement of quality can be observed in relation to a baseline system trained on the unmodified corpus. The results show a minor improvement in translation quality for the paraphrased compounds with a minor loss in overall BLEU score.

2 Background

Previous studies on the semantics of compound nouns have, at least for the English language, in general focused on finding abstract categories to distinguish different compound nouns from each other. Although different in form, the main idea is that a finite set of relations hold between the constituents of all compound nouns. Experiments have been done to analyse such categories in Girju et al. (2005), and applied studies on paraphrasing compound nouns with some form of predicative representation of these abstract categories were performed in Nakov and Hearst (2013).

Studies on Swedish compound nouns have had a slightly different angle. As Swedish noun compounding is done in a slightly different manner than in English, two nouns can be adjoined to form a third, two focal points in previous studies have been detecting compound nouns (Sjöbergh and Kann, 2004) and splitting compound nouns (Stymne and Holmqvist, 2008; Stymne, 2009).

Swedish nouns are compounded by concatenat-

[1] http://sv.wikipedia.org/

Type	Interfixes	Example
None		riskkapital (risk + kapital) *risk capital*
Additions	*-s -t*	frihetslängtan (frihet + längtan) *longing for peace*
Truncations	*-a -e*	pojkvän (pojke + vän) *boyfriend*
Combinations	*-a/-s -a/-t* *-e/-s -e/-t*	arbetsgrupp (arbete + grupp) *working group*

Table 1: Compound formation in Swedish; adapted from Stymne and Holmqvist (2008).

ing nouns to each other, creating a single unbroken unit. Compound nouns sometimes come with the interfixes *-s* or *-t*, sometimes without the trailing *-e* or *-a* from the first compounding noun, and sometimes a combination of the two. It should be noted that this is not an exhaustive list of interfixes, there are some other, more specific rules for noun compounding, justified by for example orthographic conventions, not included in Table 1, nor covered by the splitting algorithm. Table 1, adapted from Stymne and Holmqvist (2008), shows the more common modifications and their combinations.

In Koehn and Knight (2003) an algorithm for splitting compound nouns is described. The algorithm works by iterating over potential split points for all tokens of an input corpus. The geometrical mean of the frequencies of the potential constituents are then used to evaluate whether the token split actually is a compound noun or not.

3 Paraphrasing Compound Nouns

To extract candidate compound nouns for paraphrasing, we first tagged the Swedish Europarl corpus and a subset of Swedish Wikipedia using TnT (Brants, 2000) trained on the Stockholm-Umeå Corpus. The resulting corpus was used to compile a frequency dictionary and a tag dictionary, which were given as input to a modified version of the splitting algorithm from Koehn and Knight (2003), producing a list of nouns with possible split points and the constituents and their tags, if any, sorted by descending frequency. The modifications to the splitting algorithm include a lower bound, ignoring all tokens shorter than 6 characters in the corpus. This length restriction is added with the intention of removing noise and lowering running time. Another constraint added is not to consider substrings shorter than 3 characters. The third and last change to the algorithm is the addition of a length similarity bias heuristic to decide between possible split points when there are multiple candidates with a similar result, giving a higher score to a split point that generates substrings which are more similar in length.

Due to the construction of the splitting algorithm, not all split nouns are noun compounds, and without any gold standard to verify against, a set of 200 compound nouns were manually selected by choosing the top 200 valid compounds from the frequency-sorted list. The split compound nouns were then paraphrased by a native speaker of Swedish and validated by two other native speakers of Swedish. The paraphrases were required to be *exhaustive* (not leave out important semantic information), *precise* (not include irrelevant information), and *standardized* (not deviate from other paraphrases in terms of structure).

Nakov and Hearst (2013) have shown that verbal paraphrases are superior to the more sparse prepositional paraphrases, but also that prepositional paraphrases are more efficient for machine translation experiments. However, when examining the compound nouns closely it becomes obvious that the potential paraphrases fall in one of the following four categories. The first category is compound nouns that are easy to paraphrase by a prepositional phrase only, (Examples 1a, 1b), sometimes with several possible prepositions, as in the latter case.

(1) a. psalmförfattare (hymn writer)
författare av psalmer
writer of hymns

b. järnvägsstation (railway station)
station {för, på, längs} järnväg
station {for, on, along} railway

The second category overlaps somewhat with the first category in that the compound nouns could be paraphrased using only a prepositional phrase, but some meaning is undoubtedly lost in doing so. As such, the more suitable paraphrases contain both prepositional and verb phrases (Examples 2a, 2b).

(2) a. barnskådespelare (child actor)
skådespelare som är barn
actor who is child

b. studioalbum (studio album)
album inspelat i en studio
album recorded in a studio

The third and fourth category represent noun compounds that are not necessarily decomposable into their constituents. Noun compounds in the third category can be paraphrased with some difficulty using prepositional phrases, verb phrases as well as deeper knowledge of the semantics and pragmatics of Swedish (Examples 3a, 3b).

(3) a. världskrig (world war)
krig som drabbar hela världen
war that affects whole world

b. längdskidåkning (cross-country skiing)
skidåkning på plan mark
skiing on level ground

Noun compounds in the fourth category are even harder, if not impossible to paraphrase. The meaning of compound nouns that fall into this category cannot be extracted from the constituents, or the meaning has been obscured over time (Examples 4a, 4b). There is no use paraphrasing these compound nouns, and as such they are left out.

(4) a. stadsrättighet (city rights)

b. domkyrka (cathedral)

All compound nouns that are decomposable into their constituents were paraphrased according to the criteria listed above as far as possible.

4 Machine Translation Experiments

To evaluate the effect of compound paraphrasing, a phrase-based statistical machine translation system was trained on a subset of roughly 55,000 sentences from Swedish-English Europarl, with the Swedish compound nouns paraphrased before training. The system was trained using Moses (Koehn et al., 2007) with default settings, using a 5-gram language model created from the English side of the training corpus using SRILM (Stolcke, 2002). A test set was paraphrased in the same way and run through the decoder. We tested two versions of the system, one where all 200 paraphrases were used, and one where only the paraphrases in the first two categories (transparent prepositional and verb phrases) were used. As a baseline, we used a system trained with the same settings on the unmodified training corpus and applied to the unmodified test corpus.

The systems were evaluated in two ways. First, we computed standard BLEU scores. Secondly, the translation of paraphrased compounds was manually evaluated, by the author, in a random sample of 100 sentences containing one or more of the paraphrased compounds. Since the two paraphrase systems used different paraphrase sets, the manual evaluation was performed on two different samples, in both cases comparing to the baseline system. The results are shown in Table 2.

Looking first at the BLEU scores, we see that there is a small drop for both paraphrase systems. This drop in performance is most certainly a side effect of the design of the paraphrasing script. There is a certain crudeness in how inflections are handled resulting in sentences that may be ungrammatical, albeit only slightly. Inflections in the compounding nouns is retained. However, in paraphrases of category 2 and 3, the verbs are always in the present tense, as deriving the tense from the context can be hard to do with enough precision to make it worthwhile. Consequently, the slightly better score for the system that only uses paraphrases of category 1 and 2 is probably just due to the fact that fewer compounds are paraphrased with verbal paraphrases.

Turning to the manual evaluation, we see first of all that the baseline does a decent job translating the compound nouns, with 88/100 correct translations in the first sample and 81/100 in the second sample. Nevertheless, both paraphrase systems achieve slightly higher scores. The system using all paraphrases improves from 88 to 93, and the system that only uses the transparent paraphrases improves from 81 and 90. Neither of these differences is statistically significant, however. McNemar's test (McNemar, 1947) gives a p value of 0.23 for S1 and 0.11 for S2. So, even if it is likely that the paraphrase systems can improve the quality of compound translation, despite a drop in the overall BLEU score, a larger sample would be needed to fully verify this.

5 Discussion

The results from both the automatic and the manual evaluation are inconclusive. On the one hand, overall translation quality, as measured by BLEU, is lowered, if only slightly. On the other, the manual evaluation shows that, for the paraphrased

System	BLEU	Comp	
		S1	S2
Baseline	26.63	88	81
All paraphrases	26.50	93	–
Paraphrases 1–2	26.59	–	90

Table 2: Experimental results. Comp = translation of compounds; S1 = sample 1; S2 = sample 2.

compound nouns, the experimental decoders perform better than the baseline. However, this improvement cannot be established to be statistically significant. This does not necessarily mean that paraphrasing as a general concept is flawed in terms of translation quality, but judging from these preliminary results, further experiments with paraphrasing compound nouns need to address a few issues.

The lack of quality in the paraphrases, probably attributable to how inflections are handled in the paraphrasing scripts, might be the reason why the first experimental system performs worse than the second. This could indicate that there is little to be won in paraphrasing more complex compound nouns. Another possible explanation lies in the corpus. The tone in the Europarl corpus is very formal, and this is not necessarily the case with the more complex paraphrases.

The number of compound nouns actually paraphrased might also attribute to the less than stellar results. If, when training the experimental systems using the paraphrased Swedish corpora, the number of non-paraphrased compound nouns outweigh the number of paraphrased compound nouns the impact of the paraphrases might actually only distort the translation models. This could very well be the problem here, and it is hard from these experiments to judge whether or not the solution is to have more paraphrasing, or none at all.

6 Conclusion

We have reported a pilot study on using paraphrasing of compound nouns to improve the quality of machine translation from Swedish to English, building on previous work by Nakov and Hearst (2013). The experimental results are inconclusive, but there is at least weak evidence that this technique may improve translation quality specifically for compounds, although it may have a negative effect on other aspects of the translation. Further experiments could shed some light on this.

There are a couple of routes that are interesting to follow from here. In Nakov and Hearst (2013), a number of verbal and prepositional paraphrases are gathered through the means of crowd sourcing, and compared to paraphrases gathered from a simple wild card keyword search using a web based search engine. Since the paraphrases in the experiments described in this paper are done by the author and verified by no more than two other native speakers of Swedish, the paraphrases might not be generic enough. By crowd sourcing paraphrase candidates the impact of one individual's personal style and tone can be mitigated.

Another interesting topic for further research is the one of automated compound noun detection. The algorithm used for splitting compound nouns returns a confidence score which is based on the geometrical mean of the frequencies of the constituents together with some heuristics based on things such as relative length of the constituents and whether or not the constituent was found at all in the corpus. This confidence score could potentially be used for ranking not the most frequently occurring compound nouns, but the compounds where the classifier is most confident.

A number of improvements on the applied system can probably lead to a wider coverage. For one, to alter the algorithm so as to allow for recursive splitting would help in detecting and disambiguating compound nouns consisting of three or more constituents. This might be helpful since, as previously mentioned, Swedish is a highly productive language, and it is quite common to see compound nouns consisting of three or more constituents. It should be noted however, that for this to have the desired effect, the paraphrasing would have to be done recursively as well. This could potentially lead to very long sentences generated from very short ones, if the sentence includes a compound consisting of three or more parts.

Some other minor improvements or possible extensions over the current implementation includes taking into account all orthographical irregularities to get a broader coverage, running the algorithm over a more domain specific corpus to get more relevant results, and finally, automating the actual paraphrasing. This last step, however, is of course far from trivial.

References

Thorsten Brants. 2000. TnT: A statistical part-of-speech tagger. In *Proceedings of the 6th Conference on Applied Natural Language Processing*, pages 224–231.

Roxana Girju, Dan Moldovan, Marta Tatu, and Daniel Antohe. 2005. On the Semantics of Noun Compounds. *Computer Speech & Language*, 19(4):479–496.

Philipp Koehn and Kevin Knight. 2003. Empirical methods for compound splitting. In *Proceedings of the 10th Conference on European Chapter of the Association for Computational Linguistics*, pages 187–193.

Philipp Koehn, Hieu Hoang, Alexandra Birch, Chris Callison-Burch, Marcello Federico, Nicola Bertoldi, Brooke Cowan, Wade Shen, Christine Moran, and Richard Zens. 2007. Moses: Open source toolkit for statistical machine translation. In *Proceedings of the 45th Annual Meeting of the ACL on Interactive Poster and Demonstration Sessions*, pages 177–180.

Philipp Koehn. 2005. Europarl: A parallel corpus for statistical machine translation. In *Proceedings of the 10th Machine Translation Summit*, pages 79–86.

Quinn McNemar. 1947. Note on the Sampling Error of the Difference Between Correlated Proportions or Percentages. *Psychometrika*, 12(2):153–157.

Preslav I. Nakov and Marti A. Hearst. 2013. Semantic Interpretation of Noun Compounds Using Verbal and Other Paraphrases. *ACM Transactions on Speech and Language Processing*, 10(3):1–51.

Jonas Sjöbergh and Viggo Kann. 2004. Finding the correct interpretation of swedish compounds, a statistical approach. In *Proceedings of the 4th International Conference on Language Resources and Evaluation*.

Andreas Stolcke. 2002. SRILM: An extensible language modeling toolkit. In *Proceedings of the 7th International Conference on Spoken Language Processing*.

Sara Stymne and Maria Holmqvist. 2008. Processing of swedish compounds for phrase-based statistical machine translation. In *Proceedings of the 12th Annual Conference of the European Association for Machine Translation*, pages 180–189.

Sara Stymne. 2009. *Compound Processing for Phrase-Based Statistical Machine Translation*. Ph.D. thesis, Department of Computer and Information Science, Linköpings Univ.

Feature Norms of German Noun Compounds

Stephen Roller
Department of Computer Science
The University of Texas at Austin
roller@cs.utexas.edu

Sabine Schulte im Walde
Institut für Maschinelle Sprachverarbeitung
Universität Stuttgart, Germany
schulte@ims.uni-stuttgart.de

Abstract

This paper presents a new data collection of feature norms for 572 German noun-noun compounds. The feature norms complement existing data sets for the same targets, including compositionality ratings, association norms, and images. We demonstrate that the feature norms are potentially useful for research on the noun-noun compounds and their semantic transparency: The feature overlap of the compounds and their constituents correlates with human ratings on the compound–constituent degrees of compositionality, $\rho = 0.46$.

1 Introduction

Feature norms are short descriptions of typical attributes for a set of objects. They often describe the visual appearance (a firetruck *is red*), function or purpose (a cup *holds liquid*), location (mushrooms grow *in forests*), and relationships between objects (a cheetah *is a cat*). The underlying features are usually elicited by asking a subject to carefully describe a cue object, and recording their responses.

Feature norms have been widely used in psycholinguistic research on conceptual representations in semantic memory. Prominent collections have been pursued by McRae et al. (2005) for living vs. non-living basic-level concepts; by Vinson and Vigliocco (2008) for objects and events; and by Wu and Barsalou (2009) for noun and noun phrase objects. In recent years, feature norms have also acted as a loose proxy for perceptual information in data-intensive computational models of semantic tasks, in order to bridge the gap between language and the real world (Andrews et al., 2009; Silberer and Lapata, 2012; Roller and Schulte im Walde, 2013).

In this paper, we present a new resource of feature norms for a set of 572 concrete, depictable German nouns. More specifically, these nouns include 244 noun-noun compounds and their corresponding constituents. For example, we include features for *'Schneeball'* ('snowball'), *'Schnee'* ('snow'), and *'Ball'* ('ball'). Table 1 presents the most prominent features of this example compound and its constituents. Our collection complements existing data sets for the same targets, including compositionality ratings (von der Heide and Borgwaldt, 2009); associations (Schulte im Walde et al., 2012; Schulte im Walde and Borgwaldt, 2014); and images (Roller and Schulte im Walde, 2013).

The remainder of this paper details the collection process of the feature norms, discusses two forms of cleansing and normalization we employed, and performs quantitative and qualitative analyses. We find that the normalization procedures improve quality in terms of feature tokens per feature type, that the normalized feature norms have a desirable distribution of features per cue, and that the feature norms are useful in semantic models to predict compositionality.

2 Feature Norm Collection

We employ Amazon Mechanical Turk (AMT)[1] for data collection. AMT is an online crowdsourcing platform where *requesters* post small, atomic tasks which require manual completion by humans. Workers can complete these tasks, called *HITs*, in order to earn a small bounty.

2.1 Setup and Data

Workers were presented with a simple page asking them to describe the typical attributes of a given noun. They were explicitly informed in English that only native German speakers should complete

[1] http://www.mturk.com

Schneeball 'snowball'			*Schnee* 'snow'			*Ball* 'ball'		
ist kalt	'is cold'	8	*ist kalt*	'is cold'	13	*ist rund*	'is round'	14
ist rund	'is round'	7	*ist weiß*	'is white'	13	*zum Spielen*	'for playing'	4
aus Schnee	'made from snow'	7	*im Winter*	'in the winter'	6	*rollt*	'rolls'	2
ist weiß	'is white'	7	*fällt*	'falls'	3	*wird geworfen*	'is thrown'	2
formt man	'is formed'	2	*schmilzt*	'melts'	2	*ist bunt*	'is colorful'	2
wirft man	'is thrown'	2	*hat Flocken*	'has flakes'	2	*Fußball*	'football'	2
mit den Händen	'with hands'	2	*ist wässrig*	'is watery'	1	*Basketball*	'basketball'	2

Table 1: Most frequent features for example compound *Schneeball* and its constituents.

the tasks. All other instructions were given in German. Workers were given 7 example features for the nouns *'Tisch'* ('table') and *'Katze'* ('cat'), and instructed to provide typical attributes per noun. Initially, workers were required to provide 6-10 features per cue and were only paid \$0.02 per hit, but very few workers completed the hits. After lowering the requirements and increasing the reward, we received many more workers and collected the data more quickly. Workers could also mark a word as unfamiliar or provide additional commentary if desired.

We collected responses from September 21, 2012 until January 31, 2013. Workers who were obvious spammers were rejected and not rewarded payment. Typically spammers pasted text from Google, Wikipedia, or the task instructions and were easy to spot. Users who failed to follow instructions (responded in English, did not provide the minimum number of features, or gave nonsensical responses) were also rejected without payment. Users who put in a good faith effort and consistently gave reasonable responses had all of their responses accepted and rewarded.

In total, 98 different workers completed at least one accepted hit, but the top 25 workers accounted for nearly 90% of the responses. We accepted 28,404 different response tokens over 18,996 response types for 572 different cues, or roughly 50 features per cue.

3 Cleansing and Normalization

We provide two cleaned and normalized versions of our feature norms.[2] In the first version, we correct primarily orthographic mistakes such as inconsistent capitalization, spelling errors, and surface usage, but feature norms remain otherwise unchanged. This version will likely be more useful to researchers interested in more subtle variations and distinctions made by the workers.

The second version of our feature norms are more aggressively normalized, to reduce the quantity of unique and low frequency responses while maintaining the spirit of the original response. The resulting data is considerably less sparse than the orthographically normalized version. This version is likely to be more useful for research that is highly affected by sparse data, such as multimodal experiments (Andrews et al., 2009; Silberer and Lapata, 2012; Roller and Schulte im Walde, 2013).

3.1 Orthographic Normalization

Orthographic normalization is performed in four automatic passes and one manual pass in the following order:

Letter Case Normalization: Many workers inconsistently capitalize the first word of feature norms as though they are writing a complete sentence. For example, *'ist rund'* and *'Ist rund'* ('is round') were both provided for the cue *'Ball'*. We cannot normalize capitalization by simply using lowercase everywhere, as the first letter of German nouns should always be capitalized. To handle the most common instances, we lowercase the first letter of features that began with articles, modal verbs, prepositions, conjunctions, or the high-frequency verbs *'kommt'*, *'wird'*, and *'ist'*.

Umlaut Normalization: The same German word may sometimes be spelled differently because some workers use German keyboards (which have the letters ä, ö, ü, and ß), and others use English keyboards (which do not). We automatically normalize to the umlaut form (i.e. *'gruen'* to *'grün'*, *'weiss'* to *'weiß'*) whenever two workers gave *both versions for the same cue*.

Spelling Correction: We automatically correct common misspellings (such as *errecihen* $\rightarrow$ *erreichen*), using a list from previous collection experiments (Schulte im Walde et al., 2008; Schulte im Walde et al., 2012). The list was created semi-automatically, and manually corrected.

[2] The norms can be downloaded from www.ims.uni-stuttgart.de/forschung/ressourcen/experiment-daten/feature-norms.en.html.

Usage of *'ist'* and *'hat'*: Workers sometimes drop the verbs *'ist'* ('is') and *'hat'* ('has'), e.g. the worker writes only *'rund'* ('round') instead of *'ist rund'*, or *'Obst'* ('fruit') instead of *'hat Obst'*. We normalize to the *'ist'* and *'hat'* forms when two workers gave *both versions for the same cue*. Note that we cannot automatically do this across separate cues, as the relationship may change: a tree *has* fruit, but a banana *is* fruit.

Manual correction: Following the above automatic normalizations, we manually review all non-unique responses. In this pass, responses are normalized and corrected with respect to punctuation, capitalization, spelling, and orthography. Roughly 170 response types are modified in this phase.

3.2 Variant Normalization

The second manual pass consists of more aggressive normalization of expression variants. In this pass, features are manually edited to minimize the number of feature types while preserving as much semantic meaning as possible:

- Replacing plurals with singulars;
- Removing modal verbs, e.g. *'kann Kunst sein'* ('can be art') to *'ist Kunst'*;
- Removing quantifiers and hedges, e.g. *'ist meistens blau'* ('is mostly blue') to *'ist blau'*;
- Splitting into atomic norms, e.g. *'ist weiß oder schwarz'* ('is white or black') to *'ist weiß'* and *'ist schwarz'*, or *'jagt im Wald'* ('hunts in forest') to *'jagt'* and *'im Wald'*;
- Simplifying verbiage, e.g. *'ist in der Farbe schwarz'* ('is in the color black') to *'ist schwarz'*.

These selected normalizations are by no means comprehensive or exhaustive, but do handle a large portion of the cases. In total, we modify roughly 5400 tokens over 1300 types.

4 Quantitative Analysis

In the following two analyses, we explore the type and token counts of our feature norms across the steps in the cleansing process, and analyze the underlying distributions of the features per cues.

Type and Token counts Table 2 shows the token and type counts for all features in each step of the cleansing process. We also present the counts for *non-idiosyncratic* features, or features which are provided for at least two distinct cues. The orthographic normalizations generally lower the number of total and non-idiosyncratic types, and increase the number of non-idiosyncratic tokens. This indicates we are successfully identifying and correcting many simple orthographic errors, resulting in a less sparse matrix. The necessary amount of manual correction is relatively low, indicating we are able to catch the majority of mistakes using simple, automatic methods.

Data Version of Responses	Total		Non-idiosyncratic	
	Types	**Tokens**	**Types**	**Tokens**
Raw	18,996	28,404	2,029	10,675
Case	18,848	28,404	2,018	10,801
Umlaut	18,700	28,404	1,967	10,817
Spelling	18,469	28,404	1,981	11,072
ist/hat	18,317	28,404	1,924	11,075
Manual	18,261	28,404	1,889	11,106
Aggressive	17,503	28,739	1,374	11,848

Table 2: Counts in the cleansing process.

The more aggressively normalized norms are considerably different than the orthographically normalized norms. Notably, the number of total tokens increases from the atomic splits. The data is also less sparse and more robust, as indicated by the drops in both total and non-idiosyncratic types. Furthermore, the number of non-idiosyncratic tokens also increases considerably, indicating we were able to find numerous edge cases and place them in existing, frequently-used bins.

Number of Features per Cue Another important aspect of the data set is the number of features per cue. An ideal feature norm data set would contain a roughly equal number of (non-idiosyncratic) features for every cue; if most of the features are underrepresented, with a majority of the features lying in only a few cues, then our data set may only properly represent for these few, heavily represented cues.

Figure 1 shows the number of features per cue for (a) all features and (b) the non-idiosyncratic features, for the aggressively normalized data set. In the first histogram, we see a clear bimodal distribution around the number of features per cue. This is an artifact of the two parts of our collection process: the shorter, wider distribution corresponds to the first part of collection, where workers gave more responses for less reward. The taller, skinnier distribution corresponds to the second half of collection, when workers were rewarded more for less work. The second collection procedure was clearly effective in raising the number of hits completed, but resulted in fewer features per cue.

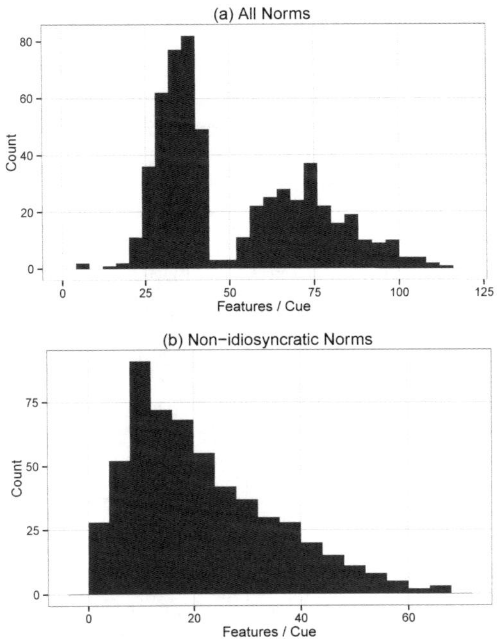

Figure 1: Distribution of features per cue.

In the second histogram, we see only the non-idiosyncratic features for each cue. Unlike the first histogram, we see only one mode with a relatively long tail. This indicates that mandating more features per worker (as in the first collection process) often results in more idiosyncratic features, and not necessarily a stronger representation of each cue. We also see that roughly 85% of the cues have at least 9 non-idiosyncratic features each. In summary, our representations are nicely distributed for the majority of cues.

5 Qualitative Analysis

Our main motivation to collect the feature norms for the German noun compounds and their constituents was that the features provide insight into the semantic properties of the compounds and their constituents and should therefore represent a valuable resource for cognitive and computational linguistics research on compositionality. The following two case studies demonstrate that the feature norms indeed have that potential.

Predicting the Compositionality The first case study relies on a simple feature overlap measure to predict the degree of compositionality of the compound–constituent pairs of nouns: We use the proportion of shared features of the compound and a constituent with respect to the total number of features of the compound. The degree of compositionality of a compound noun is calculated with respect to each constituent of the compound.

For example, if a compound noun N_0 received a total of 30 features (tokens), out of which it shares 20 with the first constituent N_1 and 10 with the second constituent N_2, the predicted degrees of compositionality are $\frac{20}{30} = 0.67$ for N_0–N_1, and $\frac{10}{30} = 0.33$ for N_0–N_2. The predicted degrees of compositionality are compared against the mean compositionality judgments as collected by von der Heide and Borgwaldt (2009), using the Spearman rank-order correlation coefficient. The resulting correlations are $\rho = 0.45, p < .000001$ for the standard normalized norms, and $\rho = 0.46, p < .000001$ for the aggressively normalized norms, which we consider a surprisingly successful result concerning our simple measure. Focusing on the compound–head pairs, the feature norms reached $\rho = 0.57$ and $\rho = 0.59$, respectively.

Perceptual Model Information As mentioned in the Introduction, feature norms have also acted as a loose proxy for perceptual information in data-intensive computational models of semantic tasks. The second case study is taken from Roller and Schulte im Walde (2013), who integrated feature norms as one type of perceptual information into an extension and variations of the LDA model by Andrews et al. (2009). A bimodal LDA model integrating textual co-occurrence features and our feature norms significantly outperformed the LDA model that only relied on the textual co-occurrence. The evaluation of the LDA models was performed on the same compositionality ratings as described in the previous paragraph.

6 Conclusion

This paper presented a new collection of feature norms for 572 German noun-noun compounds. The feature norms complement existing data sets for the same targets, including compositionality ratings, association norms, and images.

We have described our collection process, and the cleaning and normalization, and we have shown both the orthographically normalized and more aggressively normalized feature norms to be of higher quality than the raw responses in terms of types per token, and that the normalized feature norms have a desirable distribution of features per cue. We also demonstrated by two case studies that the norms represent a valuable resource for research on compositionality.

References

Mark Andrews, Gabriella Vigliocco, and David Vinson. 2009. Integrating experiential and distributional data to learn semantic representations. *Psychological Review*, 116(3):463.

Ken McRae, George S. Cree, Mark S. Seidenberg, and Chris McNorgan. 2005. Semantic feature production norms for a large set of living and nonliving things. *Behavior Research Methods*, 37(4):547–559.

Stephen Roller and Stephen Schulte im Walde. 2013. A multimodal LDA model integrating textual, cognitive and visual modalities. In *Proceedings of the 2013 Joint Conference on Empirical Methods in Natural Language Processing and Computational Natural Language Learning*, pages 1146–1157, Seattle, Washington, USA.

Sabine Schulte im Walde and Susanne Borgwaldt. 2014. Association norms for German noun compounds and their constituents. Under review.

Sabine Schulte im Walde, Alissa Melinger, Michael Roth, and Andrea Weber. 2008. An empirical characterisation of response types in German association norms. *Research on Language and Computation*, 6(2):205–238.

Sabine Schulte im Walde, Susanne Borgwaldt, and Ronny Jauch. 2012. Association norms of German noun compounds. In *Proceedings of the 8th International Conference on Language Resources and Evaluation*, pages 632–639, Istanbul, Turkey.

Carina Silberer and Mirella Lapata. 2012. Grounded models of semantic representation. In *Proceedings of the 2012 Joint Conference on Empirical Methods in Natural Language Processing and Computational Natural Language Learning*, pages 1423–1433, Jeju Island, Korea.

David Vinson and Gabriella Vigliocco. 2008. Semantic feature production norms for a large set of objects and events. *Behavior Research Methods*, 40(1):183–190.

Claudia von der Heide and Susanne Borgwaldt. 2009. Assoziationen zu Unter-, Basis- und Oberbegriffen. Eine explorative Studie. In *Proceedings of the 9th Norddeutsches Linguistisches Kolloquium*, pages 51–74.

Ling-ling Wu and Lawrence W. Barsalou. 2009. Perceptual simulation in conceptual combination: Evidence from property generation. *Acta Psychologica*, 132:173–189.

Identifying collocations using cross-lingual association measures

Lis Pereira[1], Elga Strafella[2], Kevin Duh[1] and Yuji Matsumoto[1]
[1]Nara Institute of Science and Technology, 8916-5 Takayama, Ikoma, Nara 630-0192, Japan
{lis-k, kevinduh, matsu}@is.naist.jp
[2]National Institute for Japanese Language and Linguistics, 10-2 Midoricho, Tachikawa, Tokyo 190-8561, Japan
strafelga@gmail.com

Abstract

We introduce a simple and effective cross-lingual approach to identifying collocations. This approach is based on the observation that true collocations, which cannot be translated word for word, will exhibit very different association scores before and after literal translation. Our experiments in Japanese demonstrate that our cross-lingual association measure can successfully exploit the combination of bilingual dictionary and large monolingual corpora, outperforming monolingual association measures.

1 Introduction

Collocations are part of the wide range of linguistic phenomena such as idioms (*kick the bucket*), compounds (*single-mind*) and fixed phrases (*by and large*) defined as Multiword Expressions (MWEs). MWEs, and collocations, in particular, are very pervasive not only in English, but in other languages as well. Although handling MWEs properly is crucial in many natural language processing (NLP) tasks, manually annotating them is a very costly and time consuming task.

The main goal of this work-in-progress is, therefore, to evaluate the effectiveness of a simple cross-lingual approach that allows us to automatically identify collocations in a corpus and subsequently distinguish them according to one of their intrinsic properties: the meaning of the expression cannot be predicted from the meaning of the parts, i.e. they are characterized by limited compositionality (Manning and Schütze, 1999). Given an expression, we predict whether the expression(s) resulted from the word by word translation is also commonly used in another language. If not, that might be evidence that the original expression is a collocation (or an idiom). This can be captured by the ratio of association scores, assigned by association measures, in the target vs. source language. The results indicate that our method improves the precision comparing with standard methods of MWE identification through monolingual association measures.

2 Related Work

Most previous works on MWEs and, more specifically, collocation identification (Evert, 2008; Seretan, 2011; Pecina, 2010; Ramisch, 2012) employ a standard methodology consisting of two steps: 1) candidate extraction, where candidates are extracted based on n-grams or morphosyntactic patterns and 2) candidate filtering, where association measures are applied to rank the candidates based on association scores and consequently remove noise. One drawback of such method is that association measures might not be able to perform a clear-cut distinction between collocation and non-collocations, since they only assign scores based on statistical evidence, such as co-occurrence frequency in the corpus. Our cross-lingual association measure ameliorates this problem by exploiting both corpora in two languages, one of which may be large.

A few studies have attempted to identify non-compositional MWE's using parallel corpora and dictionaries. Melamed (1997) investigates how non-compositional compounds can be detected from parallel corpus by identifying translation divergences in the component words. Pichotta and DeNero (2013) analyses the frequency statistics of an expression and its component words, using many bilingual corpora to identifying phrasal verbs in English. The disadvantage of such approach is that large-scale parallel corpora is available for only a few language pairs. On the other hand, monolingual data is largely and freely available for many languages. Our approach requires only a bilingual dictionary and non-parallel monolingual corpora in both languages.

Salehi and Cook (2013) predict the degree of compositionality using the string distance between the automatic translation into multiple languages of an expression and the individual translation of its components. They use an online database called Panlex (Baldwin et al., 2010), that can translate words and expressions from English into many languages. Tsvetkov and Wintner (2013) is probably the closest work to ours. They trained a Bayesian Network for identfying MWE's and one of the features used is a binary feature that assumes value is 1 if the literal translation of the MWE candidate occurs more than 5 times in a large English corpus.

3 Identifying Collocations

In this research, we predict whether the expression(s) resulted from the translation of the components of a Japanese collocation candidate is/are also commonly used in English. For instance, if we translate the Japanese collocation 面倒を見る *mendou-wo-miru* "to care for someone" (care-を-see)[1] into English word by word, we obtain "see care", which sounds awkward and may not appear in an English corpus very often. On the other hand, the word to word translation of the free combination 映画を見る *eiga-wo-miru* "to see a movie" (movie-を-see) is more prone to appear in an English corpus, since it corresponds to the translation of the expression as well. In our work, we focus on noun-verb expressions in Japanese. Our proposed method consists of three steps:

1) Candidate Extraction: We focus on noun-verb constructions in Japanese. We work with three construction types: object-verb, subject-verb and dative-verb constructions, represented respectively as "noun wo verb (noun-を-verb)", "noun ga verb (noun-が-verb)" and "noun ni verb (noun-に-verb)", respectively. The candidates are extracted from a Japanese corpus using a dependency parser (Kudo and Matsumoto, 2002) and ranked by frequency.

2) Translation of the component words: for each noun-verb candidate, we automatically obtain all the possible English literal translations of the noun and the verb using a Japanese/English dictionary. Using that information, all the possible verb-noun combinations in English are then generated. For instance, for the candidate 本を買う *hon-wo-kau* "to buy a book" (buy-を-book), we take the noun 本 *hon* and the verb 買う *kau* and check their translation given in the dictionary. 本 has translations like "book", "main" and "head" and 買う is translated as "buy". Based on that, possible combinations are "buy book" or "buy main" (we filter out determiners, pronouns, etc.).

3) Ranking of original and derived word to word translated expression: we compare the association score of the original expression in Japanese (calculated using a Japanese corpus) and its corresponding derived word to word translated expressions. If the original expression has a much higher score than its literal translations, it might be a good evidence that we are dealing with a collocation, instead of a free combination.

There is no defined criteria in choosing one particular association measure when applying it in a specific task, since different measures highlight different aspects of collocativity (Evert, 2008). A state-of-the-art, language independent framework that employs the standard methodology to identify MWEs is mwetoolkit (Ramisch, 2012). It ranks the extracted candidates using four different association measures: log-likelihood-ratio, Dice coefficient, pointwise mutual information and Student's *t*-score. We previously conducted experiments with these four measures for Japanese (results are ommited), and Dice coefficient performed best. Using Dice coefficient, we calculate the ratio between the score of the original expression and the average score of its literal translations. Finally, the candidates are ranked by the ratio value. Those that have a high value are expected to be collocations, while those with a low value are expected to be free combinations.

4 Experiment Setup

4.1 Data Set

The following resources were used in our experiments:

Japanese/English dictionary: we used Edict (Breen, 1995), a freely available Japanese/English Dictionary in machine-readable form, containing 110,424 entries. This dictionary was used to find all the possible translations of each Japanese word involved in the candidate (noun and verb). For our test set, all the words were covered by the dictionary. We obtained an average of 4.5 translations per word. All the translations that contains more

[1]In Japanese, を is a case marker that indicates the object-verb dependency relation.

than three words are filtered out. For the translations of the Japanese noun, we only consider the first noun appearing in each translation. For the translations of the Japanese verb, we only consider the first verb/phrasal verb appearing in each translation. For instance, in the Japanese collocation 恋に落ちる *koi-ni-ochiru* "to fall in love" (love-に-fall down)[2], the translations in the dictionary and the ones we consider (shown in bold type) of the noun 恋 *koi* "love" and the verb 落ちる *ochiru* "to fall down" are:

恋: **love** , tender **passion**
落ちる: to **fall down**, to **fail**, to **crash**, to **degenerate**, to **degrade**

Bilingual resource: we used Hiragana Times corpus, a Japanese-English bilingual corpus of magazine articles of Hiragana Times [3], a bilingual magazine written in Japanese and English to introduce Japan to non-Japanese, covering a wide range of topics (culture, society, history, politics, etc.). The corpus contains articles from 2003-2102, with a total of 117,492 sentence pairs. We used the Japanese data to extract the noun-verb collocation candidates using a dependency parser, Cabocha (Kudo and Matsumoto, 2002). For our work, we focus on the object-verb, subject-verb and dative-verb dependency relations. The corpus was also used to calculate the Dice score of each Japanese candidate, using the Japanese data.

Monolingual resource: we used 75,377 English Wikipedia articles, crawled in July 2013. It contains a total of 9.5 million sentences. The data was used to calculate the Dice score of each candidate's derived word to word translated expressions. The corpus was annotated with Part-of-Speech (POS) information, from where we defined POS patterns to extract all the verb-noun and noun-verb sequences, using the MWE toolkit (Ramisch, 2012), which is an integrated framework for MWE treatment, providing corpus preprocessing facilities.

Table 1 shows simple statistics on the Hiragana Times corpus and on the Wikipedia corpus.

4.2 Test set

In order to evaluate our system, the top 100 frequent candidates extracted from Hiragana Times corpus were manually annotated by 4 Japanese native speakers. The judges were asked to make a ternary judgment for each of the candidates on whether the candidate is a collocation, idiom or free combination. For each category, a judge was shown the definition and some examples. We defined collocations as all those expressions where one of the component words preserves its literal meaning, while the other element assumes a slightly different meaning and its use is blocked (i.e. it cannot be substituted by a synonym). Idioms were defined as the semantically and syntactically fixed expressions where all the component words loose their original meaning. Free combinations were defined as all those expressions frequently used where the components preserve their literal meaning. The inter-annotator agreement is computed using Fleiss' Kappa statistic (Fleiss, 1971), since it involves more than 2 annotators. Since our method does not differentiate collocations from idioms (although we plan to work on that as future work), we group collocations and idioms as one class. We obtained a Kappa coefficient of 0.4354, which is considered as showing *moderate* agreement according to Fleiss (1971). Only the candidates identically annotated by the majority of judges (3 or more) were added to the test set, resulting in a number of 87 candidates (36 collocations and 51 free combinations). After that, we obtained a new Kappa coefficient of 0.5427, which is also considered as showing *moderate* agreement (Fleiss, 1971).

	Hiragana Times	Wikipedia
# jp sentences	117,492	-
# en sentences	117,492	9,500,000
# jp tokens	3,949,616	-
# en tokens	2,107,613	247,355,886
# jp noun-verb	31,013	-
# en noun-verb	-	266,033
# en verb-noun	-	734,250

Table 1: Statistics on the Hiragana Times corpus and Wikipedia corpus, showing the number of sentences, number of words and number of noun-verb and verb-noun expressions in English and Japanese.

4.3 Baseline

We compare our proposed method with two baselines: an association measure based system and a Phrase-Based Statistical Machine Translation

[2]に is the dative case marker in Japanese.
[3]http://www.hiraganatimes.com

(SMT) based system.

Monolingual Association Measure: The system ranks the candidates in the test set according to their Dice score calculated using the Hiragana Times Japanese data.

Phrase-Based SMT system: a standard non-factored phrase-based SMT system was built using the open source Moses toolkit (Koehn et al., 2007) with parameters set similar to those of Neubig (2011), who provides a baseline system previously applied to a Japanese-English corpus built from Wikipedia articles. For training, we used Hiragana Times bilingual corpus. The Japanese sentences were word-segmented and the English sentences were tokenized and lowercased. All sentences with size greater than 60 tokens were previously eliminated. The whole English corpus was used as training data for a 5-gram language model built with the SRILM toolkit (Stolcke, 2002).

Similar to what we did for our proposed method, for each candidate in the test set, we find all the possible literally translated expressions (as described in Section 3). In the phrase-table generated after the training step, we look for all the entries that contain the original candidate string and check if at least one of the possible literal translations appear as their corresponding translation. For the entries found, we compute the average of the sum of the candidate's direct and inverse phrase translation probability scores. The direct phrase translation probability and the inverse phrase translation probability (Koehn et al., 2003) are respectively defined as:

$$\Phi(\overline{e}|\overline{f}) = \frac{count(\overline{f},\overline{e})}{\sum_{\overline{f}} count(\overline{f},\overline{e})} \quad (1)$$

$$\Phi(\overline{f}|\overline{e}) = \frac{count(\overline{f},\overline{e})}{\sum_{\overline{e}} count(\overline{f},\overline{e})} \quad (2)$$

Where $\overline{f}$ and $\overline{e}$ indicate a foreign phrase and a source phrase, independently.

The candidates are ranked according to the average score as described previously.

5 Evaluation

In our evaluation, we average the precision considering all true collocations and idioms as threshold points, obtaining the mean average precision (MAP). Differently from the traditional approach used to evaluate an association measure, using MAP we do not need to set a hard threshold.

Table 2 presents the MAP values for our proposed method and for the two baselines. Our cross-lingual method performs best in terms of MAP values against the two baselines. We found out that it performs statistically better only compared to the Monolingual Association Measure baseline[4]. The Monolingual Association Measure baseline performed worst, since free combinations were assigned high scores as well, and the system was not able to perform a clear separation into collocations and non-collocations. The Phrase-Based SMT system obtained a higher MAP value than Monolingual Association measure, but the score may be optimistic since we are testing in-domain. One concern is that there are only a very few bilingual/parallel corpora for the Japanese/English language pair, in case we want to test with a different domain and larger test set. The fact that our proposed method outperforms SMT implies that using such readily-available monolingual data (English Wikipedia) is a better way to exploit cross-lingual information.

Method	MAP value
Monolingual Association Measure	0.54
Phrase-Based SMT	0.67
Proposed Method	**0.71**

Table 2: Mean average precision of proposed method and baselines.

Some cases where the system could not perform well include those where a collocation can also have a literal translation. For instance, in Japanese, there is the collocation 心を開く *kokoro-wo-hiraku* "to open your heart" (heart-を-open), where the literal translation of the noun 心 *kokoro* "heart" and the verb 開く *hiraku* "open" correspond to the translation of the expression as well.

Another case is when the candidate expression has both literal and non-literal meaning. For instance, the collocation 人を見る *hito-wo-miru* (person-を-see) can mean "to see a person", which is the literal meaning, but when used together with the noun 目 *me* "eye", for instance, it can also can mean "to judge human character". When annotating the data, the judges classified as idioms some of those expressions, for instance, because the non-literal meaning is mostly used compared

[4]Statistical significance was calculated using a two-tailed t-test for a confidence interval of 95%.

with the literal meaning. However, our system found that the literal translated expressions are also commonly used in English, which caused the performance decrease.

6 Conclusion and Future Work

In this report of work in progress, we propose a method to distinguish free combinations and collocations (and idioms) by computing the ratio of association measures in source and target languages. We demonstrated that our method, which can exploit existing monolingual association measures on large monolingual corpora, performed better than techniques previously applied in MWE identification.

In the future work, we are interested in increasing the size of the corpus and test set used (for instance, include mid to low frequent MWE's), as well as applying our method to other collocational patterns like Noun-Adjective, Adjective-Noun, Adverb-Verb, in order to verify our approach. We also believe that our approach can be used for other languages as well. We intend to conduct a further investigation on how we can differentiate collocations from idioms. Another step of our research will be towards the integration of the acquired data into a web interface for language learning and learning materials for foreign learners as well.

Acknowledgments

We would like to thank Masashi Shimbo, Xiaodong Liu, Mai Omura, Yu Sawai and Yoriko Nishijima for their valuable help and anonymous reviewers for the helpful comments and advice.

References

Timothy Baldwin, Jonathan Pool, and Susan M Colowick. 2010. Panlex and lextract: Translating all words of all languages of the world. In *Proceedings of the 23rd International Conference on Computational Linguistics: Demonstrations*, pages 37–40. Association for Computational Linguistics.

Jim Breen. 1995. Building an electronic japanese-english dictionary. In *Japanese Studies Association of Australia Conference*. Citeseer.

Stefan Evert. 2008. Corpora and collocations. *Corpus Linguistics. An International Handbook*, 2.

Joseph L Fleiss. 1971. Measuring nominal scale agreement among many raters. *Psychological bulletin*, 76(5):378.

Philipp Koehn, Franz Josef Och, and Daniel Marcu. 2003. Statistical phrase-based translation. In *Proceedings of the 2003 Conference of the North American Chapter of the Association for Computational Linguistics on Human Language Technology-Volume 1*, pages 48–54. Association for Computational Linguistics.

Philipp Koehn, Hieu Hoang, Alexandra Birch, Chris Callison-Burch, Marcello Federico, Nicola Bertoldi, Brooke Cowan, Wade Shen, Christine Moran, Richard Zens, et al. 2007. Moses: Open source toolkit for statistical machine translation. In *Proceedings of the 45th Annual Meeting of the ACL on Interactive Poster and Demonstration Sessions*, pages 177–180. Association for Computational Linguistics.

Taku Kudo and Yuji Matsumoto. 2002. Japanese dependency analysis using cascaded chunking. In *proceedings of the 6th conference on Natural language learning-Volume 20*, pages 1–7. Association for Computational Linguistics.

Christopher D Manning and Hinrich Schütze. 1999. *Foundations of statistical natural language processing*, volume 999. MIT Press.

Dan Melamed. 1997. Automatic discovery of non-compositional compounds in parallel data. EMNLP.

Graham Neubig. 2011. The kyoto free translation task. *Available on line at http://www. phontron. com/kftt.*

Pavel Pecina. 2010. Lexical association measures and collocation extraction. *Language resources and evaluation*, 44(1-2):137–158.

Karl Pichotta and John DeNero. 2013. Identifying phrasal verbs using many bilingual corpora. In *Proceedings of the 2013 Conference on Empirical Methods in Natural Language Processing*, pages 636–646.

Carlos Ramisch. 2012. A generic framework for multiword expressions treatment: from acquisition to applications. In *Proceedings of ACL 2012 Student Research Workshop*, pages 61–66. Association for Computational Linguistics.

Bahar Salehi and Paul Cook. 2013. Predicting the compositionality of multiword expressions using translations in multiple languages.

Violeta Seretan. 2011. *Syntax-based collocation extraction*, volume 44. Springer.

Andreas Stolcke. 2002. Srilm-an extensible language modeling toolkit. In *INTERSPEECH*.

Yulia Tsvetkov and Shuly Wintner. 2013. Identification of multi-word expressions by combining multiple linguistic information sources.

Unsupervised Construction of a Lexicon and a Repository of Variation Patterns for Arabic Modal Multiword Expressions

Rania Al-Sabbagh†, Roxana Girju†, Jana Diesner‡
†Department of Linguistics and Beckman Institute
‡School of Library and Information Science
University of Illinois at Urbana-Champaign, USA
{alsabba1, girju, jdiesner}@illinois.edu

Abstract

We present an unsupervised approach to build a lexicon of Arabic Modal Multiword Expressions (AM-MWEs) and a repository of their variation patterns. These novel resources are likely to boost the automatic identification and extraction of AM-MWEs[1].

1 Introduction

Arabic Modal Multiword Expressions (AM-MWEs) are complex constructions that convey modality senses. We define seven modality senses, based on Palmer's (2001) cross-lingual typology, which are (un)certainty, evidentiality, obligation, permission, commitment, ability and volition.

AM-MWEs range from completely fixed, idiomatic and sometimes semantically-opaque expressions, to morphologically, syntactically and/or lexical productive constructions. As a result, the identification and extraction of AM-MWEs have to rely on both a lexicon and a repository of their variation patterns. To-date and to the best of our knowledge, neither resource is available. Furthermore, AM-MWEs are quite understudied despite the extensive research on general-purpose Arabic MWEs.

To build both the lexicon and the repository, we design a four-stage unsupervised method. **Stage 1**, we use Log-Likelihood Ratio and a root-based procedure to extract candidate AM-MWEs from large Arabic corpora. **Stage 2**, we use token level features with *k*-means clustering to construct two clusters. **Stage 3**, from the clustering output we extract patterns that describe the morphological, syntactic and semantic variations of AM-MWEs, and store them in the pattern repository. **Stage 4,** we use the most frequent variation patterns to bootstrap low-frequency and new AM-MWEs. The final lexicon and repository are manually inspected. Both resources are made publicly available.

The contributions of this paper are: (1) we address the lack of lexica and annotated resources for Arabic linguistic modality; and hence, we support NLP applications and domains that use modality to identify (un)certainty (Diab et al. 2009), detect power relations (Prabhakaran and Rambow 2013), retrieve politeness markers (Danescu-Niculescu-Mizil et al. 2013), extract and reconstruct storylines (Pareti et al. 2013) and classify request-based emails (Lampert et al. 2010); (2) we provide both a lexicon and a repository of variation patterns to help increase recall while keeping precision high for the automatic identification and extraction of productive AM-MWEs; and (3) we explore the morphological, syntactic and lexical properties of the understudied AM-MWEs.

For the rest of this paper, Section 2 defines AM-MWEs. Section 3 outlines related work. Sections 4 describes our unsupervised method. Section 5 describes manual verification and the final resulting resources.

2 What are AM-MWEs?

AM-MWEs are complex constructions that convey (un)certainty, evidentiality, obligation, permission, commitment, ability and volition. Based on their productivity, we define five types of AM-MWEs:

Type 1 includes idiomatic expressions like حتما ولابد *HtmA wlAbd* (must), لعل وعسى *lEl wEsY* (maybe) and فيما يبدو *fymA ybdw* (seemingly).

Type 2 covers morphologically productive expressions such as يرغب في *yrgb fy* (he wants to) and واثق من *wAvq mn* (sure about). They inflect

[1] Both resources are available at http://www.rania-alsabbagh.com/am-mwe.html

AM-MWEs		Unigram Synonym(s)		English Gloss
Arabic	Transliteration	Arabic	Transliteration	
عقدت العزم على	*Eqdt AlEzm ElY*	عزمت - نويت	*Ezmt - nwyt*	I intended (to)
في امكاني ان	*fy AmkAny An*	يمكنني	*ymknny*	I can/I have the ability to
لدي اعتقاد بان	*ldy AEtqAd bAn*	اعتقد	*AEtqd*	I think
هناك احتمال بان	*hnAk AHtmAl bAn*	يُحْتَمَل	*yuHotamal*	possibly/there is a possibility that

Table 1: Example AM-MWEs and their unigram synonyms

for gender, number, person, and possibly for tense, mood and aspect. Neither the head word nor the preposition is replaceable by a synonym. In the literature of MWEs, Type 2 is referred to as phrasal verbs. In the literature of modality, it is referred to as quasi-modals (i.e. modals that subcategorize for prepositions).

Type 3 comprises lexically productive expressions whose meanings rely on the head noun, adjective or verb. If the head word is replaced by another of the same grammatical category but a different meaning, the meaning of the entire expression changes. Hence, if we replace the head adjective الضروري *AlDrwry* (necessary) in من الضروري ان *mn AlDrwry An* (it is necessary to) with الممكن *Almmkn* (possible), the meaning changes from obligation to uncertainty.

Type 4 comprises syntactically productive expressions. It is similar to Type 3 except that the head words are modifiable and their arguments, especially indirect objects, can be included within the boundaries of the MWE. Thus, the same expression from Type 3 can be modified as in من الضروري جدا ان *mn AlDrwry jdA An* (it is very necessary to). Furthermore, we can have an inserted indirect object as in من الضروري للمصريين ان *mn AlDrwry llmSryyn An* (it is necessary for Egyptians to).

Type 5 includes morphologically, lexically and syntactically productive expressions like لدي يقين ان *ldy yqyn An* (I have faith that). Morphologically, the object pronoun in لدي *ldy* (I have) inflects for person, gender and number. Syntactically, the head noun can be modified by adjectives as in لدي يقين راسخ ان *ldy yqyn rAsx An* (I have a strong faith that). Lexically, the meaning of the expression relies on the head noun يقين *yqyn* (faith) which is replaceable for other modality-based nouns such as لدي نية ان *ldy nyp An* (I have an intention to).

Despite the semantic transparency and the morpho-syntactic and lexical productivity of the expressions in Types 3-5, we have three reasons to consider them as AM-MWEs:

First, although the head words in those expressions are transparent and productive, the other components, including prepositions, relative adverbials and verbs, are fixed and conventionalized. In من الضروري ان *mn AlDrwry An* (literally: from the necessary to; gloss: it is necessary to), the preposition من *mn* (from) cannot be replaced by any other preposition. In هناك احتمال بان *hnAk AHtmAl bAn* (there is a possibility that), the relative adverbial هناك *hnAk* (there is) cannot be replaced by another relative adverbial such as هنا *hnA* (there is). In يحدوني الامل في ان *yHdwny AlAml fy An* (hope derives me to), the head is the noun الامل *AlAml* (the hope). Therefore, the lexical verb يحدوني *yHdwny* (drives me) cannot be replaced by other synonymous verbs such as يقودني *yqwdqny* (leads me) or يدفعني *ydfEny* (pushes/drives me).

Second, each of those expressions has a strictly fixed word order. Even for expressions that allow the insertion of modifiers and verb/noun arguments, the inserted elements hold fixed places within the boundaries of the expression. Complex constructions that adhere to strict constraints on word order but undergo lexical variation are classified by Sag et al. (2002) as semi-fixed MWEs.

Finally, each expression of those types is lexically perceived as a one linguistic unit that can be replaced in many contexts by a unigram synonym as illustrated in Table 1. According to Stubbs (2007) and Escartín et al. (2013), the perception of complex constructions as single linguistic units is characteristic of MWEs.

3 Related Work

There is a plethora of research on general-purpose Arabic MWEs. Yet, no prior work has focused on AM-MWEs. Hawwari et al. (2012) describe the manual construction of a repository for Arabic MWEs that classifies them based on their morpho-syntactic structures.

Corpus	Token #	Types #	Description
Ajdir	113774517	2217557	a monolingual newswire corpus of Modern Standard Arabic
LDC ISI	28880558	532443	an LDC parallel Arabic-English corpus (Munteanu & Marcu 2007)
YADAC	6328248	457361	a dialectal Arabic corpus of Weblogs and tweets (Al-Sabbagh & Girju 2012)
Tashkeel	6149726	358950	a vowelized corpus of Classical and Modern Standard Arabic books
Total	**41472307**	**3566311**	

Table 2: Statistics for the extraction corpora

Attia et al. (2010) describe the construction of a lexicon of Arabic MWEs based on (1) correspondence asymmetries between Arabic Wikipedia titles and titles in 21 different languages, (2) English MWEs extracted from Princeton WordNet 3.0 and automatically translated into Arabic, and (3) lexical association measures.

Bounhas and Slimani (2009) use syntactic patterns and Log-Likelihood Ratio to extract environmental Arabic MWEs. They achieve precision rates of 0.93, 0.66 and 0.67 for bigrams, trigrams and quadrigrams, respectively.

Al-Sabbagh et al. (2013) manually build a lexicon of Arabic modals with a small portion of MWEs and quasi-modals. In this paper, quasi-modals are bigram AM-MWEs. Hence, their lexicon has 1,053 AM-MWEs.

Nissim and Zaninello (2013) build a lexicon and a repository of variation patterns for MWEs in the morphologically-rich Romance languages. Similar to our research, their motivation to represent the productivity of Romance MWEs through variation patterns is to boost their automatic identification and extraction. Another similarity is that we define variation patterns as part-of-speech sequences. The difference between their research and ours is that our variation patterns have a wider scope because we cover both the morpho-syntactic and lexical variations of AM-MWEs, whereas their variation patterns deal with morphological variation only.

4 The Unsupervised Method

4.1 Extracting AM-MWEs

4.1.1 Extraction Resources

Table 2[2] shows the token and type counts as well as the descriptions of the corpora used for extraction. For corpus preprocessing, (1) html mark-up and diacritics are removed. (2) Meta-linguistic information such as document and segment IDs, section headers, dates and sources, as well as English data are removed. (3) Punctuation marks are separated from words. (4) Words in Roman letters are removed. (5) Orthographical normalization is done so that all *alef*-letter variations are normalized to *A*, the elongation letter (ـ) and word lengthening are removed. (6) Finally, the corpus is tokenized and Part-of-Speech (POS) tagged by MADAMIRA (Pasha et a. 2014); the latest version of state-of-the-art Arabic tokenizers and POS taggers.

4.1.2 Extraction Set-up and Results

We restrict the size of AM-MWEs in this paper to quadrigrams. Counted grams include function and content words but not affixes. Working on longer AM-MWEs is left for future research.

The extraction of candidate AM-MWEs is conducted in three steps:

Step 1: we use root-based information to identify the words that can be possible derivations of modality roots. For modality roots, we use the Arabic Modality Lexicon from Al-Sabbagh et al. (2013).

In order to identify possible derivations of modality roots, we use RegExps. For instance, we use the RegExp (\w*)***m***(\w*)***k***(\w*)***n***(\w*) to identify words such as الممكن *Almmkn* (the possible), اتمكن ***Atmkn*** (I manage) and بامكاني ***bAmkAny*** (I can) which convey modality.

This RegExp-based procedure can result in noise. For instance, the aforementioned RegExp also returns the word الامريكان ***AlAmrykAn*** (Americans) which happens to have the same three letters of the root in the same order although it is not one of its derivations. Yet, the procedure still filters out many irrelevant words that have nothing to do with the modality roots.

Step 2: for the resulting words from Step 1, we extract bigrams, trigrams and quadrigrams given the frequency thresholds of 20, 15 and 10, respectively.

[2]Ajdir: http://aracorpus.e3rab.com/
Tashkeel: http://sourceforge.net/projects/tashkeela/

In previous literature on MWEs with corpora of 6-8M words, thresholds were set to 5, 8 and 10 for MWEs of different sizes. Given the large size of our corpus, we decide to use higher thresholds.

Step 3: for the extracted ngrams we use the Log-Likelihood Ratio (LLR) to measure the significance of association between the ngram words. LLR measures the deviation between the observed data and what would be expected if the words within the ngram were independent. Its results are easily interpretable: the higher the score, the less evidence there is in favor of concluding that the words are independent.

LLR is computed as in Eq. 1 where O_{ij} and E_{ij} are the observed and expected frequencies, respectively[3]. LLR is not, however, the only measure used in the literature of MWEs. Experimenting with more association measures is left for future work.

Eq. 1: $$\mathrm{LLR} = 2\ \sum_{ij} O_{ij} \log \frac{O_{ij}}{E_{ij}}$$

Table 3 shows the unique type counts of the extracted ngrams. The extracted ngrams include both modal and non-modal MWEs. For instance, both من الممكن لنا ان *mn Almmkn lnA An* (it is possible for us to) and في اقرب وقت ممكن *fy Aqrb wqt mmkn* (as soon as possible) are extracted as valid quadrigrams. Both have the word ممكن *mmkn* (possible) derived from the root *m-k-n*. Both are frequent enough to meet the frequency threshold. The words within each quadrigram are found to be significantly associated according to LLR. Nevertheless, *mn Almmkn lnA An* is an AM-MWE according to our definition in Section 2, but *fy Aqrb wqt mmkn* is not. This is because the former conveys the modality sense of possibility; whereas the latter does not. Therefore, we need the second clustering stage in our unsupervised method to distinguish modal from non-modal MWEs.

Ngram size	Unique Types
Bigrams	86645
Trigrams	43397
Quadrigrams	25634
Total	**96031**

Table 3: Statistics for the extracted MWEs

[3] We use Banerjee and Pedersen's (2003) Perl implementation of ngram association measures.

4.2 Clustering AM-MWEs

Clustering is the second stage of our unsupervised method to build the lexicon of the AM-MWEs and the repository of their variation patterns. This stage takes as input the extracted ngrams from the first extraction stage; and aims to distinguish between the ngrams that convey modality senses and the ngrams that do not.

4.2.1 Clustering Set-up

The clustering feature set includes token level morphological, syntactic, lexical and positional features. It also has a mixture of nominal and continuous-valued features as we explain in the subsequent sections.

4.2.1.1 Morphological Features

Roots used to guide the extraction of candidate AM-MWEs in Section 4.1.2 are used as clustering morphological features. The reason is that some roots have more modal derivations than others. For instance, the derivations of the root ض-ر-ر ***D-r-r*** include ضروري ***Drwry*** (necessary), بالضرورة *bAl**D**r**w**rp* (necessarily), and يضطر *y**DT**r* (he has to); all of which convey the modality sense of obligation. Consequently, to inform the clustering algorithm that a given ngram was extracted based on the root *D-r-r* indicates that it is more likely to be an AM-MWE.

4.2.1.2 Syntactic Features

In theoretical linguistics, linguists claim that Arabic modality triggers (i.e. words and phrases that convey modality senses) subcategorize for clauses, verb phrases, to-infinitives and deverbal nouns. For details, we refer the reader to Mitchell and Al-Hassan (1994), Brustad (2000), Badawi et al. (2004) and Moshref (2012).

These subcategorization frames can be partially captured at the token level. For example, clauses can be marked by complementizers, subject and demonstrative pronouns and verbs. To-infinitives in Arabic are typically marked by ان *An* (to). Even deverbal nouns can be detected with some POS tagsets such as Buckwalter's (2002) that labels them as NOUN.VN.

Based on this, we use the POS information around the extracted ngrams as contextual syntactic features for clustering. We limit the window size of the contextual syntactic features to ±1 words.

Furthermore, as we mentioned in Section 2, we define AM-MWEs as expressions with fixed word order. That is, the sequence of the POS tags that represent the internal structure of the extracted ngrams can be used as syntactic features to distinguish modal from non-modal MWEs.

4.2.1.3 Lexical Features

As we mentioned in Section 2, except for the head words of the AM-MWEs, other components are usually fixed and conventionalized. Therefore, the actual lexical words of the extracted ngrams can be distinguishing features for AM-MWEs.

4.2.1.4 Positional Features

AM-MWEs, especially trigrams and quadrigrams that scope over entire clauses, are expected to come in sentence-initial positions. Thus we use @beg (i.e. at beginning) to mark whether the extracted ngrams occur at sentence-initial positions.

4.2.1.5 Continuous Features

Except for nominal morphological and lexical features, other features are continuous. They are not extracted *per* ngram instance, but are defined as weighted features across all the instances of a target ngram.

Thus, @beg for $ngram_i$ is the probability of $ngram_i$ to occur in a sentence-initial position. It is computed as the frequency of $ngram_i$ occurring at a sentence-initial position normalized by the total number n of $ngram_i$ in the corpus.

Similarly, POS features are continuous. For instance, the probability that $ngram_i$ is followed by a deverbal noun is the frequency of its POS_{+1} tagged as a deverbal noun normalized by the total number n of $ngram_i$ in the corpus.

4.2.2 Clustering Resources

As we mentioned earlier, the extracted ngrams from the extraction stage are the input for this clustering stage. The root features are the same roots used for extraction. The POS features are extracted based on the output of MADAMIRA (Pasha et al. 2014) that is used to preprocess the corpus - Section 4.1.1. The positional features are determined based on the availability of punctuation markers for sentence boundaries.

We implement *k*-means clustering with *k* set to two and the distance metric set to the Euclidean distance[4]. The intuition for using *k*-means clustering is that we want to identify AM-MWEs against all other types of MWEs based on their morpho-syntactic, lexical and positional features. Thus the results of *k*-means clustering with *k* set to two will be easily interpretable. Other clustering algorithms might be considered for future work.

4.2.3 Clustering Evaluation and Results

4.2.3.1 Evaluation Methodology

We use precision, recall and F_1-score as evaluation metrics, with three gold sets: **BiSet**, **TriSet** and **QuadSet**, for bigrams, trigrams and quadrigrams, respectively. Each gold set has 1000 positive data points (i.e. AM-MWEs).

The gold sets are first compiled from multiple resources, including Mitchell and Al-Hassan (1994), Brustad (2000), Badawi et al. (2004) and Moshref (2012). Second, each compiled gold set is further evaluated by two expert annotators. They are instructed to decide whether a given ngram is an AM-MWE or not according to the following definitions of AM-MWEs:

- They convey modality senses - Section 1
- They have unigram synonyms
- They have fixed word orders
- Their function words are fixed

Inter-annotator kappa κ scores for the **BiSet**, **TriSet** and **QuadSet** are 0.93, 0.95 and 0.96, respectively. Most disagreement is attributed to the annotators' failure to find unigram synonyms.

The positive **BiSet** includes (1) phrasal verbs such as يتمكن من *ytmkn mn* (he manages to), يعجز عن *yEjz En* (he fails to) and يحلم ب *yHlm be* (he longs for), (2) prepositional phrases such as من الممكن *mn Almmkn* (it is possible that) and في الحقيقة *fy AlHqyqp* (actually), (3) nominal phrases such as املي هو *Amly hw* (my hope is to) and (4) AM-MWEs subcategorizing for complementizers such as يصرح بان *ySrH bAn* (he declares that) and يعرف ان *yErf An* (he knows that).

[4] We use the *k*-means clustering implementation from Orange toolkit http://orange.biolab.si/

The positive **TriSet** includes verb phrases like يفشل في ان *yf$l fy An* (he fails to) and prepositional phrases like من المستحيل ان *mn AlmstHyl An* (it is impossible to) and عندي ايمان بان *Endy AymAn bAn* (I have faith that).

The positive **QuadSet** includes verb phrases such as يحدوني الامل في ان *yHdwny AlAml fy An* (hope drives me to) and prepositional phrases such as من غير المقبول ان *mn gyr Almqbwl An* (it is unacceptable to).

With these gold sets, we first decide on the best cluster *per* ngram size. We use an all-or-nothing approach; that is, for the two clusters created for bigrams, we select the cluster with the highest exact matches with the BiSet to be the best bigram cluster. We do the same thing for the trigram and quadrigram clusters. With information about the best cluster *per* ngram size, our actual evaluation starts.

To evaluate clustered bigram AM-MWEs, we consider the output of best bigram, trigram and quadrigram clusters to allow for evaluating bigrams with gaps. We also tolerate morphological differences in terms of different conjugations for person, gender, number, tense, mood and aspect.

For example, true positives for the bigram AM-MWE يتمكن من *ytmkn mn* (he manages to) include its exact match and the morphological alternations of اتمكن من *Atmkn mn* (I manage to) and نتمكن من *ntmkn mn* (we manage to), among others. In other words, if the output of the bigram clustering has *Atmkn mn* or *ntmkn mn* but the BiSet has only *ytmkn mn*, we consider this as a true positive.

The bigram *ytmkn mn* can have a (pro)noun subject after the verb *ytmkn*: ***ytmkn*** ((pro)noun gap) ***mn***. Thus, we consider the output of the trigram best cluster. If we find instances such as يتمكن الرئيس من ***ytmkn*** *Alt}ys* ***mn*** (the president manages to) or نتمكن نحن من ***ntmkn*** *nHn* ***mn*** (we manages to), we consider them as true positives for the bigram *ytmkn mn* as long as the trigram has the two defining words of the bigram, namely the verb *ytmkn* in any of its conjugations and the preposition *mn*.

The same bigram - *ytmkn mn* - can have two gaps after the head verb *ytmkn* as in يتمكن الرئيس المصري من ***ytmkn*** *Alr}ys AlmSry* ***mn*** (the Egyptian president manages to). For that reason, we consider the best quadrigram cluster. If we find ***ytmkn*** ((pro)noun gap) ((pro)noun gap) ***mn***, we consider this as a true positive for the bigram *ytmkn mn* as long as the two boundaries of the bigrams are represented. We could not go any further with more than two gaps because we did not cluster beyond quadrigrams.

False positives for the bigram *ytmkn mn* would be the bigrams يتمكن الرئيس ***ytmkn*** *Alr}ys* (the president manages) and الرئيس من *Alr}ys* ***mn*** (the president to) in the bigram cluster where one of the bigram's components - either the verb or the preposition - is missing.

False negatives of bigrams would be those bigrams that could not be found in any of the best clusters whether with or without gaps.

Similar to evaluating bigrams, we consider the output of the trigram and quadrigram best clusters to evaluate trigram AM-MWEs. We also tolerate morphological productivity.

For instance, the trigram عندنا ايمان بان *End**nA*** *AymAn bAn* (we have faith that) conjugated for the first person plural is a true positive for the gold set trigram عندي ايمان بان *Endy AymAn bAn* (I have faith that), that is conjugated for the first person singular.

The same trigram *Endy AymAn bAn* can have two types of gaps. The first can be a noun-based indirect object after the preposition *End*. Thus, we can have عند الناس ايمان بان ***End*** *AlnAs* ***AymAn bAn*** (people have faith that). The second can be an adjective after the head noun *AymAn*. Thus we can have عندي ايمان مطلق بان ***Endy AymAn*** *mTlq* ***bAn*** (I have a strong faith that).

Consequently, in the output of the quadrigram best cluster, if we find matches to ***Endy AymAn*** (adjective gap) ***bAn*** in any conjugations of *Endy*, or if we find any matches for ***End*** (noun gap) ***AymAn bAn***, we consider them as true positives for the trigram *Endy AymAn bAn* .

If the pronoun in *End* is replaced by a noun and the adjective gap is filled, we will have a pentagram like عند الناس ايمان مطلق بان ***End*** *AlnAs* ***AymAn*** *mTlq* ***bAn*** (people have a strong faith that). Since we do not extract pentagrams, we consider chunks such as عند الناس ايمان ***End*** *AlnAs AymAn* (people have faith) and ايمان مطلق بان *AymAn mTlq* ***bAn*** (strong faith that) as false positive trigrams. This is because the former misses the complementizer بان *bAn* (in that), and the latter misses the first preposition عند *End* (literally: in; gloss: have).

Since we do not cluster pentagrams, we could not tolerate gaps in the output of the quadrigrams. We, however, tolerate morphological variation. As a result, يحدونا الامل في ان *yHdwn**A** AlAml fy An* (hope drives us to) is considered as a true positive for يحدوني الامل في ان *yHdw**ny** AlAml fy An* (hope derives me to).

It is important to note that we do not consider the next best cluster of the larger AM-MWEs unless we do not find any true positives in the AM-MWE's original cluster. For example, we do not search for bigrams' true positives in the trigram and quadrigram clusters, unless there are not any exact matches of the gold-set bigrams in the bigrams' best cluster itself. The same thing applies when evaluating trigram AM-MWEs.

4.2.3.2 Clustering Results and Error Analysis

Table 4 shows the evaluation results for bigrams, trigrams and quadrigrams. We attribute the good results to our evaluation methodology in the first place because it allows counting true positives across clusters of different ngram sizes to account for gaps and tolerates morphological variations. Our methodology captures the morphological productivity of AM-MWEs which is expected given that Arabic is morphologically-rich. It also accounts for the syntactic productivity in terms of insertion.

	Precision	Recall	F_1
Bigrams	0.663	0.776	0.715
Trigrams	0.811	0.756	0.783
Quadrigrams	0.857	0.717	0.780

Table 4: Clustering evaluation results

Long dependencies are a source of errors at the recall level. Clustering could not capture such instances as صرح الرئيس المصري حسني مبارك ب ***SrH*** *Alr}ys AlmSry Hsny mbArk* ***b*** (the Egyptian president Hosni Mubarak declared to) because they go beyond our quadrigram limit.

Another type of recall errors results from AM-MWEs that do not meet the extraction frequency threshold despite the large size of our corpus. Our positive gold sets are sampled from theoretical linguistics studies in which the included illustrative examples are not necessarily frequent. For example, we could not find instances for the volitive يتوق الى *ytwq Aly* (he longs for).

Precision errors result from the fact that our RegExp-based procedure to guide the first extraction stage is noisy. For instance, the RegExp (\w*)***t***(\w*)***w***(\w*)***q***(\w*) that was supposed to extract the volitive يتوق *ytwq* (he longs) did not return any instances for the intended modal but rather instances for يتوقف ***ytwqf*** (he stops) which interestingly subcategorizes for a preposition and a complementizer as in يتوقف عن ان *ytwqf En An* (literally: stops from to). This subcategorization frame is the same for modals such as يعجز عن ان *yEjz En An* (literally: unable from to). Consequently, يتوقف عن ان *ytwqf En An* (he stops from to) has been clustered as a trigram AM-MWE although it does not convey any modality senses. This highlights another reason for precision errors. The subcategorization frames and hence the syntactic features used for clustering are not always distinctive for AM-MWEs.

The @beg feature was the least informative among all features. In the case of bigrams, they are mostly lexical verbs that do not occur in sentence initial positions. Meanwhile, punctuation inconsistencies do not enable us to reliably mark @beg for many ngrams.

4.3 Identifying Variation Patterns

Our target is to build a lexicon and a repository of the variation patterns for AM-MWEs to boost their automatic identification and extraction, given their morpho-syntactic and lexical productivity.

In order to identify variation patterns, we use as input the best clusters from the previous clustering stage and follow these steps:

- We keep all function words *as is* with their lexical and POS representations
- We collapse all morphological tags for gender, number, person, tense, mood, aspect and case
- We add a HEAD tag to the head words (i.e. words whose roots were used for extraction)
- We add a GAP tag for adverbs, pronouns and other gap fillers to explicitly mark gap locations

An example pattern for the root ط - م - ح *T-m-H* (wish) is ((HEAD/*IV*) + (*AlY*/PREP) + (*An*/SUB_CONJ)) which reads as follows: a trigram AM-MWE whose head is a verb in any conjugation followed by the preposition *AlY* (to) and the subordinate conjunction *An* (that; to). Another pattern that results from the aforementioned steps for the same root of *T-m-H* is ((HEAD/*IV*) + (ADV/GAP) + (*AlY*/PREP) + (An/SUB_CONJ)). It means that an adverb can be inserted in-between the HEAD and the preposition *AlY* (to).

4.4 Bootstrapping AM-MWEs

We use the patterns identified in the previous stage in two ways: first, to extract low-frequency AM-MWEs whose HEADs have the same roots as the pattern's HEAD; and second, to extract AM-MWEs that have the same lexical, POS patterns but are not necessarily derived from the modality roots we used in extraction.

For example, from the previous section we used ((HEAD/*IV*) + (*AlY*/PREP) + (*An*/SUB_CONJ)) to extract the third person feminine plural conjugation of the root *T-m-H* in the trigram يطمحن الى ان *yTmHn AlY An* (they wish for) that occurred only once in the corpus. We used the same pattern to extract يصبو الى ان *ySbw AlY An* (he longs for) that has the same pattern but whose HEAD'S root *S-b-b* was not in our list of modality roots.

Among the new extracted AM-MWEs are the expressions من الواضح ان *mn AlmwADH An* (it is clear that) and من الطبيعي ان *mn AlTbyEy An* (it is normal that) that share the same pattern with من الممكن ان *mn Almmkn An* (it is possible that). We decide to consider those expressions as AM-MWEs although they are not epistemic in the conventional sense. That is, they do not evaluate the truth value of their clause-based propositions, but rather presuppose the proposition as true, and express the speakers' sentiment towards it.

This bootstrapping stage results in 358 AM-MWEs. They are inspected during manual verification.

5 Manual Verification and Final Results

We manually verify the best clusters, the bootstrapped AM-MWEs and the constructed patterns before including them in the final lexicon and repository to guarantee accuracy. Besides, we manually add modality senses to the lexicon entries. We also manually complete the morphological paradigms of the morphologically productive AM-MWEs. That is, if we only have the bigram يرغب في *yrgb fy* (he longs for) conjugated for the third singular masculine person, we manually add the rest of the conjugations.

The final lexicon is represented in XML and is organized by modality senses and then roots within each sense. The lexicon comprises 10,664 entries. The XML fields describe: the Arabic string, the size of the AM-MWE, the corpus frequency and the pattern ID. The pattern ID is the link between the lexicon and the repository because it maps each lexicon entry to its lexical, POS pattern in the repository.

Roots		Senses		Sizes	
A-m-l	710	Epistemic	4233	Bigrams	4806
A-k-d	693	Evidential	811	Trigrams	3244
r-g-b	396	Obligative	748	Quadrigrams	2614
$-E-r	378	Permissive	755		
H-s-s	370	Commissive	111		
q-n-E	312	Abilitive	676		
E-q-d	293	Volitive	3330		
Total: 10,664					

Table 5: Statistics for the AM-MWE lexicon for the top 7 roots and the distributions of modality senses and AM-MWE sizes

If a lexicon entry is manually added, the tag MANUAL is used for the corpus frequency field. Table 5 gives more statistics about the lexicon in terms of modality senses, AM-MWE sizes and the top 7 frequent modality roots.

The XML repository is given in the three POS tagsets supported by MADAMIRA. The XML fields describe: the pattern's ID, the POS of the head and the pattern itself with the HEADs and GAPs marked. Appendices A and B give snapshots of the lexicon and the repository in Buckwalter's POS tagset.

6 Conclusion and Outlook

We described the unsupervised construction of a lexicon and a repository of variation patterns for AM-MWEs to boost their automatic identification and extraction. In addition to the creation of novel resources, our research gives insights about the morphological, syntactic and lexical properties of such expressions. We also propose an evaluation methodology that accounts for the productive insertion patterns of AM-MWEs and their morphological variations.

For future work, we will work on larger AM-MWEs to cover insertion patterns that we could not cover in this paper. We will experiment with different association measures such as point-wise mutual information. We will also try different clustering algorithms.

Acknowledgement

This work was supported by grant NPRP 09-410-1-069 of the Qatar National Research Fund. We would also like to thank the four anonymous reviewers for their constructive comments.

References

Rania Al-Sabbagh and Roxana Girju. 2012. YADAC: Yet another Dialectal Arabic Corpus. *Proc. of LREC'12*, Istanbul, Turkey, May 23-25 2012

Rania Al-Sabbagh, Jana Diesner and Roxana Girju. 2013. Using the Semantic-Syntactic Interface for Reliable Arabic Modality Annotation. *Proc. of IJCNLP'13*, Nagoya, Japan, October 14-18 2013

Mohammed Attia, Antonio Toral, Lamia Tounsi, Pavel Pecina and Josef van Genbith. 2010. Automatic Extraction of Arabic Multiword Expressions. *Proc. of the Workshop on MWE 2010*, Beijing, August 2010

Elsaid Badawi, M.G. Carter and Adrian Gully. 2004. *Modern Written Arabic: A Comprehensive Grammar*. UK: MPG Books Ltd

Satanjeev Banerjee and Ted Pedersen. 2003. The Design, Implementation, and Use of the Ngram Statistic Package. *Proc. of CiCling'03*, Mexico City, USA

Ibrahim Bounhas and Yahya Slimani. 2009. A Hybrid Approach for Arabic Multi-Word Term Extraction. *Proceedings of NLP-KE 2009*, Dalian, China, September 24-27 2009

Kristen E. Brustad. 2000. *The Syntax of Spoken Arabic: A Comparative Study of Moroccan, Egyptian, Syrian and Kuwaiti Dialects*. Georgetown Uni. Press, Washington DC, USA

Tim Buckwalter. 2002. Arabic Morphological Analyzer. Technical Report, Linguistic Data Consortium, Philadelphia

Cristian Danescu-Niculescu-Mizil, Moritz Sudhof, Dan Jurafsky, Jure Leskovec and Christopher Potts. 2013. A Computational Approach to Politeness with Application to Social Factors. *Proc. of the 51st ACL*, , Sofia, Bulgaria, August 4-9 2013

Mona Diab, Lori Levin, Teruko Mitamura, Owen Rambow, Vinodkumar Prabhakaran, and Weiwei Guo. 2009. Committed Belief Annotation and Tagging. *Proc. of the 3rd LAW Workshop, ACL-IJCNLP'09*, pp. 68-73, Singapore

Carla Parra Escartín, Gyri Smørdal Losnegaard, Gunn Inger Lyse Samdal and Pedro Patiño García. 2013. Representing Multiword Expressions in Lexical and Terminological Resources: An Analysis for Natural Language Processing Purposes. *Proc. of eLex 2013*, pages 338-357, Tallinn, Estonia, October 17-19 2013

Abdelati Hawwari, Kfir Bar and Mona Diab. 2012. Building an Arabic Multiword Expressions Repository. *Proc. of the 50th ACL*, pages 24-29, Jeju, Republic of Korea, July 12 2012

Andrew Lampert, Robert Dale and Cecile Paris. 2010, Detecting Emails Containing Requests for Action. *Proc. of the 2010 ACL*, pages 984-992, Los Angeles, California, June 2010

F. Mitchell and S. A. Al-Hassan. 1994. *Modality, Mood and Aspect in Spoken Arabic with Special Reference to Egypt and the Levant.* London and NY: Kegan Paul International

Ola Moshref. 2012. Corpus Study of Tense, Aspect, and Modality in Diglossic Speech in Cairene Arabic. PhD Thesis. University of Illinois at Urbana-Champaign

Dragos Stefan Munteanu and Daniel Marcu. 2007. ISI Arabic-English Automatically Extracted Parallel Text, Linguistic Data Consortium, Philadelphia

Malvin Nissim and Andrea Zaninello. 2013. A Repository of Variation Patterns for Multiword Expressions. *Proc. of the 9th Workshop of MWE*, pp. 101-105, Atlanta, Georgia, June 13-14 2013

Frank R. Palmer. 2001. *Mood and Modality*. 2nd Edition. Cambridge University Press, Cambridge, UK

Silvia Pareti, Tim O'Keefe, Ioannis Konstas, James R. Curran and Irena Koprinska. 2013. *Automatically Detecting and Attributing Indirect Quotations. Proc. of the 2013 EMNLP,* pages. 989-1000, Washington, USA, October 18-21 2013

Arfath Pasha, Mohamed Al-Badrashiny, Ahmed El Kholy, Ramy Eskander, Mona Diab, Nizar Habash, Manoj Pooleery, Owen Rambow and Ryan Roth. 2014. MADAMIRA: A Fast, Comprehensive Tool for Morphological Analysis and Disambiguation of Arabic. *Proc. of the 9th International Conference on Language Resources and Evaluation,* Reykjavik, Iceland, May 26-31 2014

Vinodkumar Prabhakaran and Owen Rambow. 2013. Written Dialog and Social Power: Manifestations of Different Types of Power in Dialog Behavior. *Proceedings of the 6th IJCNLP*, pp. 216-224, Nagoya, Japan, October 14-18 2013

Ivan Sag, Timothy Baldwin, Francis Bond, Ann Copestake and Dan Flickinger. 2002. Multiword Expressions: A Pain in the Neck for NLP. *Proceedings of CiCling 2002*, pages 1-15, Mexico City, Mexico

Michael Stubbs. 2007. An Example of Frequent English Phraseology: Distributions, Structures and

Functions. *Language and Computers: Corpus Linguistics 25 Years on*, pages 89-105, (17)

Appendix A: A snapshot of the XML lexicon


```
<lexicon name="AM-MWE Lexicon v1.0">
    <modality sense="abilitive">
      <head root="q-d-r">
        <am-mwe string="قادر على" len="2" freq="283" patternID="23"> </am-mwe>
        <am-mwe string="لديه القدرة على" len="3" freq="7" patternID="45"> </am-mwe>
        ...
      </head>
    </modality>
    <modality sense="epistemic">
      <head root="g-l-b">
        <am-mwe string="في الغالب" len="2" freq="122" patternID="15"> </am-mwe>
        ...
      </head>
      <head root="H-w-l">
        <am-mwe string="يستحيل ان" len="2" freq="70" patternID="10"> </am-mwe>
        ...
      </head>
      <head root="n-Z-r">
        <am-mwe string="من المنتظر ايضا ان " len="4" freq="38" patternID="50"> </am-mwe>
        ...
      </head>
    </modality>
</lexicon>
```


Appendix B: A snapshot of the XML repository


```
<repository name="AM-MWE Variation Patterns v1.0">
   <tagset name="Buckwalter" pos-tagger="MADAMIRA v1.0">
      ...
      <pattern ID="10" head-pos="*+IV+*" pos="(HEAD)+ (An/SUB_CONJ)"></pattern>
      ...
      <pattern ID="15" head-pos="DET+NOUN+*" pos="(fy/PREP)+(HEAD)"></pattern>
      ...
      <pattern ID="23" head-pos="ADJ+*" pos="(HEAD)+(ElY/PREP)"> </pattern>
      ...
      <pattern ID="45" head-pos="DET+NOUN+*" pos="(lyd/NOUN)+(PRON*/GAP)*+(HEAD)+(ElY/PREP)">
      </pattern>
      ...
      <pattern ID="50" head-pos="DET+NOUN+*" pos="(mn/PREP)+(HEAD)+(ADV/GAP)*+(An/SUB_CONJ)">
      </pattern>
      ....
   </tagset>
</repository>
```

Issues in Translating Verb-Particle Constructions from German to English

Nina Schottmüller
Uppsala University
Department of Linguistics and Philology
nschottmueller@gmail.com

Joakim Nivre
Uppsala University
Department of Linguistics and Philology
joakim.nivre@lingfil.uu.se

Abstract

In this paper, we investigate difficulties in translating verb-particle constructions from German to English. We analyse the structure of German VPCs and compare them to VPCs in English. In order to find out if and to what degree the presence of VPCs causes problems for statistical machine translation systems, we collected a set of 59 verb pairs, each consisting of a German VPC and a synonymous simplex verb. With this data, we constructed a test suite of 236 sentences where the simplex verb and VPC are completely substitutable. We then translated this dataset to English using Google Translate and Bing Translator. Through an analysis of the resulting translations we are able to show that the quality decreases when translating sentences that contain VPCs instead of simplex verbs. The test suite is made freely available to the community.

1 Introduction

In this paper, we analyse and discuss German verb-particle constructions (VPCs). VPCs are a type of multiword expressions (MWEs) which are defined by Sag et al. (2002) to be "idiosyncratic interpretations that cross word bounderies (or spaces)". Kim and Baldwin (2010) extend this explanation in their definition of MWEs being "lexical items consisting of multiple simplex words that display lexical, syntactic, semantic and/or statistical idiosyncrasies".

VPCs are made up of a base verb and a particle. In contrast to English, where the particle is always separated from the verb, German VPCs are separable, meaning that the particle can either be attached as a prefix to the verb or stand separate from it, depending on factors such as tense and voice, along with whether the VPC is found in a main clause or subordinate clause.

The fact that German VPCs are separable means that word order differences between the source and target language can occur in statistical machine translation (SMT). It has been shown that the translation quality of translation systems can suffer from such differences in word order (Holmqvist et al., 2012). Since VPCs make up for a significant amount of verbs in English, as well as in German, they are a likely source for translation errors. This makes it essential to analyse any issues with VPCs that occur while translating, in order to be able to develop possible improvements.

In our approach, we investigate if the presence of VPCs causes translation errors. We do this by creating and utilising a dataset of 236 sentences, using a collection of 59 German verb pairs, each consisting of a VPC and a synonymous simplex verb, a test suite that is made freely available. We discuss the English translation results generated by the popular translation systems Google Translate and Bing Translator and show that the presence of VPCs can harm translation quality.

We begin this paper by stating important related work in the fields related to VPCs in Section 2 and continue with a detailed analysis of VPCs in German in Section 3. In Section 4, we describe how the data used for evaluation was compiled, and in Section 5, we give further details on the evaluation in terms of metrics and systems tested. Section 6 gives an overview of the results, as well as their discussion, where we present possible reasons why VPCs performed worse in the experiments, which finally leads to our conclusions in Section 7. An appendix lists all the verb pairs used to construct the test suite.

2 Related Work

A lot of research has been done on the identification, classification, and extraction of VPCs, with the majority of work done on English. For example, Villavicencio (2005) presents a study about the availability of VPCs in lexical resources and proposes an approach to use semantic classification to identify as many VPC candidates as possible. She then validates these candidates using the retrieved results from online search engines.

Many linguistic studies analyse VPCs in German, or English, respectively, mostly discussing the grammar theory that underlies the compositionality of MWEs in general or presenting more particular studies such as theories and experiments about language acquisition. An example would be the work of Behrens (1998), in which she contrasts how German, English and Dutch children acquire complex verbs when they learn to speak, focusing on the differences in the acquisition of VPCs and prefix verbs. In another article in this field by Müller (2002), the author focuses on non-transparent readings of German VPCs and describes the phenomenon of how particles can be fronted.

Furthermore, there has been some research dealing with VPCs in machine translation as well. In a study by Chatterjee and Balyan (2011), several rule-based solutions are proposed for how to translate English VPCs to Hindi, using their surrounding entities. Another paper in this field by Collins et al. (2005) presents an approach to clause restructuring for statistical machine translation from German to English in which one step consists of moving the particle of a particle verb directly in front of the verb. Moreover, even though their work does not directly target VPCs, Holmqvist et al. (2012) present a method for improving word alignment quality by reordering the source text according to the target word order, where they also mention that their approach is supposed to help with different word order caused by finite verbs in German, similar to the phenomenon of differing word order caused by VPCs.

3 German Verb-Particle Constructions

VPCs in German are made up of a base verb and a particle. In contrast to English, German VPCs are separable, meaning that they can occur separated, but do not necessarily have to. This applies only for main clauses, as VPCs can never be separated in German subordinate clauses. Depending on the conjugation of the verb, the particle can a) be attached to the front of the verb as prefix, either directly or with an additional morpheme, or b) be completely separated from the verb. The particle is directly prefixed to the verb if it is an infinitive construction, for example within an active voice present tense sentence using an auxiliary (e.g., *muss herausnehmen*). It is also attached directly to the conjugated base verb when using a past participle form to indicate passive voice or perfect tense (e.g., *herausgenommen*), or if a morpheme is inserted to build an infinitive construction using *zu* (e.g., *herauszunehmen*). The particle is separated from the verb root in finite main clauses where the particle verb is the main verb of the sentence (e.g., *nimmt heraus*). The following examples serve to illustrate the aforementioned three forms of the non-separated case and the one separated case.

Attached:
Du musst das **herausnehmen**.
*You have to **take** this **out**.*

Attached+perfect:
Ich habe es **herausgenommen**.
*I have **taken** it **out**.*

Attached+*zu*:
Es ist nicht erlaubt, das **herauszunehmen**.
*It is not allowed to **take** that **out**.*

Separated:
Ich **nehme** es **heraus**.
*I **take** it **out**.*

Just like simplex verbs, VPCs can be transitive or intransitive. For the separated case, a transitive VPC's base verb and particle are always split and the object has to be positioned between them, despite the generally freer word order of German. For the non-separated case, the object is found between the finite verb (normally an auxiliary) and the VPC.

Separated transitive:
Sie **nahm** die Klamotten **heraus**.
*Sie **nahm heraus** die Klamotten.
*She **took** [**out**] the clothes [**out**].*

Non-separated transitive:
Sie will die Klamotten **herausnehmen**.
*Sie will **herausnehmen** die Klamotten.
*She wants to **take** [**out**] the clothes [**out**].*

Similar to English, a three-fold classification can be applied to German VPCs. Depending on their formation, they can either be classified as a) compositional, e.g., *herausnehmen* (to take out), b) idiomatic, e.g., *ablehnen* (to turn down, literally: to lean down), or c) aspectual, e.g., *aufessen* (to eat up), as proposed in Villavicencio (2005) and Dehé (2002).

Compositional:
Sie **nahm** die Klamotten **heraus**.
*She **took out** the clothes.*

Idiomatic:
Er **lehnt** das Jobangebot **ab**.
*He **turns down** the job offer.*

Aspectual:
Sie **aß** den Kuchen **auf**.
*She **ate up** the cake.*

There is another group of verbs in German which look similar to VPCs. Inseparable prefix verbs consist of a derivational prefix and a verb root. In some cases, these prefixes and verb particles can look the same and can only be distinguished in spoken language. For instance, the infinitive verb *umfahren* can have the following translations, depending on which syllable is stressed.

VPC:
umfahren
to knock down sth./so. (in traffic)

Inseparable prefix verb:
um**fah**ren
to drive around sth./so.

As mentioned before, there is a clear difference between these two seemingly identical verbs in spoken German. In written German, however, the plain infinitive forms of the respective verbs are the same. In most cases, context and use of finite verb forms reveal the correct meaning.

VPC:
Sie **fuhr** den Mann **um**.
*She **knocked down** the man (with her car).*

Inseparable prefix verb:
Sie **umfuhr** das Hindernis.
*She **drove around** the obstacle.*

For reasons of similarity, VPCs and inseparable prefix verbs are sometimes grouped together under the term prefix verbs, in which case VPCs are then called separable prefix verbs. However, since the behaviour of inseparable prefix verbs is like that of normal verbs, they will not be treated differently throughout this paper and will only serve as comparison to VPCs in the same way that any other inseparable verbs do.

	Simplex	VPC	Total
Finite sentence	59	59	118
Auxiliary sentence	59	59	118
Total	118	118	236

Table 1: Types and number of sentences in the test suite.

4 Test Suite

In order to find out how translation quality is influenced by the presence of VPCs, we are in need of a suitable dataset to evaluate the translation results of sentences containing both particle verbs and synonymous simplex verbs. Since it seems that there is no suitable dataset available for this purpose, we decided to compile one ourselves.

With the help of several online dictionary resources, we first collected a list of candidate VPCs, based on their particle, so that as many different particles as possible were present in the initial set of verbs, while making sure that each particle was only sampled a handful of times. We then checked each of the VPCs for suitable simplex verb synonyms, finally resulting in a set of 59 verb pairs, each consisting of a simplex verb and a synonymous German VPC (see Appendix A for a full list). We allowed the two verbs of a verb pair to be partially synonymous as long as both their subcategorization frame and meaning was identical for some cases.

For each verb pair, we constructed two German sentences in which the verbs were syntactically and semantically interchangeable. The first sentence for each pair had to be a finite construction, where the respective simplex or particle verb was the main verb, containing a direct object or any kind of adverb to ensure that the particle of the particle verb is properly separated from the verb root. For the second sentence, an auxiliary with the infinitive form of the respective verb was used to enforce the non-separated case, where the particle is attached to the front of the verb.

Using both verbs of each verb pair, this resulted in a test suite consisting of a total of 236 sentences (see Table 1 for an overview). The following example serves to illustrate the approach for the verb pair *kultivieren - anbauen* (to grow).

> Finite:
> Viele Bauern in dieser Gegend **kultivieren** Raps. (simplex)
> Viele Bauern in dieser Gegend **bauen** Raps **an**. (VPC)
> *Many farmers in this area* ***grow*** *rapeseed.*
>
> Auxiliary:
> Kann man Steinpilze **kultivieren**? (simplex)
> Kann man Steinpilze **anbauen**? (VPC)
> *Can you* ***grow*** *porcini mushrooms?*

The sentences were partly taken from online texts, or constructed by a native speaker. They were set to be at most 12 words long and the position of the simplex verb and VPC had to be in the main clause to ensure comparability by avoiding too complex constructions. Furthermore, the sentences could be declarative, imperative, or interrogative, as long as they conformed to the requirements stated above. The full test suite of 236 sentences is made freely available to the community.[1]

5 Evaluation

Two popular SMT systems, namely Google Translate[2] and Bing Translator,[3] were utilised to perform German to English translation on the test suite. The translation results were then manually evaluated under the following criteria:

- Translation of the sentence: The translation of the whole sentence was judged to be either correct or incorrect. Translations were judged to be incorrect if they contained any kind of error, for instance grammatical mistakes (e.g., tense), misspellings (e.g., wrong use of capitalisation), or translation errors (e.g., inappropriate word choices).

- Translation of the verb: The translation of the verb in each sentence was judged to be correct or incorrect, depending on whether or not the translated verb was appropriate in the context of the sentence. It was also judged to be incorrect if for instance only the base verb was translated and the particle was ignored, or if the translation did not contain a verb.

- Translation of the base verb: Furthermore, the translation of the base verb was judged to be either correct or incorrect in order to show if the particle of an incorrectly translated VPC was ignored, or if the verb was translated incorrectly for any other reason. For VPCs, this was judged to be correct if either the VPC, or at least the base verb was translated correctly. For simplex verbs, the judgement for the translation of the verb and the translation of the base verb was always judged the same, since they do not contain separable particles.

The evaluation was carried out by a native speaker of German and was validated by a second German native speaker, both proficient in English.

6 Results and Discussion

The results of the evaluation can be seen in Table 2. In this table, we merged the results for Google and Bing to present the key results clearly. For a more detailed overview of the results, including the individual scores for both Google Translate and Bing Translator, see Table 3.

In the total results, we can see that on average 48.3% of the 236 sentences were translated correctly, while a correct target translation for the sentence's main verb was found in 81.1% of all cases. Moreover, 92.2% of the base verb translations were judged to be correct.

By looking at the results for VPCs and simplex verbs separately, we are able to break down the total figures and compare them. The first thing to note is that only 43.2% of the sentences containing VPCs were translated correctly, while the systems managed to successfully translate 53.4% of the simplex verb sentences, showing a difference of around 10% absolute. The results for the verb transitions in these sentences differ even further with 71.6% of all VPC translations being judged to be correct and 90.7% of the simplex translations judged to be acceptable, revealing a difference of around 20% absolute.

Another interesting result is the translation of the base verb, where a correct translation was found in 93.6% of the cases for VPCs, meaning that in 22.0% of the sentences the systems made a mistake with a particle verb, but got the meaning of the base verb right. This indicates that the usually different meaning of the base verb can be misleading when translating a sentence that contains

[1] http://stp.lingfil.uu.se/~ninas/testsuite.txt
[2] http://www.translate.google.com
[3] http://www.bing.com/translator

	Sentence (%)	Verb (%)	Base V. (%)
VPC	102 (43.2%)	169 (71.6%)	221 (93.6%)
Finite	47 (39.8%)	80 (67.8%)	114 (96.6%)
Infinitive	55 (46.6%)	89 (75.4%)	107 (90.7%)
Simplex	126 (53.4%)	214 (90.7%)	214 (90.7%)
Finite	59 (50.0%)	103 (87.3%)	103 (87.3%)
Infinitive	67 (56.8%)	111 (94.1%)	111 (94.1%)
Total	228 (48.3%)	381 (81.1%)	435 (92.2%)

Table 2: Translation results for the test suite summed over both Google Translate and Bing Translator; absolute numbers with percentages in brackets. Sentence = correctly translated sentences, Verb = correctly translated verbs, Base V. = correctly translated base verbs, Simplex = sentences containing simplex verbs, VPC = sentences containing VPCs, Finite = sentences where the target verb is finite, Infinitive = sentences where the target verb is in the infinitive.

a VPC, causing a too literal translation. Interestingly, many of the cases where the resulting English translation was too literal are sentences that contain idiomatic VPCs rather than compositional or aspectual ones, such as *vorführen* (to demonstrate, literally: to lead ahead/before).

In general, the sentences that contained finite verb forms achieved worse results than the ones containing infinitives. However, the differences are only around 7% and seem to be constant between VPC and simplex verb sentences. Taking into account that the sentences of each sentence pair should not differ too much in terms of complexity, this could be a hint that finite verb forms are harder to translate than auxiliary constructions, but no definite conclusions can be drawn from these results.

Looking at the individual results for Google and Bing, however, we can see that Bing's results show only a small difference between finite and infinitive verbs, whereas the scores for Google vary much more. Even though the overall results are still rather worse than Google's, Bing Translator gets a slightly better result on both finite simplex verbs and VPCs, which could mean that the system is better when it comes to identifying the separated particle that belongs to a particle verb. Google Translate, on the other hand, gets a noticeably low score on finite VPC translations, namely 59.3% compared to 86.4% for finite simplex verbs, or to Bing's result of 76.3%, which clearly shows that separated VPCs are a possible cause for translation error.

The following examples serve to illustrate the different kinds of problems that were encountered during translation.

> Ich **lege** manchmal Gurken **ein**.
>
> Google: *Sometimes I **put** a cucumber.*
> Bing: *I sometimes **put** a cucumber.*

A correct translation for *einlegen* would be *to pickle* or *to preserve*. Here, both Google Translate and Bing Translator seem to have used only the base verb *legen* (to put, to lay) for translation and completely ignored its particle.

> Ich **pflanze** Chilis **an**.
>
> Google: ***I plant to** Chilis.*
> Bing: ***I plant** chilies.*

Here, Google Translate translated the base verb of the VPC *anpflanzen* to *plant*, which corresponds to the translation of *pflanzen*. The VPC's particle was apparently interpreted as the preposition *to*. Furthermore, Google encountered problems translating *Chilis*, as this word should not be written with a capital letter in English and the commonly used plural form would be *chillies*, *chilies*, or *chili peppers*. Bing Translator managed to translate the noun correctly, but simply ignored the particle and only translated the base verb, providing a much better translation than Google, even though *to grow* would have been a more accurate choice of word.

> Der Lehrer **führt** das Vorgehen an einem Beispiel **vor**.
>
> Google: *The teacher **leads** the procedure **before** an example.*
> Bing: *The teacher **introduces** the approach with an example.*

	Google			Bing		
	Sentence (%)	Verb (%)	Base V. (%)	Sentence (%)	Verb(%)	Base V. (%)
VPC	56 (47.5%)	83 (70.3%)	112 (94.9%)	46 (39.0%)	86 (72.9%)	109 (92.4%)
Finite	24 (40.7%)	35 (59.3%)	57 (96.6%)	23 (39.0%)	45 (76.3%)	57 (96.6%)
Infinitive	32 (54.2%)	48 (81.4%)	55 (93.2%)	23 (39.0%)	41 (69.5%)	52 (88.1%)
Simplex	63 (53.4%)	108 (91.5%)	108 (91.5%)	63 (53.4%)	106 (89.8%)	106 (89.8%)
Finite	28 (47.5%)	51 (86.4%)	51 (86.4%)	32 (54.2%)	54 (91.5%)	54 (91.5%)
Infinitive	35 (59.3%)	57 (96.6%)	57 (96.6%)	31 (52.5%)	52 (88.1%)	52 (88.1%)
Total	119 (50.4%)	191 (80.9%)	220 (93.2%)	109 (46.2%)	192 (81.4%)	215 (91.1%)

Table 3: Separate results for Google Translate and Bing Translator; absolute numbers with percentages in brackets. Sentence = correctly translated sentences, Verb = correctly translated verbs, Base V. = correctly translated base verbs, Simplex = sentences containing simplex verbs, VPC = sentences containing VPCs, Finite = sentences where the target verb is finite, Infinitive = sentences where the target verb is in the infinitive.

This example shows another too literal translation of the idiomatic VPC *vorführen* (to show, to demonstrate). Google's translation system translated the base verb *führen* as *to lead* and the separated particle *vor* as the preposition *before*. Bing managed to translate *vorführen* to *to introduce* which could be correct in a certain context. However, in other cases this would be an inaccurate or even incorrect translation, for example if that teacher demonstrated the approach for the second time. It might be that Bing drew a connection to the similar VPC *einführen* which would be a suitable translation for *to introduce*.

Er **macht** schon wieder **blau**.

Google: *He's already* ***blue****.*
Bing: *He is again* ***blue****.*

In this case, the particle of the VPC *blaumachen* (to play truant, to throw a sickie) was translated as if it were the adjective *blau* (blue). Since *He makes blue again* is not a valid English sentence, the language model of the translation system probably took a less probable translation of *machen* (to do, to make) and translated it to the third person singular form of *to be*.

These results imply that both translation systems rely too much on translating the base verb that underlies a VPC, as well as its particle separately instead of resolving their connection first. While this would still be a working approach for compositional constructions such as *wegrennen* (to run away), this procedure causes the translations of idiomatic VPCs like *einlegen* (to pickle) to be incorrect.

7 Conclusions

This paper presented an analysis of how VPCs affect translation quality in SMT. We illustrated the similarities and differences between English and German VPCs. In order to investigate how these differences influence the quality of SMT systems, we collected a set of 59 verb pairs, each consisting of a German VPC and a simplex verb that are synonyms. Then, we constructed a test suite of 118 sentences in which the simplex verb and VPC are completely substitutable and analysed the resulting English translations in Google Translate and Bing Translator. The results showed that especially separated VPCs can affect the translation quality of SMT systems and cause different kinds of mistakes, such as too literal translations of idiomatic expressions or the omittance of particles. The test suite that was created in the process of this study is made accessible online, thus providing a valuable resource for future research in this field.

This study focused on the identification and analysis of issues in translating texts that contain VPCs. Therefore, practical solutions to tackle these problems were not in the scope of this project, but would certainly be an interesting topic for future work. For instance, the work of Collins et al. (2005) and Holmqvist et al. (2012) could be used as a foundation for future research on how to avoid literal translations of VPCs by doing some kind of reordering first, to avoid errors caused by the translations system not being able to identify the base verb and the particle to be connected.

Furthermore, the sentences used in this work were rather simple and certainly did not cover all the possible issues that can be caused by VPCs, since the data was created manually by one person. Therefore, it would be desirable to compile a more realistic dataset to be able to analyse the phenomenon of VPCs more thoroughly, as well as employing additional people to ensure the quality of both, the dataset and the evaluation.

Moreover, it would be important to see the influence of other grammatical alternations of VPCs as well, as we only covered auxiliary infinitive constructions and finite forms in this study. Another interesting aspect to analyse in more detail would be if some of the errors are specifically related to only one class of VPCs, e.g., if idiomatic VPCs perform worse than compositional and aspectual ones. However, this would again require a revised dataset, where the proportion of each of the three verb classes is about the same to ensure comparability. In this study, the proportion of VPCs that exhibited an at least slightly idiomatic meaning was higher than for the other two verb classes.

Finally, it would be interesting to see if the results also apply to other language pairs where VPCs can be found, as well as to change the translation direction and investigate if it is an even greater challenge to translate English VPCs into German, considering that it is presumably harder to predict the correct position of verb and particle.

References

Heike Behrens. How difficult are complex verbs? Evidence from German, Dutch and English. *Linguistics*, 36(4):679–712, 1998.

Niladri Chatterjee and Renu Balyan. Context Resolution of Verb Particle Constructions for English to Hindi Translation. In Helena Hong Gao and Minghui Dong, editors, PACLIC, pages 140–149. Digital Enhancement of Cognitive Development, Waseda University, 2011.

Michael Collins, Philipp Koehn, and Ivona Kucerov. Clause restructuring for statistical machine translation. In *Proceedings of the 43rd Annual Meeting on Association for Computational Linguistics*, ACL'05, pages 531–540, Stroudsburg, PA, USA, 2005. Association for Computational Linguistics.

Nicole Dehé. *Particle Verbs in English: Syntax, Information Structure, and Intonation.* John Benjamins Publishing Co, 2002.

Maria Holmqvist, Sara Stymne, Lars Ahrenberg, and Magnus Merkel. Alignment-based reordering for SMT. In Nicoletta Calzolari (Conference Chair), Khalid Choukri, Thierry Declerck, Mehmet Uur Doan, Bente Maegaard, Joseph Mariani, Jan Odijk, and Stelios Piperidis, editors, *Proceedings of the Eight International Conference on Language Resources and Evaluation*, LREC'12, Istanbul, Turkey, 2012. European Language Resources Association (ELRA).

Su Nam Kim and Timothy Baldwin. How to Pick out Token Instances of English Verb-Particle Constructions. *Language Resources and Evaluation*, 44(1-2):97–113, 2010.

Stefan Müller. Syntax or morphology: German particle verbs revisited. In Nicole Dehé, Ray Jackendoff, Andrew McIntyre, and Silke Urban, editors, *Verb-Particle Explorations*, volume 1 of *Interface Explorations*, pages 119–139. Mouton de Gruyter, 2002.

Ivan A. Sag, Timothy Baldwin, Francis Bond, Ann Copestake, and Dan Flickinger. Multiword Expressions: A Pain in the Neck for NLP. In *Proceedings of the Third International Conference on Computational Linguistics and Intelligent Text Processing*, CICLing'02, pages 1–15, 2002.

Aline Villavicencio. The availability of verb-particle constructions in lexical resources: How much is enough? *Computer Speech & Language*, 19(4):415–432, 2005.

Appendix A. Verb Pairs

antworten - zurückschreiben; bedecken - abdecken; befestigen - anbringen; beginnen - anfangen; begutachten - anschauen; beruhigen - abregen; bewilligen - zulassen; bitten - einladen; demonstrieren - vorführen; dulden - zulassen; emigrieren - auswandern; entkommen - weglaufen; entkräften - auslaugen; entscheiden - festlegen; erlauben - zulassen; erschießen - abknallen; erwähnen - anführen; existieren - vorkommen; explodieren - hochgehen; fehlen - fernbleiben; entlassen - rauswerfen; fliehen - wegrennen; imitieren - nachahmen; immigrieren - einwandern; inhalieren - einatmen; kapitulieren - aufgeben; kentern - umkippen; konservieren - einlegen; kultivieren - anbauen; lehren - beibringen; öffnen - aufmachen; produzieren - herstellen; scheitern - schiefgehen; schließen - ableiten; schwänzen - blaumachen; sinken - abnehmen; sinken - untergehen; spendieren - ausgeben; starten - abheben; sterben - abkratzen; stürzen - hinfallen; subtrahieren - abziehen; tagen - zusammenkommen; testen - ausprobieren; überfahren - umfahren; übergeben - aushändigen; übermitteln - durchgeben; unterscheiden - auseinanderhalten; verfallen - ablaufen; verjagen - fortjagen; vermelden - mitteilen; verreisen - wegfahren; verschenken - weggeben; verschieben

- aufschieben; verstehen - einsehen; wachsen - zunehmen; wenden - umdrehen; zerlegen - auseinandernehmen; züchten - anpflanzen.

URL to test suite:
http://stp.lingfil.uu.se/~ninas/testsuite.txt

Author Index